HISTORY OF MODERN SLOVAKIA

JOZEF LETTRICH

HISTORY
OF
MODERN
SLOVAKIA

FREDERICK A. PRAEGER
New York

BOOKS THAT MATTER

Published in the United States of America in 1955 by
Frederick A. Praeger, Inc., Publishers,
105 West 40th Street, New York 18, New York

Library of Congress Catalog Card Number: 55-7562

Printed in the United States of America

CONTENTS

Chapter   *Page*
     Preface: What This Book is About   1

Part I—THREE PERIODS OF SLOVAK HISTORY

1   The Pre-Hungarian Period   11
2   Under the Magyars   18
3   In Czechoslovakia   43

Part II—PRODUCTS OF SLOVAK RADICALISM

1   Autonomism   67
2   Separatism   85
3   Totalitarianism   110

Part III—THE SLOVAK STATE

1   The Protectorate   123
2   Under the Swastika   142
3   In Germany's Grip   157
4   Anti-Semitism   174

Part IV—STRUGGLE FOR LIBERTY

1   The Resistance against German Domination   193
2   The Struggle for Democracy   228
3   The Resistance against Communist Domination   261

    Documents   285

    Bibliography   319

    Index   325

    Illustrations

WHAT THIS BOOK IS ABOUT

On March 15, 1939, the day Czechoslovakia's frontiers were flagrantly violated by an armed German invasion, the British Prime Minister, Neville Chamberlain, announced to the House of Commons that the British Government did not feel bound by the supplementary accord to the Munich Agreement guaranteeing Czechoslovakia her frontiers, given her on September 29, 1938, less than six months before, because by "the proclamation of the independence of Slovakia by the Slovak Diet," Czechoslovakia had disintegrated from the inside.

This statement by the British Prime Minister was not founded on fact. Internal political conditions were not the cause of the fall of the Czechoslovak Republic. The Slovak Diet was not a freely elected legislative body of the Slovak people, consequently it was not authorized to speak for Slovakia. When the Slovak Diet proclaimed its secession from Czechoslovakia on March 14, 1939, it was not expressing its own free will. It was yielding to German pressure, to an ultimatum by Adolf Hitler. After the so-called Declaration of Independence, Slovakia was neither a free nor an independent state. It was a vassal of Hitler's Germany.

Many far-reaching changes have occurred since that fateful statement by Neville Chamberlain. Germany launched the Second World War which was to end in her defeat and that of her satellites. In the war Czechoslovakia was an ally of the

1

Western Powers, while the Slovak State was a member of the Hitlerite coalition. In the Fall of 1944, long before the war's end, the Slovak people rose in arms against the regime of the Slovak State, overthrew it, and renewed Czechoslovak sovereignty on the territory of Slovakia. With Germany's defeat the Slovak State was also defeated and Czechoslovakia was resuscitated in her pre-Munich border, with the exception of Subcarpathian Ruthenia which was annexed by the USSR.

Largely as a result of the activities of the International Military Tribunal in Nuremberg the essential details of the aggressive policies of the Third Reich were brought to light. The trials also disclosed the effective help given German imperialism by its fifth column abroad which, in the case of Czechoslovakia, was represented by Henlein's Sudeten-German Party and by the Slovak Separatists. And yet, to this day, one hears repeated over and over again the arguments of Neville Chamberlain. As a result, Western public opinion has no clear understanding of what preceded the proclamation of Slovak independence, of what really went on in Slovakia under the Slovak State, of what Slovak Autonomism and Slovak Separatism really stood for. Who are these Slovaks; what are their aspirations?

The purpose of this book is to answer these questions by presenting documentary evidence, and thereby to contribute to the better understanding of the Slovaks, of Slovakia, and the Czechoslovak Republic. These answers are today often hidden under a dense fog of political propaganda. In compiling the material for this work, the author has been guided by the desire to present the facts to the reader and to let him make his own inferences. The author's comments on historic events have therefore been kept to a minimum.

The Slovaks are one of the old European nations with Western orientation and culture. Their history reaches back to their common ancestry with the Czechs. Long before the arrival of the Magyars in the Central European lowlands they had already developed two Mid-European empires of their own (the Empire of Samo and that of Great Moravia). The Slovaks accepted the Western Christian rites as early as the middle of the ninth century and thereby extended the influence of West European culture into the Carpathian regions. At the beginning of the tenth century the Magyars destroyed the Great Moravian Empire and separated Slovaks and Czechs by force. The separate political, cultural and national life of the Slovaks and Czechs lasted a full ten centuries. While living under Magyar rule in Hungary, the Slovaks had to fight for mere survival—for the preservation of their language and national consciousness, animated by their love of freedom. Yet, not even that long period of separation deprived Slovaks and Czechs of their awareness of common racial and national origins, common cultural and spiritual life. The Czechs and Slovaks shared the leaders of their national rebirth and had, until the middle of the last century, a common literary language. Slovaks, like Czechs, at first sought to satisfy their national aspirations within the framework of Austria-Hungary, which they hoped would develop into a federative state of free and equal nations. When Germans and Hungarians agreed to divide all political powers in the Monarchy between themselves in the famous "Settlement" of 1867, Vienna and Budapest replied to the federalist plans of the Czechs and Slovaks with persecution. Czechs and Slovaks thereupon decided on separation from the Habsburg Monarchy. Their ideal became a common Czechoslovak State. Their efforts were crowned with success at the end of World War I, thanks largely to the support of the Western Powers. Czechs and Slovaks, and a little later the Subcarpathian Ruthenians, exercised their right of self-determination and proclaimed the creation of the Czechoslovak Republic. The new state had only the twenty years between the two World Wars in which to build its house upon firm foundations, but in the two decades, the Slovaks achieved a unique cultural, national, political, economic, and social progress.

The Czechoslovak Republic also had to face many internal problems of every description, from the very beginning. One of these problems was the adjustment of relations between Slovaks and Czechs as partners in creating and maintaining the state. This problem must, however, be viewed in the light of the preceding historical period. Two decades could not remove what centuries had piled up between the Czechs and Slovaks. Numerous political mistakes were made by both Czechs and Slovaks, especially the centralization of state powers in one place.

One of the influences on Czech-Slovak relations was Slovak Autonomism, the opposition to Czechoslovak Centralism. The leader of the Autonomists was Msgr. Andrej Hlinka. However, he aimed at satisfying his political ambitions entirely within the framework of Czechoslovakia. With the approaching international crisis which culminated in Munich, the Slovak Autonomists of Hlinka's Slovak People's Party fell more and more under the control of the young radicals, many of whom were not only ideological adherents of Hitler's National Socialism but also were its actual agents. They made no secret of their adherence to Hitler's program of destroying Czechoslovakia. They joined forces with the Henlein Party, the Trojan Horse of the German National Socialists, turned away from the program of Autonomy and openly proclaimed that they wished to create an independent Slovakia under Hitler's protection. They were Separatists, not Autonomists. The vast majority of the Slovak people did not approve of the political extremism of the Slovak Separatists. They could carry out their treasonable plans only by first establishing a political dictatorship, which would enable them to rule without the approval—in fact, against the express will—of the Slovak people.

Czechoslovakia at the time of the Munich crisis found herself wedged between two grindstones. From abroad, she was harassed by the coalition of foreign dictators: Adolf Hitler, Miklós Horthy, the Hungarian, and the Polish Colonel, Joseph Beck. On the domestic front the Slovak Separatists joined the disloyal German and Magyar minorities. All these forces joined on September 29, 1938, a day which became a black day in Czechoslovakia and European history. On that day Germany, Great Britain, France and Italy signed an agreement in Munich which handed the so-called Sudeten-German areas of Czechoslovakia to Germany. It was, in effect, the first partition of Czechoslovakia and the beginning of a great international conflict. After Munich, the Slovak Separatists suppressed the democratic institutions of Slovakia and established a dictatorship of the Slovak People's Party. They formed a Slovak Government, in which they themselves oc-cupied the majority of seats, strangled all political opposition, organized armed Party troops called Hlinka Guards (HG), provoked anti-Czech and anti-Jewish feeling and introduced political terror. In that atmosphere they then proceeded to hold undemocratic and controlled elections with a single list of candidates for the Slovak Diet. The Czechoslovak Republic, deprived of much of its territory, politically and economically shaken to its foundations, was at the mercy of Hitler, and Slovakia at the mercy of the Separatist radicals. It was now only a matter of time before Hitler would occupy and partition the remaining parts of Czechoslovakia.

Hitler's emissaries and his Slovak and German agents in Slovakia had prepared everything beforehand. Hitler invited the ex-premier of the Slovak Government, Jozef Tiso, to a meeting in Berlin on March 13, 1939, and presented the question of Slovakia's secession from the Czech lands of the Republic in the form of an ultimatum. The Slovak Diet complied with Hitler's ultimatum and proclaimed the Slovak State on the following day. On March 15, 1939, German troops crossed the Czechoslovak frontiers and began the occupation of Bohemia, Moravia, Silesia and of Western Slovakia. On the same day Hungarian troops entered Subcarpathian Ruthenia. Czechoslovakia was partitioned for the second time and ceased to exist. Plato's words, "a tyrant, after he has made his first appearance, always presents himself as a protector," fully applies to Hitler. Three days later he took the Slovak State under his protection. According to the Treaty of Protection, Slovakia renounced an independent foreign policy and became a German Protectorate.

The Slovak State could exist only in the shadow of Hitlerite Germany. Its authoritarian regime became still more rigid. The Slovak Government established the first concentration camp in Slovakia's entire history. Government by the Führer-principle was introduced, under the "Leader" Jozef Tiso, who first became Prime Minister, then Chairman of the totalitarian Slovak People's Party, and later President of the State. Slovak National Socialism became the official ideology, a faithful reproduction of Nazism. The regime embarked on a ruthless persecution of Jews. In the year 1942 alone, some 68,000 Jews were deported from Slovakia to Germany, where nearly all were slaughtered.

As a vassal state of the German Reich, Slovakia took part in all of Hitler's wartime adventures—against Poland, the USSR, Great Britain and the United States. Slovakia formally adhered to the Tripartite Pact. Germany also obtained rich economic spoils from Slovakia.

The overwhelming majority of the Slovak people was opposed to the Munich settlement. They were equally opposed to the policies of the Slovak Separatists. They refused to accept political dictatorship, or anti-Czech and anti-Jewish actions and repudiated the Slovak State, its government and its regime. The Slovak people remained unalterably loyal to the Czechoslovak idea of statehood, to their Slovak national, democratic and Western ideals. When the people could no longer stand up openly for these principles, they launched an underground struggle. From the time of the Munich Agreement, a widespread movement of underground resistance began to develop in Slovakia, which operated in complete accord with the Czechoslovak liberation movement abroad, whose leaders were in London. The Resistance at home was governed by the following objectives: to weaken the German war effort; to provoke difficulties that would prevent the consolidation of the Slovak Government; to keep alive faith in the renewal of Czechoslovak independence; and finally to prepare an armed uprising against the Germans and their Slovak Quislings. To achieve this, a unified command of the underground resistance was established in Slovakia in Autumn 1943. When Jozef Tiso called in the German Army, on August 29, 1944, to restore order in Slovakia, the country was completely disorganized by partisans, the Slovak Army and the Slovak people who refused to obey the puppet government. At that moment the leaders of the resistance at home issued orders for an armed insurrection. This led to the Slovak National Uprising which lasted two months; Slovak military units and partisans continued, however, to battle with the Germans until the end of World War II. During the uprising, the Slovak Government lost all control over insurgent Slovak territory and the insurgents established their own legislative and executive organs. The Germans and the Slovak Government ordered widespread reprisals against participants in the uprising and against all Jews. Thousands of persons were put to death in Slovakia and in concentration camps in Germany, without a hearing and without trial. Among the victims were both military commanders of the insurgent forces, Generals Ján Golian and Rudolf Viest, numerous political and military leaders, and also 15 members of the American Military Mission captured on Slovak territory.

Under an agreement between the three Allied Great Powers, Czechoslovakia was liberated by Soviet, not by Western Armies. Moscow made the maximum use of the country's liberation and placed Communists in key economic and administrative positions in the Czechoslovak government. Thus Czechoslovakia fell under the influence of the Communists working as a Fifth Column for Moscow. First, the Communists tried to use Slovakia as the springboard to seize power in all of Czechoslovakia. There was bitter fighting from 1945 by the minority for control of the state's democratic institutions. In the 1946 election, the anti-Communist parties obtained 70% of votes and the Communists 30%. The Communists could not achieve their aims in Slovakia and therefore prepared a political coup in Prague, which they carried out in February 1948. Czechoslovakia was taken behind the Iron Curtain.

The Communist dictatorship forced systematic Sovietization of Czechoslovak public life, but it also brought to life an anti-Communist resistance movement. The Communist enslavement of Czechoslovakia has, in many ways, proved to be worse than the Nazi occupation—especially as to the political terror it has introduced, its subjugation of the Churches, the economic persecution of entire classes of society. A great many political leaders and tens of thousands of ordinary citizens escaped from Czechoslovakia to the West, and in exile immediately began organizing a new liberation movement abroad, the purpose of which is the defeat of Communist and Soviet rule and the restoration of the freedom and independence of a democratic Czechoslovakia. The Council of Free Czechoslovakia, established in February, 1949, in Washington, D. C., has become the focal point of all these efforts.

Numerous representatives of Slovak Separatism and political officials of the Slovak State escaped to Austria and Germany even before the end of World War II, and many of them eventually reached overseas havens. In time, in spite of their defeat in the war on the side of Hitler, they again started a political campaign aimed against the existence of Czechoslovakia and in favor of a renewal of the Slovak State.

* * *

This work makes no claim to complete coverage of source material, which is extensive and often difficult, if not impossible, to obtain abroad. Attitudes and opinions on current matters are not and cannot be final. It is for future historians, working in times far removed from actual events, and having full access to sources to speak with finality.

I should like to express my sincere gratitude to all who rendered me much valuable assistance in writing and publishing this book. I am particularly indebted to my friends—Mr. Matej Josko for his invaluable aid in collecting the very extensive source of materials used and to Messrs. Peter Zenkl and Juraj Slávik for their magnanimous support in making this work possible. I am also obliged very much to Mrs. Helen Kiernan-Váša, Miss Vlasta Vráz and Mr. Virgil L. Peacock for their inestimable technical help.

J. L.

Washington, D. C., Spring, 1954.

PART 1

THREE PERIODS OF SLOVAK HISTORY

Chapter One

THE PRE-HUNGARIAN PERIOD

The Moravians — The Empire of Samo — The Principality of Nitra — Prince Pribina — The Great Moravian Empire — The Princes Mojmír I. and Rastislav — The Missionaries Constantine-Cyril and Methodius — Prince Svätopluk and His Sons — The Coming of the Magyars — The End of Great Moravia.

Slovakia lies in the heart of Europe. On the South flows the river Danube and in the West and East there are the mountain ranges of the Carpathians. In classical times these natural barriers were the strategic frontier of the Roman Empire. The geographic position of Slovakia has been a decisive influence upon the political and cultural fortunes of all known races that settled in this region, from prehistoric times until this day. Since the earliest beginnings of civilization in the Danubian basin, Slovakia has straddled the important European trade routes leading from the South to the North and from the East to the West. Because of the favorable economic conditions which prevailed there, the good trade routes and the strategic position of the South Slovakian lowland, its history has been especially colorful. It has been a coveted prize of aggressive nations pushing toward the West from the East and it has been the battleground of the prolonged struggle between Romans and barbarians. After the fall of Rome, the Avars fought the Slavs and the Franks in these lands, and later—Franks fought Slavs. This turbulent era ended with the invasion of the Magyars at the end of the ninth century.

Slavs entered this area in the course of the great migration of East-European nations into the Danubian basin in the fifth and sixth centuries. These Slavs were the common ancestors of present-day Czechs and Slovaks. They settled on the left bank of the Danube and along the Moravia River and its tributaries and became known as Moravians. These western-most Slavic peoples, with their distinct characteristics and a highly developed Greco-Roman culture, rapidly adapted themselves to their new surroundings. Under the leadership of the Frankish merchant Samo they established their own powerful Central European empire in the seventh century. It fell apart when Samo died. After the Franks had defeated and exterminated the warlike Avars, a struggle broke out between the West-Frankish and East-Roman (Byzantine) Empires for dominion over Central Europe. It was at this critical moment of struggle between Western and Eastern Europe, and precisely in the area where cultural influences and power politics of the two great adversaries of that period came to grips with one another, that the Moravians began laying the foundations of their own independent political existence. As a result of this, the Moravians found themselves confronted with a fateful dilemma—which side to choose, with which of their powerful neighbors to ally themselves—whether to join the camp of the West Frankish Empire with its Western (Roman) orientation or the East-Roman Empire, with its Eastern (Byzantine) traditions. The Eastern-Roman Empire, with its seat in Byzantium, observed the Eastern Orthodox rites. The Western Roman Empire, with Rome for its capital, to which the Franks also belonged, accepted the Western (Catholic) rites. In the early medieval age, the sword came with the cross—Christianity also meant political subjugation. This was especially true of the small nation which accepted Christianity from a great power, as in the case of the Moravians on the one hand, and the Western Franks and the Eastern Roman Empire on the other. The Moravians chose the middle of the road. They tried to remain politically independent from both, and culturally they accepted the Western (Roman Catholic) rite from the East, from Byzantium.

During the first half of the ninth century the Nitranian Slovaks, led by their Prince Pribina, achieved prominence among the several Moravian tribes. A notable cultural event is linked with the name of Pribina: the dedication of a Christian Church in Nitra by the Archbishop Adalram of Salzburg in the year 835 A.D. That was the first Christian church not only in the lands occupied by Slovakia, or by present Czechoslovakia, but in all the regions occupied by Western Slavs. Pribina became a fervent protector of Christianity and consequently also a protagonist of Frankish cultural and political influence in the Nitranian principality. This attitude brought him into sharp conflict with the Moravian Prince Mojmir I., who drove him out of Nitra and united the Moravian Slav tribes in a new Slav state which has gone down in history as the Great Moravian Empire. All through the reign of Mojmir I., who never accepted the Christian faith, Great Moravia successfully resisted the pressure of the East Frankish Empire. As a result, the Byzantine Empire became interested in this area and extended its influence further to the West. Of course, the policy of independence on the part of the Great Moravian Empire could not fail to provoke repeated attempts by the East Frankish Empire to subjugate and destroy the Great Moravians. At the same time the Western tribes of the Great Moravians, the Czechs, began showing tendencies aimed at establishing their own independent state, and Great Moravia became the focal point of internal and external difficulties. At this point the East Frankish King, Louis the German, intervened and deposed Mojmir I. in 846 A.D. Mojmir was succeeded by his nephew, Prince Rastislav, who tried hard to maintain a policy of strict neutrality toward his more powerful neighbors. Nevertheless the Franks continued to press hard upon the country. For a while Rastislav managed to fight them off and preserve his independence from Louis the German, but in the end he was captured and died a prisoner in Bavaria in 870 A.D.

The painful experience of the Moravian princes with East-Franks, who had persistently brought with them not only the cross but also the sword, gave Rastislav a bold idea. He first turned to Rome with a request that Christian missionaries be sent to Great Moravia, and when his request was left unanswered he made the same proposition to the Byzantine Emperor Michael III. The Emperor gladly agreed because this offered him a unique opportunity for gaining a cultural and political foothold in the vital area to the North of the middle Danube. Some time about the year 863 A.D. the Emperor Michael III, therefore sent two learned brothers, Constantine and Methodius, from Thessalonike to Great Moravia. The missionaries had thoroughly prepared themselves for their mission in Rastislav's empire; they had created a new Slavonic alphabet, the Glagolica, and translated liturgic writings into the Slav language spoken in the Thessalonike region. In Great Moravia, Constantine and Methodius set to work with great zeal and soon baptized a large number of Moravians. This, however, provoked the jealousy of the German priests who denounced the brothers from Thessalonike to Pope Nicolas I. in Rome.

The Pope summoned them to Rome to justify their conduct. Constantine and Methodius obeyed the Pope's order, but by the time they reached Rome, Pope Nicolas had been succeeded by Hadrian II. The new Pope approved their teaching in the year 868 A.D. and made Constantine a Bishop. Constantine took on the new name of Cyril and decided to remain in Rome where he died on the 14th of February 869 A.D. Meanwhile, Methodius returned to Great Moravia as Bishop of Moravia, accompanied by a number of disciples. He found the county in the throes of internal difficulties and threatened by German attack. Consequently he decided to leave and went to Pannonia, South of the Danube, and there was made an Archbishop. Yet even his voluntary departure failed to placate the jealousies of the German clergy who continued to attack the Slav apostles of the faith, especially Methodius. They once more denounced him in Rome and by their vindictive intrigues succeeded in inducing Pope John VIII, to forbid the Slav liturgy introduced by Constantine-Cyril and Methodius, and to summon Methodius a second time to answer accusations before the Papal Tribunal. Methodius was again submitted to a lengthy investigation, but when he answered all the accusations, the Pope again permitted worship in the Slav language, although not without limitations. Methodius died in 880 A.D. exhausted and discouraged by the incessant attacks of the German clergy, and it was not long before his disciples were also forced to leave Great Moravia. From then on the work of bringing the Christian faith to those lands, which had been started by Constantin-Cyril and Methodius, continued along two separate lines. Christian teaching according to the Latin rite rapidly gained momentum whereas the Slavic rites kept losing ground among the Western Slav nations and eventually disappeared entirely. Yet the mission of the brothers from Thessalonike did not fail to leave its deep mark on the spiritual, religious and cultural life of Slovaks and Czechs. It was as the result of their first efforts that the complete conversion of Slovaks and Czechs to the Christian faith was accomplished in the end. It was this conversion which definitely settled not only the cultural but also the political orientation of the Western Slavs. Slovaks and Czechs have been moving along that same road, throughout their history, until the present day.

Rastislav was succeeded on the princely throne of Great Moravia by his nephew Svätopluk, who, at the beginning of his reign, enjoyed the good will of the Court of the East-Frankish Empire. This was not to last. The Germans captured him, held him a prisoner for some time and, in 874 A.D., forced him to sign a peace treaty which was very unfavorable to him. Nevertheless, Svätopluk succeeded in purchasing a temporary respite from the attacks of his aggressive neighbors and made use of the time to set his own house in order. Later he decided on expansion to the South-East, toward Pannonia beyond the Danube which brought him once more into conflict with the German Emperor Charles III and with the Regent of Pannonia who was later to become the German Emperor Arnulf. In the end these conflicts with the Germans were to prove fatal to the Great Moravian Empire which, under the rule of Svätopluk, had developed into an advanced and powerful state. That state comprised the territory of the western regions of present day Slovakia, Moravia, a part of Austria, Bohemia, Silesia, western Poland and even a part of the lands beyond the Danube.

Svätopluk died in the year 894 A.D. having divided his empire between his two sons, Mojmir II and Svätopluk II. His death marked the beginning of the dissolution of the Great Moravian Empire. Pannonia, on the other side of the Danube, was the first to secede and then Bohemia, Moravia and Silesia were lost. Svätopluk's sons began to fight among themselves; thus the destruction of the empire was completed. In his struggle with his brother Mojmir II, Svätopluk II turned for help to the German Emperor Arnulf who was quick to respond. He immediately attacked Mojmir II, but when his attacks failed, Arnulf secured the help of the nomad Magyar tribes who had recently migrated from Eastern Europe into the regions beyond the Danube. After repeated invasions, the Magyars finally succeeded in defeating Mojmir II sometime around 906-908 A.D. and destroyed the Great Moravian Empire. Upon the ruins they eventually built a new state known as Hungary. The end of the Great Moravian Empire and the growth of Hungary in Central Europe produced a number of entirely new and more complicated problems which have defied solution in the ten centuries that have elapsed since.

As a result of the fall of the Great Moravian Empire and the establishment of Hungary, an artificial boundary was defined along the West Carpathian Mountains between Slovaks and Czechs who, until then, had been culturally and politically united in a single state. The Slovaks lost their political independence and national freedom. They came under the domination of the Magyars who, though constituting a minority, became the ruling element in the multilingual State of Hungary.

It was the first division forced upon Slovaks and Czechs. With the disappearance of the Great Moravian Empire the attempt of Western Slavs to build a powerful Mid-European State came to an end, an attempt which, had it succeeded, would certainly have changed the course of European history.[1]

---

[1] František Bokes: Dejiny Slovákov a Slovenska, Slovenská vlastiveda, (History of the Slovaks and of Slovakia, Studies in Slovak Statehood), IV. Bratislava, 1946. pp. 9-13, 18-25. Francis Dvornik: The Making of Central and Eastern Europe, London, 1949, pp. 1-19. S. Harrison Thomson: Czechoslovakia in European History, Princeton, N. J. 1953, pp. 7-14, 238-241. J. C. Street: Slovakia Past and Present, London, 1928, pp. 7-8.

Chapter Two

UNDER THE MAGYARS

Magyar Attacks upon the West — Saint Stephen — Feudal Hungary — Composition of Population — Invasions of the Tatars, Hussites and Turks — German Colonization — Turkish Rule — Reformation and Religious Struggles — The Counter Reformation — Germanization and Magyarization — The Literary Slovak Language — The 1848 Revolution — The Slovak National Memorandum — The Slovak "Matica" — The Austrian-Hungarian Settlement — Persecution — Passive Resistance — Political Activity — Election Terror — Černová — World War I — Situation of the Slovaks in Hungary

Two new kingdoms arose on the territory of the former Great Moravian Empire, that of the Czechs called Bohemia, and that of the Magyars called Hungary. The Czech Kingdom, comprising Bohemia, Moravia, Silesia and Lusatia, organized itself fairly soon as a Czech national state which, during the first centuries of its existence, was to a large extent dependent upon Germany.

More than a half century had to pass before the Magyars settled down somewhat more permanently on the great plains between the rivers Danube and Tisa and Pannonia. Even after the destruction of the Great Moravian Empire the Magyars continued to ravage the West on foraging expeditions up the Valley of the Danube and seriously to threaten the German territories on the Upper Danube. In the year 955 A.D. they penetrated into Bavaria and Swabia and put entire regions to the torch. Emperor Otto I put an end to these invasions. He defeated the Magyars in the battle of the Lech

Meadows on August 10, 955, and forced them to withdraw to the middle reaches of the Danube. There they eventually settled down and slowly acquired the more civilized customs of the nations they had subdued, especially the Moravians. Still another half century had to elapse, however, before the first Hungarian king, Stephen, achieved a semblance of political consolidation in the Kingdom of Hungary. The Danubian Basin in the tenth century was marked by political confusion, incessant changes and general insecurity. The Magyars accepted the Christian faith only toward the end of the tenth century, largely through the influence of the Moravians, the predecessors of the Slovaks. Together with Christianity the Magyars also accepted a Western cultural and political orientation.

The Hungarian King Stephen, who was later canonized, introduced a feudal system of the West-European pattern into Hungary. Ownership of land, especially of extensive estates, privileges granted by the ruler as reward for services rendered, the existence of a clerical and secular nobility, all tended to create a political and cultural division of the people into two castes—the nobility with the king at its head, which amounted to a powerful oligarchy, and the common people who were the "plebs misera contribuens" living in utter servitude and abject poverty. All power was concentrated in the hands of the king and the aristocracy. They alone participated in legislative deliberations and judicial actions, regardless of nationality, which, at that time, seemed of no relevance. Later on another privileged class was added, consisting of officials and inferior members of the King's retinue, of deserving warriors, and of the lower clergy. These were the lower nobility. Once cities were founded and vested with royal privileges, a third privileged class came into being, that of the freeman of the boroughs. From the fourteenth century on these three privileged classes, aristocracy, lower nobility and burghers were the only ones represented in the Hungarian Assembly, or Diet. Until the 1848 Revolution the common people had no access to the National Assembly or to county and municipal administrative bodies. All nationalities of the Kingdom were treated alike in this respect, whether they were Magyars, Slovaks, Ruthenians, Croatians, Rumanians or Germans. Not nationality but social position or membership in the Estates of the Kingdom was the yardstick of political rights. The ideological and cultural character of the state was determined by the privileged Estates, without regard to the numerous nationalities of Hungary. Although the Magyars were, until the disintegration of Hungary, only a minority compared to the other nationalities, they nevertheless were the dominant nationality from the outset. They could play this dominant role in the Middle Ages thanks to the support of the Church, to the aristocracy and the burghers, and, in more modern times, the intelligentsia, all of whom were mostly of Magyar nationality. Apart from Magyars, Hungary comprised solid groups of Slovaks, Croatians, Ruthenians, Serbs, Rumanians, Germans and Jews. With the exception of the Croatians, who were given territorial autonomy, the other non-Magyar nationalities were first subjected to social discrimination, then to national and, in the end, to political oppression, which grew more and more intense.

Apart from the Ruthenians and Jews who constituted the smallest groups, the worst treatment was given the Slovaks. The reason for this may be found in the circumstance that the greatest part, perhaps nearly all of the population of Slovakia, consisted of peasants who were held in serfdom by alien landlords. No Slovaks were appointed to the aristocracy, and what Slovaks there were among the lower nobility and in the cities, had acquired those positions only relatively late. Thus the Slovaks were practically without rights, living completely at the mercy of local feudal lords. Conditions were further aggravated by two circumstances: the relatively sparse population of the mountainous regions inhabited by the Slovaks; and the cosmopolitan character of Hungary. Owing to the influence of the Roman Catholic Church, which in a country that called itself the Apostolic Kingdom or the Regnum Marianum had a very privileged position. Latin became the official and literary language of polyglot Hungary. National elements were of little concern. That is why there are relatively few historical references to Slovak or other national achievements in the cultural life of Hungary.

Fundamental changes occurred in the national and social composition of the population of Hungary after the Tatar invasion in the middle of the thirteenth century. These had their greatest effect in Slovakia. The Slovak mountain regions lent themselves particularly well to defense against the frequent invasions of Hungary by foreign nations, especially Tatars and Turks. Large areas were unpopulated, but natural resources such as precious metals, copper and iron-ore in the area, made the mountains particularly suitable for colonization. The Hungarian rulers invited Germans to settle in Slovakia and Transylvania. The Germans, given protection and privileges, founded a number of cities, mostly mining communities, which developed into centers not only of trade but of culture. Out of the wealthy merchants, artisans, clerks, printers, teachers, professors and miners a burghers' class gradually developed. Churches, schools, monasteries, castles and fortresses were built and around them new life developed. The Slovak element slowly penetrated into the cities which began to take on a Slovak character. The same happened with the rural gentry, with the teachers, clergy and officials who had been educated at Western universities. When a university was founded in Prague by King Charles IV in 1348, numerous Slovaks went to study there, and several became professors at that university. In this manner the cultural relations between

Slovaks and Czechs, which had been forcibly interrupted, were reestablished. They were to play a vital role in the spiritual development of the two peoples. The most powerful influence that united them was the written Czechoslovak language which continued to be common to both. In the first half of the fifteenth century the armies of the Czech Hussite warriors penetrated into Slovakia, under the command of Ján Žižka of Trocnov and Jan Jiskra of Brandýs. The Hussite forces came to help the disunited Hungarian nobility fighting for the Crown of Hungary. They introduced a new spirit of independence from Rome. Above all, they once again strengthened the ties of a common language and culture between Czechs and Slovaks.

Still greater changes were to occur in the life of Hungary after the Turkish invasions and the defeat of the Hungarian forces under King Louis II by the Turks at Mohács in 1526. Hungary broke into three parts. The central part was occupied by the Turks, Transylvania became autonomous while Slovakia, with the Trans-Danubian Province, remained under Habsburg rule. This situation continued until the second half of the seventeenth century, when the Turks were finally defeated at Vienna and chased out of Hungary. During that long period, Slovakia became the center of political, cultural, and economic life of the Kingdom of Hungary and retained this position until well into the nineteenth century. Bratislava, the present capital of Slovakia, was the capital of the Hungarian realm. It was the city where the kings of Hungary were crowned, where the Diet convened and where the principal government offices were located. The first university in the Hungarian Kingdom, the "Academia Istropolitana," was founded in Bratislava on June 5, 1467.

The Lutheran religious reformation spread into Slovakia almost at the same time and fell upon fertile soil. Noblemen, clergy, and commoners, first the Germans and then Slovaks and Magyars, flocked to the banners of the new faith. The Renaissance and Reformation made their influence felt even in the social and political sphere in Hungary and breathed new life into the national consciousness of its people. To counter these, the King, the church hierarchy, and the aristocrats who had remained loyal to the Roman Catholic Church, forced the Diet to pass legislation to stifle Protestantism. Nevertheless a number of influential families of aristocrats also became adherents of the new faith. They included the Thurzos, Tökölys, Révays and others. The persecuted Protestants, whose faith had produced a new emphasis on national languages, were inevitably joined by the forces resisting national and spiritual subjugation. The desperate struggle against the Habsburgs for religious freedom and equal rights for Protestants was fought mostly on Slovak territory, reaching its bitterest phase during the Counter-Reformation in the seventeenth century. The struggle ended with a number of religious Peace Agreements between the Habsburgs and the leaders of Protestant Resistance. Once the agreements were signed, the Habsburgs broke them. The result was civil war. The insurgents were led first by Count Štefan Bočkay, then by Count Gabriel Bethlen and finally by Count Emery Tököly. In those days Slovakia witnessed religious revolts and conspiracies as well as repeated armed campaigns against the Habsburg rulers, provoked by the deep-rooted dissatisfaction that held the country in its grip. One of these conspiracies was organized by Count Francis Vesselényi in the second half of the seventeenth century; early in the eighteenth century Count Francis Rákóczy II. led an uprising against the Royal Court. The people of Slovakia suffered indescribable spiritual and material hardship and unbelievable social misery, aggravated by religious persecution, repeated bad harvests and pestilence. Such turbulent times and such abject poverty called for radical relief. Eventually liberal ideas from the West reached the lands of the Austro-Hungarian Empire. Ideas of the natural rights of man, regardless of his origin or religion, penetrated these regions of medieval feudalism and tyranny and broke down the opposition to economic, cultural, and administrative reforms. They produced a revival of national consciousness. This heralded a new chapter in the history to the nations of the monarchy, including the Slovaks.

The middle ages did not know the concept of Nation and knew no nationality questions. The idea of the nation would have meant the denial of the idea of Christian universality. According to those notions, the Hungarian political nation consisted of the ruler and the privileged Estates, symbolized by the idea of the Hungarian "Holy Crown." The common people, most of whom were serfs, were not considered to be members of the political nation. The people had no political rights whatever. They had only duties; the duty to render military service, to perform physical tasks, to pay taxes, and to provide labor. Such was the fate of the overwhelming majority of the Slovak people. Yet neither political nor social servitude could prevent them from acquiring an education through the church and schools, from acquiring national consciousness and from national awakening. Much of the credit for this must go to West-European spiritual trends. Apart from the Renaissance, Reformation, and the period of Enlightenment it was, above all, the spiritual movement called Romanticism which helped to achieve this. All these forces combined to bring about the rebirth of the Slovak nation. The Reformation not only helped to give new life to religion, but also increased the appreciation of the fact that the language spoken by the people had become the instrument of culture. A further step was made in this era of Enlightenment —the language of the people was introduced into public life. Romanticism finally focused attention on the nation. This last development completed the national and political awakening of the people of Central, Eastern, and Southern Europe. The modern nationalistic trends destroyed the artificial notion of the "Hungarian Nation" which laid claim to an undefined combination of territory and Estates, and which tried to identify the multinational Hungarian State with a "Hungarian Nation." According to this theory, every inhabitant of Hungary was a Hungarian, regardless of nationality, whether he was a Magyar, a Slovak, a Croatian, a Ruthenian, a Rumanian, or a German. On April 16, 1784, the Austrian Emperor, Joseph II, who was a great champion of Enlightenment, made German the official language of the Monarchy. He thereby cast aside Latin as the official language and provoked violent resentment on the part of the non-German nationalities of Austria-Hungary, especially of the Magyars who ostentatiously began using the Magyar language instead of Latin and German. Following the national awakening of the Magyars in Hungary, an interesting development set in. In the eighteenth century the Magyars began to claim for themselves the leading position in the country as a result of their deliberate identification of the medieval "Natio Hungarica" with the Magyar Nation. According to them a Slovak, Ruthenian, Croatian, Rumanian, or German in Hungary was a Hungarian and a Hungarian was a Magyar. It was this twisted ideology which justified the systematic attempt to denationalize the non-Magyar nations of Hungary, provoking dissatisfaction, political tension, and perpetual crises. In the end it was responsible for the fall of Hungary and for the disintegration of the Austro-Hungarian Monarchy. It was a theory which refused to recognize facts. It was based on a fiction. Scarcely had the first serious blow shaken the foundations of the kingdom, than it had to succumb to the living forces of the national organisms which demanded their natural rights.

Slovak National Rebirth followed the path of the German philosophers of Romanticism, Herder and Hegel, who in turn had drawn on the philosophy of the Great French Revolution which proclaimed civic and human rights. Here, too, Czechoslovak spiritual and cultural unity proved that it had survived the centuries which had passed since the beginnings of the common cultural traditions, its common historic origins, and the common history of Great Moravia. As late as the eighteenth and nineteenth centuries Czechoslovak unity was a reality. This was evident by the existence of a common literary language, the "Language of the Bible," as it had been established by the sixteenth century translation of the "Kralice Bible," as well as by the common champions of Czechoslovak National Rebirth, the Slovaks Ján Kollár and Pavel Jozef Šafárik and the Moravian František Palacký. Ján Kollár moved from the field of Slavic unity aimed at a spiritual rebirth of all Slav nations, all of whom, with the exception of the Russians, were at that time under foreign national and political domination. Kollár's Slavism was purely spiritual and humanitarian.

A new movement was under way in Slovakia in Kollár's days, a product of the philosophy of Enlightenment. Enlightened Slovak Catholics were attempting to replace the old-fashioned literary language of the Kralice Bible by the living Slovak language. For this purpose they chose to proceed from the West-Slovak dialect. Simultaneously with their national rebirth the Slovaks were engaged in a serious cultural argument over their literary language. The argument also had religious overtones. Slovak Protestants, however, wished to retain the Czechoslovak written language, the language of the Kralice Bible, which was the language of Protestant liturgy. The Catholics supported the movement for an independent literary language. Ján Kollár belonged to the party which defended the biblical language and opposed a separate Slovak language of literature. He was a Slovak Protestant clergyman in Budapest and later a professor at the Faculty of Theology of the University of Vienna. What finally decided the argument between the two Slovak camps in favor of a separate Slovak language and united all Slovaks, regardless of religion, was the aggressiveness of Magyar nationalism. Ever since that time, religious questions have played a very important role in Slovak national and political life.

A law was passed in 1836 making the Magyar language the official language of administration and teaching in all Hungary. At the same time the Magyars began forcing the Magyar language upon the churches, primarily upon the Protestant Churches which were autonomous and had been employing the national language in their official dealings and rites. This presented a serious threat to the Slovaks, and especially to the Slovak Protestants. They protested against these attempts at Magyarization and demanded protection from the Imperial Court in Vienna. It was of no avail and the danger of forcible Magyarization eventually united all Slovaks, whether Catholics or Protestants, whether they were in favor of a separate Slovak literary language or against it. The result was an agreement by a large majority of Slovaks of both camps to establish an independent Slovak language of writing, not however based on the West Slovak dialect but upon the Slovak dialect spoken in Central Slovakia. The decisive factor in bringing this about was the need for a more effective resistance to the increasing Magyar pressure upon Slovak political and cultural positions. In 1845, the great Slovak national, cultural, and political leader, the Protestant L'udovit Štúr, began publishing the important periodical "Slovenskje Narodňje Novini" (Slovak National Newspaper) in the Slovak language of Central Slovakia. This was the first act of establishing the new Slovak language of literature. Its introduction was highly beneficial. It eliminated damaging cultural struggles, encouraged the development of Slovak literature and culture, and helped to keep alive Slovak national consciousness in the difficult seventy years which still lay ahead for the Slovak people in Hungary. But the split with the Czechoslovak language also had some ominous effects. It caused some estrangement between Czechs and Slovaks and resulted in the elimination of some notable men of letters from Slovak literature. The advantages, however, outweighed the disadvantages. Thanks to the fact that the Slovaks had managed to iron out their problem of language, they were better prepared to meet the critical events of the revolutionary years of 1848-49.

The national rebirth of the Magyars, coupled with their stubborn desire to force the Habsburg ruler to grant them a privileged position in Hungary, struck a serious blow at the absolutist and aristocratic structure of the Empire. In 1848-49 the Magyars forced an abandonment of the political structure which had been based on the Estates and proclaimed the equality of the citizens. Legislative and executive powers thereby passed from the king to parliamentary government in which, together with the all-powerful aristocracy, the people now also had some say. These reforms were nevertheless still far from establishing a democratic form of government and as political conditions improved, the status of the nationalities deteriorated. Open conflict developed between the Magyars on one side, and the several nationalities on the other as to the structure and internal policy of Hungary. As opposed to the Magyar theory of a one-nation national state of Hungarians, a term which for all practical purposes was to comprise only Magyars, the non-Magyar nationalities proclaimed that the state consisted of several nations, and that each nation should possess national and territorial autonomy. Neither the Magyars nor the Court could solve this conflict peacefully. The Magyars in Hungary and the Germans in Austria, relying upon the powerful forces of the Dynasty, of the aristocracy, of bureaucracy, the officer-caste, and the Church, flatly repudiated the idea of equal national rights under a federal form of government, as had been proposed by all the national groups, in particular by the leader of the Czechs, František Palacký. As soon as these oppressed nationalities came to realize that their national aspirations would never be satisfied within the framework of the Austro-Hungarian Monarchy, they turned toward the principle of national self-determination. At the end of World War I, the struggle was decided in favor of the non-Magyar and non-German nationalities. As a result, the Monarchy fell apart.

Changed political conditions in Hungary after 1848/1849 forced the Slovaks to voice their demands time and again to the Imperial Court of Vienna, in the Diet in Bratislava and to the Budapest Government. They claimed recognition of the Slovaks as a national entity as well as equal rights with the other nationalities. Although these demands were limited to what were considered fundamental and self-evident matters, such as the use of Slovak in schools, government offices and courts of justice in Slovakia, they fell upon deaf ears everywhere. The Hungarian Government denounced these claims as "Pan-Slav," anti-Hungarian, and treasonable tendencies. One of the most insistent opponents of Slovak national demands was the Magyar liberal, Louis Kossuth, who eventually became a political exile himself.

Since the demands of the Slovaks remained unheeded, Slovak patriots convened in Liptovský Sväty Mikuláš on May 10, 1848, and voted a petition called "Demands of the Slovak Nation." It embodied the first formal political program of Slovaks in modern times. Therein the Slovaks, having overcome more than nine centuries of social and political subjugation, and having achieved a new national consciousness, proclaimed their demands for rights and liberties. They demanded that all nationalities have the right to be heard in their own language in debates in the Hungarian Diet. They asked for legislative assemblies for each nation. They wanted the ethnographic borders of each national group determined. They claimed the right for each nation to instruct its representatives in parliament as to the way they should vote. The languages of the nationalities were to become the language of schools and administrative offices and the Magyar Language Statute was to be amended accordingly. The Slovaks demanded the right to raise the national colors, to have Slovak commanders of the National Guards, and to use Slovak as the language of command. The petition stipulated the democratic right of the vote for all citizens. Only persons who were nationally conscious were to be given jobs in the administration. It proposed recognition of the freedom of the press, of the right of assembly, and the individual right to safety of the person. They asked that the land which peasants had occupied during the revolution be deeded to them, that the laws regulating urban pastures and forests be liberalized, and that the same rights be granted to other oppressed nationalities, particularly the Poles of Galicia.

All subsequent Slovak national declarations were founded on this basic political program. It was clearly a modern, democratic program, based on respect for the integrity of the Monarchy, demanding only decentralization instead of centralization, a state which would be fair to its several nationalities. It was through no fault of the injured nationalities that their relations with the Monarchy progressively deteriorated and loosened, and that serious cracks began to show up in the fabric of the state.[1]

The Hungarian Government took a hostile view of the "Demands." It declared martial law and started criminal proceedings against its authors, L'udovít Štúr, Jozef Miloslav Hurban, and Michal Miloslav Hodža. They escaped to Prague.

[1] Reginald D. Lang: European Federalism, European Ideologies, New York, 1948 pp. 978-983.

To try to counteract the effect of Slovak national aspirations, the Hungarian Government proceeded to publish a periodical, printed in Slovak, but with an anti-Slovak tendency. All attempted political and legal remedies having failed, the Slovaks, profiting by the tension that had developed between Budapest and Vienna, decided on an armed insurrection against the Hungarian Government. At the head of this action stood the Slovak National Council. The revolt was centered in Western Slovakia. The forces of the insurgents also included Czechs, both among the officers and the ranks. It was another demonstration of Czechoslovak community. In the course of the revolt, more · radical demands were advanced, including the demand for complete Slovak independence from Hungary. The Hungarian Government immediately sent armies to suppress the uprising. After several indecisive battles, the Slovak insurgents finally succumbed to superior force. Some insurgents escaped to the neighboring territory of Moravia, others were subjected to cruel retribution, to persecution, trials and death sentences. Revolutionary disturbances also occurred in Central Slovakia. These were coordinated with simultaneous military action undertaken by the Viennese Court against Budapest, and Slovak insurgents, who found themselves on the Austrian side of the Monarchy, joined Austrian troops marching into Hungary against the revolting Magyars. The revolutionary turmoil in Hungary lasted from the Fall of 1848 until Spring, 1849, when the Magyar revolution was liquidated with the assistance of Russian troops.

The Slovaks tried to benefit from the situation. On March 19, 1849, they submitted a petition to the Emperor Francis Joseph I in Vienna, asking for autonomy under the direct control of Vienna, instead of Budapest, as well as for the granting of the same national rights to Slovaks as to the other nationalities. The Emperor agreed to receive a delegation with the petition and agreed to it in principle, but it soon became evident that the Imperial Court of Vienna was not a reliable ally. As soon as it had succeeded in pacifying the Magyars, neither the Emperor nor the Austrian Government felt they needed any further support from the nationalities of the Monarchy. They pigeonholed the Slovak petition for the next decade and initiated a stiff absolutist regime in the Monarchy.

After these painful experiences with Vienna, the Slovaks once more turned to Budapest, hoping to come to an agreement with the Magyars. In 1861 they took part in the national elections, together with the Subcarpathian Ruthenians, but failed to obtain a single representative in the Hungarian Diet. The Ruthenians got one representative, A. I. Dobrjansky. The attitude of the Hungarian Parliament was inimical to the nationalities, who had stated their points of view in a series of large national rallies. The Slovaks had their rally in Turčiansky Svätý Martin on June 6 and 7, 1861, which became known as the "Slovak National Rally." It passed the famous "Memorandum of the Slovak Nation" according to a draft prepared by Štefan Marko Daxner. (See Document No. 1). In this Memorandum, the Slovaks asked that the Slovak nation be recognized as having the same rights as the other nationalities and that Slovak be accepted as the official language in the "Slovak regions," that is to say in those areas where they "live as a coherent mass." They further demanded the right to a Slovak system of schools, societies, periodicals, and Slovak representation in public institutions, the abolition of statutes supporting Magyarization, and a chair of Slovak language and literature at the University of Budapest. The Memorandum was submitted to the Budapest Diet and a record of the Rally was sent to the Ruthenians, Rumanians, Serbs, and Croatians. It was also resolved to establish the "Matica" of Slovakia which was to become the principal Slovak cultural foundation.

The resolutions of the Slovak National Rally provoked resentment among the Magyars and Hungarian officials who organized meetings of protest against the Slovak demands. The meetings were called by the representatives of the Hungarian authorities in the Slovak communities. These officially inspired protests were alleged to have been made by "Magyars with Magyar hearts, having Slovak tongues." The Hungarian Diet also declared itself opposed to the demands of the Memorandum, insisting that not the nationalities but the individual citizens were endowed with political rights in the Realm and that all of them together were the united and indivisible Hungarian Nation. This Hungarian Diet was itself short-lived. The Austrian Emperor dissolved it because of its attitude regarding the settlement of the differences between Austria and Hungary and reintroduced an absolutist regime. This situation seemed once more temporarily favorable to the Slovaks who decided to send a new delegation to Vienna to plead for their cause. The delegation was led by the Roman Catholic Bishop Štefan Moysés and the Bishop of the Protestant Church, Karol Kuzmány, who were received by the Emperor on December 12, 1861. They presented the ruler with a new Memorandum, more or less identical with the "Memorandum of the Slovak Nation," except that it included the request for a "Monarch's Privilege," that is to say that the Emperor should enact the demands of the Memorandum by a solemn Imperial Decision. The Memorandum also specified the "Slovak regions" which were to be administered within the domain of the Hungarian Kingdom. The Emperor passed the Memorandum to the Austrian Government which in turn forwarded it to the Chancery of the Court in Budapest. The Chancery of the Court replied that the authors of the Memorandum were bent on subversion against Hungary and that they were to be refused. The Viennese Government accepted this opinion. Once more the Slovaks had to revert to their original plan of seeking recognition of their national rights in Budapest. At the same time they decided to go ahead with the immediate creation of the "Slovak Matica" (Slovak Foundation).

The Charter of the Slovak Matica was confirmed by the Emperor himself, and public subscriptions were launched among Slovaks to raise the required funds. The objectives of the Matica were to foster Slovak education, to encourage literature and the arts, and to improve the material welfare of the nation. The Constituent General Assembly of the Slovak Matica was held in Turčiansky Svätý Martin on August 4, 1863, and even the Emperor made an act of grace on this occasion by donating 1000 Florins. Bishop Štefan Moyses was elected the first chairman of the Matica and Karol Kuzmány his deputy. It was the most momentous cultural and political success of the Slovaks in Hungary since the Revolution of 1848-49.

As a result of the defeat of the Austro-Hungarian armies by the Prussians, at Sadova, in 1866, the Monarchy lost much of its international prestige. To counteract that, the Emperor now began looking for ways to mend the rift that had developed between Austria and Hungary as an outcome of the ill-fated Hungarian revolt of 1848-49. In 1865 the Emperor decided to end the rule of absolutism and ordered the convocation of the Hungarian Diet. The Slovaks tried hard for representation in the Diet, but failed. Once again Magyar interference with elections by force of arms prevented the Slovaks from obtaining a single representative. The Diet then proceeded to enact far-reaching constitutional changes which transformed the Monarchy. Under the new arrangement the Austro-Hungarian Empire became a Dual-Monarchy, the two parts of which were united by a common ruler and by a joint administration of certain affairs. Apart from that, both Austria and Hungary each had its separate Parliament, its own government, its own administration, and its own judicial system.

Germans became the masters in the part that was to be Austrian and Magyars in that which was Hungary. The new arrangement came into force in 1867, and became known as the Austrian-Hungarian Settlement. A year later, the Hungarian Parliament passed the notorious Nationalities Act, by which the Magyar language was established as the exclusive official language of the "United Hungarian Nation." True, this law did permit the use of the languages of the several nationalities under certain circumstances in administration and the courts, but the privilege was accorded only to individuals, not to national entities. Moreover, one of the conditions was that the use of any other language was to be in no way detrimental to the exclusively official character of the Magyar language. The Slovaks failed to gain recognition as a national entity and the immediate result of the Austrian-Hungarian Settlement was that they were entirely delivered to the arbitrary will of the Magyars. They were soon to feel the consequences of the change.

The first consequence was the sentencing to jail and fining of one of the most outstanding figures of Slovak public life, Jozef Miloslav Hurban. Another result was that in the next elections to the Hungarian Parliament in 1869 only three Slovak representatives managed to get elected. After that the Association of Slovak youth, the Slovenská Omladina, was outlawed. In the elections of 1872 the Slovaks got only two representatives and these felt little solidarity with the Slovak people. At the same time Magyarization proceeded in Slovakia according to a master-plan. Its first victims were three Slovak Senior High Schools, the denominational "Gymnasia" in Revúca, Turčiansky Svätý Martin and Kláštor pod Znievom which were being operated with private Slovak funds. The Hungarian Government closed them in 1874. In 1875 the government dissolved the Slovak Matica and confiscated all its assets, justifying its acting by alleging that the foundation had been "guilty of un-Hungarian and subversive activities." According to its Charter, the assets of the Slovak Matica were to go to the Slovak Nation if it were ever liquidated, but the Hungarian Prime Minister, Count Koloman Tisza, thought otherwise. He declared that "under Hungarian laws there was no Slovak Nation." When the Slovaks tried to complain to the Emperor, the Magyars stopped them.

The end of the three Slovak Gymnasia and the Slovak Matica was a grievous blow to the nation. The government, of course, refused to provide any state-supported Slovak schools and cultural institutes. The Slovaks lost the last media of higher education in the native tongue. They were now faced with the impossible dilemma of choosing beween loyalty to themselves as a nation and foregoing higher education, or sending their children to Magyar schools at the risk of losing their national identity.

Elementary schools maintained by the Churches still taught in Slovak. The regime soon turned upon these. A law was passed in 1879 making the Magyar language a mandatory subject in all elementary church-schools, including Slovak schools. In 1883 all high schools were changed into Magyar schools. There were 39 high schools in Slovakia at the time, but none of them taught any Slovak. In 1902 it was decreed that Slovak elementary church-schools were to teach 18 to 20 hours of Magyar language per week. Then in 1907 Count Albert Apponyi's notorious School Laws were passed, according to which all teachers, whether in state or church schools, were to educate their pupils to love the Magyar Nation and the Hungarian State. The state was authorized to change even Slovak church schools to Magyar schools if they included a minority of Magyar pupils. Teachers who neglected to teach the Magyar language could be summarily dismissed, and for the same cause the state had the right to close down a school entirely. The schools became the most potent weapons of denationalization. By 1914 there were 42,186 elementary schools for 1,107,497 Magyar children in Hungary but only 365 for 256,020 Slovak children. In 1918 Hungarian statistics listed no more than 30,118 children of Slovak nationality. In the school year 1913-14 there were 229 secondary schools in Hungary with 77,636 students. Of these 1,620 declared themselves to be of Slovak nationality, but they had no Slovak schools at all, whether secondary, senior high schools or trade schools, or universities.[2] In view of such discrimination against Slovaks it is hardly surprising that statistics in the year 1910 stated that 26.8% of the children in Slovakia were illiterate.[3]

The Slovaks suffered no less in the political field. Hungary never knew the right of universal, direct, equal, and secret suffrage. In the year 1901 for example, no more than 6.1% of the population of Hungary had the right to vote, regardless of nationality. The remaining 93.9% had no vote at all. This undemocratic system of voting was a remnant of the feudal system which Hungary never discarded completely. The Slovaks could hardly qualify for the vote, which required the fulfilment of certain conditions of birth, property, taxes, and personal qualifications, and they therefore had only a negligible number of votes. The allocation of representatives was still more absurd. Slovak constituencies sent 58 representatives to Parliament. Between 1867 the year of the Austrian-Hungarian Settlement and 1918, when Hungary disintegrated, there were nine parliamentary elections. The results were as follows: in the elections of 1869, 1875, 1878 and 1881 the Slovaks obtained no seat at all in Parliament. All 58 seats went to Magyars. In 1872, 1905 and 1910, the Slovaks received two seats each time. In 1901 the Slovaks had 4 and the Magyars 54 representatives from Slovak constituencies,

---

2 Anton Štefánek: Zur Soziographie der geistigen Kultur in der Slovakei (Acta Academiae Scientiarum et Artium Slovacae, X.,) Bratislava, 1943-44, pp. 379-433.
3 Štatistická príručka Slovenska, 1948, (Statistical Yearbook of Slovakia) Bratislava, 1948, p. 254.

and in 1907 they secured 7 as compared to 51 Magyar seats.[4] These results were brought about by unfair, oppressive, and corrupt voting procedures, which were eloquently described by the distinguished writer R. W. Seton-Watson.[5] The Slovaks tried by every possible means to improve these intolerable political conditions. They knocked at the door of the Emperor in Vienna, they appealed to the Hungarian Parliament and Government, they tried passive resistance, then political activism, and finally, joined with the leaders of the other oppressed nationalities. They had very little success. Slovak demands were answered by intimidation, by removal from jobs, by trials, fines and jail. Between 1906 and 1908 alone, 560 Slovaks were sentenced for political crimes to a total of 91 years in jail and fines of 42,000 Crowns. National persecution reached its climax with the bloodshed of Černová and the ensuing trials. On October 27, 1907, a Roman Catholic church was to be consecrated in Černová, a small community near Ružomberok. It had been built with money of the poor villagers and with the help of the great native of that village, Father Andrej Hlinka, a priest in Ružomberok and a leading Slovak public figure, who had been subjected to much persecution by the authorities of the state and of the church. At that time Hlinka was forbidden to exercise his clerical functions and the parishioners therefore petitioned Bishop Alexander Párvy to cancel Hlinka's suspension and permit him to participate in the consecration ceremonies. The Bishop granted permission for the ceremonies but neither lifted Hlinka's suspension from office nor allowed him to participate. The parishioners were deeply hurt and decided to have the ceremony postponed, but the Bishop, a Slovak-baiting Magyar nationalist, now insisted that the church be dedicated as planned. The authorities dispatched a strong force of troops

---

[4] C. J. C. Street: Hungary and Democracy, London, 1923, pp. 55-60.
[5] "Racial Problems in Hungary," London, 1908.

to occupy the village on the day of the ceremony, but when the uninvited priests arrived to perform the rites, the parishioners obstructed their entry. Thereupon the troops opened fire, killing 15 outright and wounding several scores. Not even this seemed to satisfy the vindictive Budapest Government. Another 55 villagers were sentenced to a total of 37 years in jail and when the Slovak representative in the Budapest Parliament, Milan Hodža, demanded that the incident be investigated and those responsible punished, he was shouted down by the Magyar Members of Parliament. Nevertheless the matter attracted wide attention at home and abroad since it permitted a glimpse behind the scenes of the allegedly liberal Hungarian nationality policy. At the time of the Černová bloodshed, Andrej Hlinka was not in Slovakia, but that did not seem to prevent his persecution for it. In the end, after he had served a two year prison sentence and after Bishop Párvy had been forced by the Vatican to lift Hlinka's suspension from office, he consecrated the Černová church himself on June 29, 1910.[6]

Social conditions among the Slovaks in Hungary were equally unhappy. They had no nobility of their own, no commerce, no banking, no schools, no intelligentsia. They lived mostly as peasants or industrial laborers. Their standard of living was low. The state was not interested in their social welfare. Their prospects were meager. Statistical records eloquently prove this point. In 1918, when Slovakia obtained its independence with the creation of the Czechoslovak Republic, there were 12,447 Hungarian civil servants on Slovak territory. Only 35 offered their services to the new Republic. The others, being of Magyar nationality, refused to serve. Of 948 county officials, only 18 remained to serve the Czechoslovak state; only 11 of the 823 city officials, 33 of the 1,133 District

6 Karol Sidor: Masakra v Černovej, (The Massacre of Černová), Scranton, Pa., 1947 pp. 1-42.

officials, 10 of the 660 high school teachers and college-professors, 1 of the 464 judges offered their services to the new Republic. State and public offices had been closed to Slovaks in Hungary. Serious unemployment and perpetual depression reigned in Slovakia from the Austrian-Hungarian Settlement in 1867, until the outbreak of World War I. In that period ¾ of a million Slovaks emigrated to earn their bread abroad, mostly to the United States.

After a phase of national passivity which had brought them no gain the Slovaks toward the end of the nineteenth century changed their tactics to political activism. This change was produced by a number of causes. One was a new ideologic orientation of young Slovaks. Another was a political trial of Transylvanian Rumanians which led to the creation of an Interim Committee of Rumanian-Slovak-Serb Unity and to the calling of a rally of these nationalities at Budapest in 1895. The Interim Committee and the Rally of Nationalities proclaimed the unity of purpose of these three nationalities in resisting forced Magyarization in Hungary. The Magyars replied by organizing large celebrations of the "Millenium," of the thousand years that had passed since they migrated into the Danubian Basin, as well as by introducing further measures of Magyarization. On February 18, 1905, the representatives in Parliament of the non-Magyar nations founded a Joint Parliamentary Club in the new spirit of cooperation they had established among themselves.[7] In the same year, Andrej Hlinka was elected a priest in the city of Ružomberok and the Slovak People's Party was founded on December 5. The new party declared a positive National-Slovak program, along conservative lines, and aimed at championing the rights of Slovak Catholics. The oldest Slovak political party was the Slovak National Party, with a nationalist and conservative

[7] Milan Hodža: Die Slowakisch-Rumänische Zusammenarbeit im Budapester Parlament, Praha, 1935, p. 3-11.

program. There was a third party, the Social Democrats, which was a regional branch of the Hungarian Social Democrats, with an industrial labor membership.

Political activities such as these breathed new life into Slovak national affairs and strengthened the people for the remaining two decades of living under the Magyars which were to be the most trying of all. The dark clouds of an approaching World conflict were already discernible over Austria-Hungary. The internal difficulties of the Monarchy were now aggravated by problems of foreign policy, and matters reached a point where neither the reforms attempted by the Crown Prince Francis Ferdinand with a view to reorganizing the Monarchy, nor belated attempts by the Hungarian Government to solve the problem of nationalities could save the situation. Neither Slovaks, nor any of the nationalities expected any favorable results from these last minute efforts. They rather relied on the trends set in motion by the assassination of the Crown Prince Francis Ferdinand and his wife in June, 1914, in Sarajevo. The First World War sealed the fate of the Monarchy. The Slovaks contributed their share to its destruction. The Habsburg Empire had proved itself incapable of dealing with its nationalities. It remained true to the principle expressed by the Austrian Prime Minister, Count Frederick Ferdinand Beust, when he advised the Magyars at the time of the Austrian-Hungarian Settlement "to look after your hordes, as we'll look after ours." Under the Magyars, the Slovaks were moving along the road to physical extinction. Between 1840 and 1880 the population of Hungary increased from 11,274,676 to 13,749,603, that is to say by 21.9% and to 18,264,533 by 1910 that is by a further 33.6%.[8] Compared with this, the population of Slovakia increased by only 20,862 between the years 1848 and 1880,

8 Révai Nagy Lexikona, (Encyclopedia), Budapest, 1910 and subsequent, XIII/200.

i.e. by a mere 0.8% and from 1880 to 1910 by 458,350 (18.7%) while the population of the Czech provinces for example increased by almost 50% between 1848 and 1910.[9] The balance-sheet of the thousand years of Magyar rule of the Slovaks is unbelievably in the red. The Slovaks suffered irreplaceable losses in their national potential, especially in physical substance, in political and cultural development, and in economic and social strength. These were the facts which brought about the fundamental change in the Slovak attitude toward Austria-Hungary—the abandonment of the earlier desire to reorganize the Monarchy into the common home of equal and contented nationalities, and the formation of an unshakable resolution to leave the Monarchy and the Magyars and to join their political future with that of the Czechs in the Czechoslovak Republic.

Liberation came at the eleventh hour.[10]

[9] Štatistická príručka Slovenska (Slovak Statistical Yearbook) 1948, Bratislava, pp. 11-13.

[10] Dr. František Bokes: Dejiny Slovákov a Slovenska, Slovenská vlastiveda, (History of the Slovaks and of Slovakia), IV. Bratislava, 1946, pp. 53-339. S. Harrison Thomson: Czechoslovakia in European History, Princeton, N. J., 1953, pp. 238-275.

IN CZECHOSLOVAKIA

Ideological Trends in Slovak Politics — Czechoslovak Internal Re-
sistance in Slovakia — Slovak-Czech Contacts — The Mikuláš As-
sembly — The Martin Declaration — Slovaks in the Czechoslovak
Movement for Liberation Abroad — The American Slovaks — The
Cleveland and Pittsburgh Agreements — The Czechoslovak National
Council — Creation of the Czechoslovak Republic — The Foundations
of a New Life — The 1920 Constitution — National Minorities —
Administration in Slovakia — Growth of Slovakia During 20 years
of the Czechoslovak Republic.

Following the Austrian-Hungarian Settlement the Slovaks
were forced to review their attitude toward the Monarchy
and the Magyars. In view of the prevailing anti-Slovak denationalization policy, they lost all hope of satisfying their
national aspirations within the Hungarian Kingdom. Yet they
lacked a specific political program. The domestic and foreign
political situation was not ripe for such a program. At first
the Slovaks moved along the lines of opposition to the government, of mere passive resistance and non-participation in
elections but in the end they chose a program of self-determination and of separation from Hungary and the Monarchy. Such
a development required half a century to mature.

Until the end of the nineteenth century there were no
ideologic or party differences among Slovaks. The none too
large intelligentsia of both religious faiths—Catholics and
Protestants—as well as the people who had a national consciousness, adhered to the principles of the Memorandum and

the Slovak Matica, as represented by the Slovak National Party and its newspaper, the Národnie Noviny (National News). The city of Turčiansky Svätý Martin became the center of Slovak national life. Basically, these principles represented a nationalistic and conservative political and cultural attitude, aiming to maintain and to develop Slovak national and cultural values, the Slovak language, traditions and customs, and to assure progress politically, culturally and economically. Slovaks in those days were enthusiastic supporters of the idea of Slav cooperation. They were looking to the Russian Czars for the liberation of Slovakia. The most prominent representative of these ideas was the poet, author, journalist and patriot, Svetozár Hurban-Vajanský.

Cultural and personal contact between Czechs and Slovaks, especially the frequent visits by Thomas G. Masaryk to Slovakia, acted as a stimulant to Slovak ideas and brought about Slovak political and cultural activism. The young Slovak intelligentsia embraced the new trend, young men who had gathered around the revue "Hlas" (Voice) and who became known as the "Hlasists." Unlike the conservative Slovak National Party and later on the Slovak People's Party, the Hlasists aimed at liberating Slovakia in close cooperation with the Czech nation. They also proclaimed the need for new methods of political work, for a grass-roots activity among the people, for self-help, progress, and democracy.

The Hlasists justified their Czechoslovak orientation not only by pointing to the bonds of blood and of a wealth of common political and spiritual traditions, but by showing that their fortunes in the past and the present interests of Slovaks and Czechs were identical. They pointed to the common Czecho-Slovak literary language as one of the most powerful bonds, to the indelible marks left on Slovak history by the memory of Great Moravia, to the influence of Charles University in Prague, to the expeditions of the Czech Hussite warriors to Slovakia, to the influence of the Reformation and the Kralice Bible, to the work of Juraj Tranovský and Ján Ámos Komenský, to the great men who had helped to bring about a rebirth of both nations and to the political support the Slovaks had received from the Czechs in the revolutionary years of 1848-1849 and after. The most convincing argument of the Hlasists was that unless the Slovaks and the Czechs cooperated closely and mutually supported one another, they would inevitably succumb to the Germanizing and Magyarizing pressure of their respective governments and would never be able to bring about a common national liberation. Slovaks and Czechs were—according to the Hlasists—to rely on one another and on their own strength, rather than upon the Russian Czar.

Their criticism was aimed at the Slovaks themselves, especially at the leaders of Slovak national life. The differences of opinion led to a public controversy between the older and the younger generations which, in the end, proved highly beneficial in the struggle for Slovak independence. A number of aggressive periodicals were born of the controversy, such as the Hlas, Milan Hodža's outstanding Slovenský Týždenník (Slovak Weekly), The Slovenský Denník (Slovak Daily), Robotnícke Noviny (Workers' News), and Prúdy (Currents). Slovak politicians once more took up the fight. Economic self-aid organizations were set up and farm cooperatives were created. Slovak youths were helped to go to study at Czech secondary and professional schools and at the Czech University of Prague. The Slovak fight with Budapest became more overt, better organized and more aggressive. Political and cultural cooperation with the Czech provinces of Moravia and Bohemia in the West was progressively expanded and coordinated more efficiently. Thanks to the Czechs, the Slovaks could now voice their grievances in the two important cities of Prague and Vienna. The Vienna and Budapest Governments failed to prevent this rebirth of cooperation between Czechs and Slovaks.

Soon all Slovak patriots, whether Catholic or Protestant, conservative or progressive, old or young, embraced the idea of Slovak-Czech ideological, political, and cultural cooperation. This was to be of vital importance during World War I when the struggle for the liberation of the Czech and Slovak Nations reached its culmination point, both at home and outside the borders of Austria-Hungary.

The Slovaks welcomed World War I as the long-awaited opportunity for remedying conditions in the Danubian Basin and also as bringing their liberation. It was generally felt that the Monarchy would not survive the war, although nobody could as yet foresee what would happen afterward. Nothing could now subdue the hope for freedom, not even such serious blows as the conscription of practically all Slovak national leaders into the armies of the Monarchy, the intensified pressure of Magyarization and increased oppression resulting from the false self-confidence of the rulers after initial military successes, the death of the great leader Svetozár Hurban-Vajanský, and the restriction of political and cultural activities to a minimum. From the beginning of the war, the Slovaks started organizing their secret resistance. Several centers were established where leaders could meet, exchange information and discuss the implications of events upon the military and post-war situation, and establish contact with Czech leaders. One important center of Slovak resistance was established in Vienna, where Milan Hodža, Kornel Stodola, Ivan Dérer and Ján Cablk maintained permanent contacts with Czech political leaders. Another was in Prague, maintained by Jaroslav Vlček, Anton Štefánek, and František Votruba. Emil Stodola was at work in Budapest, Milan Ivanka in Bratislava. In Turčiansky Svätý Martin, the center of the Movement for liberation, the underground group consisted of Matúš Dula, Ján Vanovič, Jozef Škultéty and many others; to the underground group in Ružomberok belonged Dr. Vavro Šrobár, Andrej Hlinka, Metod Bella and Vladimír Makovický. There was not a town or village in which a Slovak priest, lawyer, or teacher did not conduct some quiet political activity. Regular contact was maintained by couriers among the several centers.

As the war dragged on, views about the life that was to follow the war began taking shape. At home, at the front, and above all in the United States, Slovaks unanimously accepted the idea of the Czechoslovak State. Indeed, it was now some of the Slovak leaders who had to argue with some of their Czech colleagues at home that the latter should discard their idea of establishing a Czech State without Slovakia, and accept the program of a Czechoslovak State. Thanks to the efforts of Milan Hodža, Dr. Vavro Šrobár, and František Votruba, a Declaration by the Union of Czechs, read in the Viennese Imperial Council by the Czech Representative František Staněk on May 30, 1917, specifically mentions "the joining of all branches of the Czechoslovak Nation," which meant not only Czechs, but also Slovaks. It was the first proclamation of a Czechoslovak program in the Parliament of Austria. The next, even more determined statement of this kind was the "Twelfth-Night Declaration" of the Czech Union of Representatives in the Austrian Parliament, on January 6, 1918, in which the Slovaks and Slovakia were repeatedly mentioned as a branch of the Czechoslovak Nation for whom the Declaration claimed the rights of self-determination. Later, Dr. Vavro Šrobár made sure that the "Oath of the Czechoslovak Nation" of April 13, 1918 once more emphasized the problem of Slovak liberation. In this manner the Slovaks, who could not bring their national problem before the Hungarian parliament forum, were represented in the Austrian half of the Monarchy by the relatively less oppressed Czechs who voiced the Slovak desires in the Austrian Parliament. The resistance in Slovakia also spoke through these Czech political statements. Indicative of Slovakia was the fact that as early as Spring 1918 Milan Hodža was already drawing up the lists of the Slovaks who were to participate in the administration of the future Czechoslovakia.

The actions of the leaders of the Movement for Liberation were eventually reinforced by major popular manifestations. At the beginning of the war the Slovak National Party had officially discontinued its overt political activities, for tactical reasons, and to avoid increased persecution, though it did not remain silent. From the beginning of 1918, however, there was an increasing popular demand for the Slovak National Party also to step into the open. Before it could do so, Slovak workmen had taken matters into their own hands and convoked a mass rally in Liptovský Svätý Mikuláš on May 1, 1918. The principal speaker was Dr. Vavro Šrobár who sharply criticized the conditions under which the Slovaks had to live during the war and who voiced certain demands embodied in a resolution. It was passed with tremendous enthusiasm. The "Liptovský Svätý Mikuláš Resolution" (See Document No. 2) described the Slovaks as "the branch of the Czechoslovak family in Hungary." It demanded the "unconditional recognition of the right of self-determination of all nations," including those of "the branch of the Czechoslovak family in Hungary." The Resolution was received with exceptional favor in Slovakia, in the Czech provinces, and even among Slovaks in the United States. It caused consternation among Hungarian officials who retaliated against those who had called the meeting and against the authors of the Resolution by initiating criminal proceedings for high treason against them. Scarcely had the tumult calmed down when 22 leading Slovaks made another gesture of defiance by going to Prague to take part in the fiftieth anniversary celebrations of the laying of the cornerstone of the Czech National Theater, which were held from May 15 to 20, 1918. Because of their presence and the fiery oratory of the Slovak poet Pavel Országh-Hviezdoslav, the Prague festivities became a political demonstration for Czechoslovak unity. After the festivities, Czech and Slovak leaders discussed their common political future. The Hungarian authorities started criminal proceedings against the Slovak participants of the Prague celebrations. Dr. Vavro Šrobár was arrested and imprisoned.

On May 24, 1918 it was the Slovak National Party's turn to call a political meeting to Turčiansky Svätý Martin. The meeting arrived at the unanimous decision to part with Austria-Hungary, to demand "the unconditional and complete right of self-determination for the Slovak Nation," to participate "in the establishment of an independent state, consisting of Slovakia, Bohemia, Moravia and Silesia," and to bring these points to the notice of "the Czech representatives in Prague." (See Document No. 3). Andrej Hlinka took part in the meeting of the Slovak National Party. His words well expressed the prevailing political mood in Slovakia. He said, "This is the moment for action. We must clearly state whether we shall go with the Czechs. Let us not evade the issue. The thousand years of marriage to the Magyars failed. We must part." The traditional national festivities were to be celebrated in Turčiansky Svätý Martin on August 26, 1918. Had they not been forbidden by the authorities, they would certainly have been in the same spirit.

Meanwhile events were rushing on at home and abroad. The Central Powers were suffering on all fronts and the Austro-Hungarian Monarchy was on its last legs. The Slovaks, although still constantly attacked and intimidated, were getting ready for the coming of freedom. A further political meeting was held on September 12, 1918, in Budapest at which it was decided to form a Slovak National Council to act as the political representative of all Slovak political parties and trends. The President-elect of the Council, Matúš Dula, sent out a circular letter of September 23, informing Slovak leaders of the decision and asking for approval and comment. At last, a meeting of the committee of the Slovak National Party was called on October 24. It convened in Turčiansky Svätý Martin on October 30, 1918 to discuss the creation of the Slovak National Council. Simultaneously with these events, the only Slovak representative in the Hungarian Parliament, Ferdiš Juriga, bade farewell to the Magyars and to Austria-Hungary on behalf of the Slovak National Council, on October 19, 1918. Juriga described the injustices which had been committed against the nations of Hungary, in particular against the Slovaks, and denied Hungary's right "to represent the interests of the Slovak Nation at a coming Peace-Congress." He declared that that would be the exclusive right of the "Slovak National Council." In the end he stated that the right to self-determination was a self-evident attribute of all the nationalities in Hungary. As could be expected, Juriga was immediately attacked with ruthless ferocity by the Magyar Members of Parliament who refused to realize that this was to be the last session of the last Parliament.

The final chapter of Slovak participation in the Czechoslovak Movement of Liberation at home was the memorable Declaration Assembly in Turčiansky Svätý Martin on October 30, 1918, which carried the "Declaration of the Slovak Nation." (See Document No. 4). Therein the Slovaks proclaimed their secession from Hungary, as had been decided by them on May 24, 1918. The Declaration states "in the name of the Czechoslovak Nation, living within the borders of Hungary" that only the Slovak National Council had the right to speak for this nation, not the Hungarian Government. The Declaration also affirmed that by virtue of the principle of self-determination, the Slovaks were uniting with the Czechs in a common state. The second chapter of Slovak history had ended, the chapter that had been the longest and the most painful.[1]

A no less important part was played by the Slovaks in the Czechoslovak Movement of Liberation Abroad, led by the Czechoslovak National Council, created in Paris in 1916 for the purpose of defeating Austria-Hungary and establishing a Czechoslovak Republic. The Czechs were represented in the Council by Thomas G. Masaryk and Edvard Beneš, the Slovaks by Milan Rastislav Štefánik. This council had a branch in Russia, which included the Slovaks Ivan Markovič, Vladimír Hurban, Ján Jesenský and Jozef Országh, Sr. As soon as Legions of Czechoslovak volunteers were formed on the side of the Allies, Slovaks who had been taken prisoners of war by the Allied armies joined these Legions and participated in the fighting. The Czechoslovak Legions in Russia included some 5,000 Slovaks, those in France more that 1,600 and in Italy about 1,000, a total of some 8,000 volunteers.[2]

Even before the Czechoslovak National Council came into being, Slovaks living abroad raised their voices in favor of Czech and Slovak liberation and their union in a common state. This happened first in Russia and then in the United States. As soon as war broke out, the Slovak Association in Russia presented a memorandum to the Government of Russia drawing attention to the fate of the Czechs and Slovaks in the Austro-Hungarian Monarchy and to the need for libera-

[1] Dr. Martin Grečo: Martinská deklarácia (The Martin Declaration), Bratislava, 1939, 1939, pp. 7-144; Dr. František Bokes: Dejiny Slovákov a Slovenska (History of the Slovaks and of Slovakia), IV., Bratislava, 1946, pp. 347-364; S. Harrison Thomson: Czechoslovaia in European History, Princeton, N. J., 1953, p. 321; C. J. C. Street: Slovakia Past and Present, London, 1928, pp. 38-41.

[2] Dr. Ivan Markovič: The Cooperation of Slovaks and Czechs in War and Revolution (reprinted in R. W. Seton-Watson: Slovakia Then and Now), London, 1931, pp. 104-105; Dr. Ivan Markovič: Slováci v zahraničnom odboji (Slovaks in the Resistance Abroad), Praha, 1923, pp. 1-102.

ting them. On September 18, 1914, Czar Nicolas received the Chairman of the Slovak Society in Warsaw, Jozef Országh, Sr., and asked to be briefed about the Slovaks in Hungary. In 1915, the Slovak-Russian Society in Moscow came out in favor of joining Slovakia to Russia. On August 29, 1916, the Representatives of the Czechoslovak National Council in Paris concluded an agreement with the Union of Czechoslovak Societies in Russia, which declared among other things their common will to fight for the liberation of Czechs and Slovaks from Austria-Hungary. With the failure of the Russian Armies on the battlefront and the ever increasing internal difficulties of the Czarist regime in Russia, the political importance of the Slovaks living in Russia waned. Their role was taken over by Slovaks of America who replaced them as the primary political element of the movement of liberation abroad. Spokesman for the American Slovaks at the time was the Slovak League in America, which also issued a memorandum at the end of 1914. The memorandum demanded "complete autonomy and self-determination on behalf of the Slovaks in Hungary." Representatives of the Slovak League and of the Czech Alliance reached an agreement in Cleveland, Ohio, on October 22, 1915, in which they demanded the liberation of the Czech and Slovak nations and their union "in a federative form of state, with complete Slovak national autonomy for Slovakia, with its own parliament and administration, with complete cultural freedom, with full right to use the Slovak language, with its own political and financial administration having Slovak as the language of the state." On April 12, 1916, the Slovak League in America resolved in Pittsburgh, Pa., to send Štefan Osuský and Gustáv Košík as its representatives to Europe to inform the political leaders of the Quadruple Alliance of the Slovak demands. When Thomas G. Masaryk arrived in America in May 1918, American Slovaks demanded that matters pertaining to the future national and political existence of Slovaks in Czechoslovakia be satisfactorily settled. The outcome of the discussions was embodied in the "Czecho-Slovak Agreement" of Pittsburgh. (See Document No. 5). This Agreement was concluded by the representatives of Slovak and Czech organizations—of the Slovak League of America, the Czech National Alliance and the Czech Catholic Alliance —in the presence of T. G. Masaryk. It dealt with the "Czecho-Slovak question" and "statements of program made heretofore." The Agreement approved the political program of a union of Czechs and Slovaks in an independent state, and Slovakia was promised its own administration, parliament and judiciary system. According to the Agreement, Slovak was to be the language of administration and teaching. Cooperation between Czechs and Slovaks was to be developed and regulated by mutual agreement. Details concerning the organization of Czechoslovakia were, however, to be left to the decision of Czechs and Slovaks and to their legitimate representatives after liberation. After the Pittsburgh Agreement was signed, the Slovaks in the United States began to recruit volunteers for the Czechoslovak Legions and to collect money for the Czechoslovak Liberation Movement Abroad. They collected a total of $800,911.00.[3]

The success of the Czechoslovak Legions on the Allied fronts, the agreement of Czechs and Slovaks in America to support the leaders of the Movement of Liberation Abroad, and their moral, political, and material support all worked together to earn Allied recognition of the Czechoslovak National Council as a provisional Czechoslovak Government.[4]

Essential as the role of Czechs and Slovaks in the resistance at home and abroad had been, their efforts would clearly

[3] Peter P. Yurchak: The Slovaks, Their History and Traditions, Whiting, Ind., 1946, pp. 190-191.
[4] František Bokes: opus cit. pp. 340-345, 350-354; S. Harrison Thomson, opus cit. pp. 276-325.

not have sufficed to defeat the Austro-Hungarian Monarchy and establish the Czechoslovak Republic. The essential factor was the war-effort of the Allies, especially those of the West, who defeated the Central Powers and won World War I. The United States in particular, led by President Woodrow Wilson, took a decisive stand in favor of the right of self-determination and the freedom and independence of the subjugated nations. In his address to Congress on January 8, 1918, President Wilson outlined his 14 point "Program of World Peace." In point 10 he declared: "The nations of Austria-Hungary, whose place alongside other nations we wish to guarantee and safeguard, must be given the greatest freedom of independent development." He later qualified this demand by stating that only the nations of Austria-Hungary themselves have the right to decide "to what extent the Austro-Hungarian Government satisfies their aspirations and rights." The non-German and non-Magyar nations of the Habsburg Monarchy decided that what they aspired to was independence. Of the original Empire there remained a small independent Austria and a small independent Hungary. Three new states were created: Czechoslovakia, Poland and Yugoslavia, and Rumania was enlarged by the addition of Transylvania. Although allied governments one after another had extended recognition as a provisional Czechoslovak Government to the Czechoslovak National Council in Paris, from June 1918 on, it is October 28, 1918 which has come to be regarded as the date of the foundation of the Republic. On that day, the Austro-Hungarian armies capitulated and the establishment of the new state was proclaimed in Prague. The Slovak member of the National Committee which issued the proclamation was Dr. Vavro Šrobár. Soon afterwards the first Czechoslovak Government on national territory was formed, with Karel Kramář as Prime Minister. The Slovaks had two members in that cabinet, M. R.

Štefánik became Minister of War and V. Šrobár Minister of Health.

A vast array of problems of domestic and foreign policy lay ahead of the new Republic. Numerous questions of frightening complexity had to be solved: the young state had to have a solid foundation with its frontiers defined and secured; the economic burden of the war had to be liquidated. All these things demanded quick stabilization so that a democratic and socially just political system could be established. The new leaders of the nation could draw upon the ideals of free states as examples toward which to strive, and profiting by the past lessons of the Austro-Hungarian Monarchy, avoid making the same mistakes. Apart from problems common to both, the Slovaks were also saddled with the initial problem of taking over the administration from the former Hungarian civil service and of filling thousands of jobs which required experienced administrators, of fixing the boundary between Hungary and Slovakia and of defending it against invasion by the new Hungarian Bolshevik regime.

The new Hungarian state came out of the war greatly reduced in size, weakened, defeated, and confused, but it refused to face facts: it would not give up Slovakia without a fight. Hungarian troops, which found themselves on Slovak soil at the moment of liberation, refused to submit to the authority of the Czechoslovak Government. Hungarian officials, teachers, and judges obstructed the functioning of the new government in Slovakia. The Hungarian Government began negotiations with the Slovak National Council and made various tempting offers, but, when it failed to gain back the Slovaks, it tried to get at least as favorable a frontier as possible. Until Spring 1919 Slovakia was being perpetually embarrassed by Hungary. Then a Communist dictatorship under the notorious Béla Kún got the upper hand in Hungary and promptly invaded Slovakia. The young Czechoslovak army and Czech and Slovak volunteers resisted. Only the Peace Treaty of Trianon, on June 4, 1919, finally put an end to Magyar intrigues and invasions. Meanwhile Slovakia had lost valuable time required for internal stabilization.

In the midst of these emergencies a new political life began to develop in Czechoslovakia. From the outset it had to adjust itself to a number of difficult fundamental conditions. To mention but a few, there was the national composition, with the different historical evolution of the Czechs, the Slovaks, and later, the Ruthenians; the very differences in cultural, economic and social development in the Western and Eastern parts of the states and, not least among these problems, the fundamentally uncooperative attitude of the population toward the government and state authority in general, an attitude it had developed through centuries of dealing with unfriendly, alien officials of the Austrian and Hungarian oppressors. Notwithstanding all these gigantic obstacles, the Czechoslovakian leaders resolved to establish republican and democratic institutions from the outset, according to the pattern of the Western democracies, to carry out a sensible land-reform, to pass far reaching and modern social legislation, to adhere to a liberal policy toward national minorities, and to permit private enterprise to flourish to the utmost. These tendencies were reflected in the new Constitution, and in the political practices which developed from the beginning of the Republic until the Munich crisis, 20 years later. Those twenty years of development reflected the traditional ideals of the Czech and Slovak nation, ideals which were democratic in the best sense of the word. Above all, the young Republic was fortunate in having that great democrat, Thomas G. Masaryk, as its first President.

As regards the structure of the state, the idea of a national state with a centralized government gained the upper hand over that of a decentralized state of several nationalities. This idea of a homogenous state naturally led to the notion of one Czechoslovak Nation and language, consisting of two national and linguistic branches—Czech and Slovak. This notion had been incorporated in the creed of the leaders of the Czechoslovak resistance abroad during the war and now it became an objective of state policy. One might mention as one of the documentary examples of this way of thinking the "Declaration of Independence of the Czechoslovak Nation issued by its Provisional Government on October 18, 1918"—the "Washington Declaration"—drafted by T. G. Masaryk. It states: "We demand the right for the Czechs to be united with their Slav brothers in Slovakia, which had once been a part of our national state." Czechoslovakia is mentioned there as a "free and independent nation and state." General M. R. Štefánik, who before the war had been one of the Hlasists, regarded the Czechs and Slovaks as one nation. In the "Twelfth-Night Declaration" of January 6, 1918, the Union of Czech Members of Parliament spoke of the Slovaks as of "a branch of the Czechoslovak Nation." Because of foreign policy considerations all who participated in drafting the Declaration of Turčiansky Svätý Martin on October 30, 1918, also adopted this idea. In this "Declaration of the Slovak Nation" the Slovaks proclaimed themselves to be the representatives of the "Czechoslovak Nation living within the borders of Hungary." The preamble to the Czechoslovak Constitution of February 29, 1920, begins with the words: "We, the Czechoslovak Nation . . ." The constitution then lays down the supreme law of the land in accordance with this principle. It introduces a centralized system of state administration, with a single parliament, a single government and one supreme tribunal. Simultaneously with the Constitution the basic Language Law was also enacted, stipulating that the "Czechoslovak language is the official language of the Republic" with the proviso that official procedure in the Czech lands is to be "usually in Czech" and in Slovakia "usually in Slo-vak." It was this notion of a single Czechoslovak Nation and language which eventually aroused Slovak nationalism and became one of the causes of Slovak autonomism.

In a very short time Czechoslovakia presented herself to the family of nations as a democratic state with modern ınstitutions, a highly developed economy, and an adequate standard of living. The people had really become the source of supreme power in the state. It elected its representatives freely, directly, and by secret ballot. Everybody had the right to vote, regardless of sex. The head of the state was the President, elected by Parliament, and executive powers were exercised by a government responsible to Parliament. Legisla-tive, executive, and judicial powers were strictly separated. Justice was administered by independent judges. All privileges of sex, ancestry, or profession were abolished. All inhabitants of the state had the same rights, regardless of origin, citizen-ship, language, race or religion. Rights and freedoms of the individual were protected by law and respected. The rights of national minorities, which were on the whole very liberal, were incorporated in the legal system. This system soon gained the loyal adherence of the large majority of the Czechoslovak population, which began to realize that this was indeed their own Republic, their own state which assured them protection and free institutions, which facilitated free and unfettered spiritual and material development, and which was devoted to internal and external peace. Needless to say, Czechoslo-vakia also suffered from problems and defects, but all these could have been remedied by her own efforts, without having to shake the very foundations of the state. One of these problems was the presence of national minorities inside the borders of the Republic especially Germans and Magyars, a carry-over from the Austro-Hungarian Empire in which these nations had ruled supreme. The census of 1921 showed that there were 3,123,750 Germans in Czechoslovakia (23.36% of the total population) and 744,621 Magyars (5.57%). In 1930 there were 3,318,445 (22.53%) Germans and 719,569 (4.89%) Magyars.

Czechoslovakia endeavoured to comply with all justified national, cultural, and economic demands of the national minorities. She consequently fulfilled the stipulations of the Peace Treaty of Saint-Germain of September 10, 1919, concerning the protection of minorities. From 1926 to 1938 these political parties of the German minority, which maintained a constructive attitude toward the new Republic, had several cabinet ministers in the Czechoslovak Government and their representatives in Parliament and usually supported the government's policies. For the benefit of its German minority the Czechoslovak Government maintained a complete German University and two Technical Institutes of university level.

At that time Slovakia had no Technical Institute at all! Citizens of German nationality could thus obtain an education in German, from elementary school all the way through university, earn a professional degree, and enter any profession without as much as knowing the official language of the Czechoslovak State. These Germans had an endless number of national or cultural associations, innumerable periodicals of every kind, an active political life and were among the most advanced and wealthiest citizens of the Republic. A large proportion of the country's banks, industries, foundries, mines, and cooperatives were owned by Czechoslovak citizens of German stock. Of the 300 seats in the Prague Parliament the German minority had one fourth, almost double the number of Slovak seats. The position of the Magyar minority was similar, though less significant. In 1930 there were 571,988 members of the Magyar minority in Slovakia, i.e., 17.179% of the total population. They had 9 members in the Czechoslovak Parliament in Prague. (Let us remember that in 1918 two million Slovaks had only 2 seats in the Hungarian Parliament in Budapest.) In 1937 there were the following state schools, paid for and maintained by the government for the benefit of the Magyar minority in Slovakia: 20 high schools, with 3,719 pupils, 10 trade schools with 467 pupils, 21 lower secondary schools with 4399 pupils and 745 elementary schools with 85,507 pupils.[5] The Magyars, too, had their own political, cultural, and economic periodicals, dailies, weeklies, and monthlies, their own publishing houses, their own associations, cooperatives, and business enterprises—assets such as the Slovaks, of whom there were four times as many, never dared dream of in old Hungary. Withall, a large proportion of the Magyars and the majority of Germans maintained an attitude of opposition, obstruction, and disloyalty to Czechoslovakia. They accepted the Hungarian and German "irredenta" propaganda and joined forces with anti-Czechoslovak aggression from abroad. German national-socialist imperialism and Hungarian revisionism found a willing fifth column in these minorities inside Czechoslovakia. Satisfaction of the demands of minorities within Czechoslovakia was not their aim, the destruction of the Republic was what they were after. Faced with such an attitude, not even the Government's most liberal minority policy could pacify the minorities. The outcome was "Munich," which temporarily destroyed Czechoslovakia but which was to be no less fateful to the minorities themselves.

Another fundamental problem that had to be solved by the Republic was the organization of a new political structure for Slovakia, to settle its constitutional position in the state, and to regulate the relations between Czechs and Slovaks. A complete administration, a new system of schools, and courts

[5] Anton Štefánek: Zur Soziographie des geistigen Kultur in der Slovakei (Acta Academiae Scientiarum et Artium Slovacae, X,) Bratislava, 1943-44, pp. 407-408.

of law had to be created. Slovak officials and civil servants had to be found and trained at a time when there was an acute shortage of qualified professional personnel and experts. Worse still, every problem was made more difficult by the emergency conditions which existed at the end of the war and all solutions had to be sought under the greatest pressure of time. Much had inevitably to be improvised, temporary measures had to take precedence over final solutions, and many mistakes were made on both sides, by the Slovaks as well as by the Czechs.

Problems of personalities, nationalities, ideologies, politics and religion came to the fore.

Dr. Vavro Šrobár became the first administrative chief of liberated Slovakia. He had proved himself a man of exceptional energy, courage, and experience, acquired in the prolonged struggle for national liberation. He was a man of progressive ideals and devoted to the Czechoslovak idea of national and linguistic unity. He became the Slovak member of the National Committee in Prague on its day of creation, October 28, 1918, and on December 10, 1918, was appointed Minister Plenipotentiary for Slovakia. He selected 14 officials to assist him in the exercise of these exceptional, almost autocratic powers. Dr. Šrobár certainly contributed largely to stabilizing conditions in post-war Slovakia, but unfortunately somewhat spoiled the promising beginnings of his political career in the liberated country by becoming involved in controversies with two no less distinguished Slovak political leaders, Milan Hodža and Andrej Hlinka. The controversies were reflected in the two new political parties: Hodža's Slovak Agrarian Party and Hlinka's Slovak People's (Catholic) Party. Apart from these complications, Dr. Šrobár was compelled to fill a large number of jobs in the administration, schools, and the judicial branch with Czech officials, without whose aid he would have been utterly unable to cope with the problems he was facing. Alas, the presence of these large numbers of Czech officials and employees in Slovakia eventually developed into a very touchy problem between Slovaks and Czechs. Czech officials and Czech teachers naturally spoke Czech in their jobs in Slovakia and Czech workers continued to flock into Slovakia and take every type of job, even the quite menial ones of mailmen, railwaymen, and messengers in government offices, even after a sufficient number of Slovak applicants became available. This provoked friction and some justified complaint which fanned the flames of the movement for national autonomy in Slovakia.

With the creation of a Ministry Plenipotentiary for Slovakia, Slovakia acquired the character of an administrative unit, which had a different administration from that of the Czech lands. Basically that was a sensible measure, because there did exist fundamental differences and divergent traditions between the two parts of the Republic and these could not be eliminated at one stroke. Unfortunately the Prague Ministries failed to respect the full powers given to Dr. Šrobár. They interfered with the jurisdiction of the Bratislava Ministry, took over one of its function after another, or reserved themselves the right to approve its decision which relegated the Office of the Minister Plenipotentiary for Slovakia to a role of subordination to the Government Departments in Prague. All this seemed to be justified on the theory of a unified and centrally administered state. A county (župa) administrative system was introduced in Slovakia but without the Country League which had been provided for by law. This reform, which was to emphasize the administrative individuality of Slovakia, was soon abolished. The Counties were cancelled in 1927 and a Provincial Administration created which while making Slovakia a territorially autonomous entity failed to provide it with legislative or executive authority. After the events of "Munich," when Hlinka's Slovak

People's Party usurped all political power in Slovakia, the "Autonomy of the Land of Slovakia" was enacted on November 22, 1938, and Slovakia obtained a Diet and a Slovak Government. The Czechoslovak Republic was transformed from a centralized state into a decentralized federative entity, which consisted of three autonomous units: the Czech lands; Slovakia; and Subcarpathian Ruthenia (Ukraine). This far-reaching change, however, came too late. It could no longer satisfy the nationalist extremists of Hlinka's Slovak People's Party who were not interested in a program of Slovak Autonomy but wanted an independent Slovakia according to the pattern that had been drawn up for them in Berlin.

The unlimited possibilities for political self-expression had produced a number of political parties in Slovakia, parties that were Czechoslovak and whose activities extended over the entire Republic, parties limited to Slovakia only, parties of the minorities, of the conservative element, and of the socialists. No matter whether they approved government policies or whether they were in the opposition, they all stood on political platforms which accepted the fundamental idea of the Czechoslovak Republic. Not until the time immediately preceeding the Munich crisis did the German and Hungarian extreme nationalist parties openly attack the existence of the state. They were then joined by the radical wing of the younger members of the Slovak People's Party. It was recognized by the majority of the Slovak population that in the short twenty years of existence of the Czechoslovak State, thanks to the constructive political powers of the Slovaks, their admirable creative urge, and to the immense help given them by the Czechs, Slovakia had undergone incredible changes in every field of human endeavor. The progress she made in these twenty years had never been surpassed in any phase of Slovak history. Let us look at a few examples.

Foremost among these was the growth of population. Notwithstanding that tens of thousands still emigrated abroad, the population increased from 2,993,859 in 1921 to 3,324,111 by 1930, that is by 11% and to 3,421,144 in 1947, after the spontaneous departure of a part of Magyars and after the transfer of the Germans, that is by a further 3.2%. The growth of some of the cities of Slovakia was even more rapid. Bratislava had 78,000 inhabitants in 1919 and 184,400 in 1948. In the same period Košice grew from 44,000 to 60,700 inhabitants, Nitra from 16,500 to 20,500, Žilina from 9,000 to 18,000, Turčiansky Svätý Martin from 3,000 to 20,000 and so on.[6]

Many of the complaints voiced by the Slovaks against the policy of employment of Slovaks in government jobs between 1918 and 1938 were justified. Yet even in this field the achievements were not inconsiderable. By 1938 there were 2,957 Slovaks, not including 900 community clerks (notaries), in administrative jobs, 1,133 in the rural police force, 5,626 in the postal service, and there were 227 Slovak judges and 81 judges awaiting permanent appointment. The Czecho-slovak State Railroads employed 14,562 Slovaks.

The most impressive advances were made in Slovakia in the field of education. By 1940 there were only 5.4% illiterate persons above six years of age in Slovakia. Of these remnants more than ⅘ (83.1%) were persons who had passed school age before 1920, that is to say the vast majority had missed all education while still under the Magyars. In the school year 1946-47 there were 601 nursery schools and kinder-gartens in Slovakia, with 38,839 children and 838 supervisors or teachers; 3,585 grade schools with 380,966 pupils and 9,728 teachers; 21 institutes for retarded children with 1,489 children and 125 instructors; 61 senior high schools with 30,426 pupils and 1,299 teachers; 18 normal schools and

[6] Waller Wynne, Jr.: The Population of Czechoslovakia, Washington, 1953, pp. 48-57.

colleges for teachers with 3,173 students and 260 professors; 3 institutes for training kindergarten personnel, with 156 students; 177 trade and apprentice schools with 34,947 pupils and 2,007 teachers. There were at the same time 5 universities, or independent university colleges in Slovakia, with 11,466 students and 340 professors. On April 1, 1948, there were 196,746 radio sets in Slovak homes and 234 community movie theatres. There were 265 periodicals, 5 permanent legitimate theaters, presenting 1,261 shows per year—689 plays, 219 opers and 344 other forms of entertainment. There were innumerable societies for education, culture, science and research, and the arts.

In the field of public health, by 1947, there were 67 institutes for the treatment of the sick in Slovakia, with 15,411 beds, 695 doctors, and 2,065 nurses, who cared for 244,914 patients. In 1948 there were 1,894 doctors in Slovakia.[7]

Great improvements were also achieved in the economic and social life of Slovakia, even though the developments were not always entirely satisfactory. The first step was land reform by which 686,000 hektares of farmland from former larger estates were distributed to 198,786 families of small-holders, greatly invigorating the Slovak farmer class. No less remarkable was the increase and development of trade and industry, commerce and banking, although they had to pass through numerous critical periods. In Slovakia, greatest increase in industry occurred after World War II which radically changed the economic and social structure of the country. Slovakia lost its character of a predominantly agricultural land, and became an industrialized country with a modern light and heavy industry capable of giving bread to the majority of the people.

It would involve too many details if we were to mention

[7] Štatistická príručka Slovenska (Slovak Statistical Handbook) 1948, Bratislava, 1948, pp. 253-262.

the vigorous building activity between 1921 and 1930, which produced 91,450 new houses, or the expansion of electrification which is today at least 20 times that of 1919. Even transportation underwent radical changes; from 1920 to 1937 more than 400 kilometers of new railroads were built, and twice as much again since that time. 1,216 kilometers of new highways were constructed in that same period and about twice as much again since.

Within the Czechoslovak Republic, Slovakia grew from a neglected, backward and spiritually and economically oppressed land into a modern highly developed area. The progress it made in those 30 years has seldom been equalled even during several generations in states that had been free for centuries. These were the blessings of liberty the Slovaks found in the Czechoslovak Republic, as well as the fruits of the vitality and hard work of the people, supported in every respect by the Czech Nation, which, in turn, derived great benefit from its unity with the Slovaks. And yet, economic development was greatly hindered at that time by an endless chain of obstacles such as the consequences of the First World War, the depression in the thirties, an attitude of opposition on the part of a considerable group of Slovaks, the exorbitant costs of armaments during the years that preceded the Second World War, the territorial losses suffered by Slovakia after Munich, the Nazi occupation of Czechoslovakia, the Second World War which made all Slovakia a battlefield and then the final blow of Communist dictatorship. Without such obstacles, who knows how much greater still this development would have been?

What was achieved splendidly justified Slovak liberation from Magyar misrule. It justified the creation of the Czechoslovak Republic. The twenty-years of the Czechoslovak Republic were the finest in Slovak history.

PART II

PRODUCTS OF SLOVAK RADICALISM

Chapter One

AUTONOMISM

Beginnings — The Council of Priests — The Hlinka-Šrobár Contro-
versy — The Founding of Hlinka's Slovak Peoples' Party — Hlinka's
Journey to Paris — The Program of Autonomism — Vojtech Tuka —
The "Rodobrana" — "Vacuum Juris" — The Tuka Trial — The
Elections of 1925 and 1929 — The "Nástup"-ists — Populist Ag-
gressivity — The 1935 Elections — The Piešťany Convention —
Agreement with the Henlein Party — The Bratislava Demonstration
— Hlinka's Death — At the Crossroads

Slovak Autonomism was a political movement which developed in Slovakia after the establishment of the Czechoslovak
Republic. It was an outgrowth of Slovak nationalism, represented by two Slovak political parties, Hlinka's Slovak
People's Party and the Slovak National Party. Their objectives had not been stated with any clarity until 1938. From
1919 to 1938 autonomism was expressed by general cliches
such as "Slovakia for the Slovaks," "Slovak Autonomy,"
"Incorporate the Pittsburgh Agreement into the Czechoslovak Constitution" and the like. What the Autonomists wanted
was the fulfilment of certain demands, some stated in the negative form, others positive but undefined. They were opposed
to the idea of a homogenous Czechoslovak Nation and to a
centralist regime. What they wanted was a recognition of
the Slovak national entity and autonomy for Slovakia with
its own Diet and executive, but within the framework of the
Czechoslovak Republic. They wished to change the single,
centrally administered state into a decentralized and federal

one. It took two decades for these ideas and concepts to crystalize.

True, there had been similar political ambitions before. The Slovaks in Hungary had claimed autonomy for Slovakia in the middle of the 19th century and during the First World War. Slovaks in Russia and in the United States had repeatedly insisted on Slovak administrative autonomy within Czechoslovakia. Nevertheless Slovak autonomism as a movement developed independently from the past or from the attitudes of nations living abroad. Its motivation was local.

The first symptoms of Slovak autonomism became discernible at the Turčiansky Svätý Martin Declaration Rally. Some of the signers of the Declaration had a private discussion on October 31, 1918, presided over by Emil Stodola. The topic was how to administer Slovakia. Stodola made the suggestion that autonomy might be one way to solve the administrative problem. Others suggested that Slovakia be administered on a temporary basis for the first ten years after which elected representatives of Slovakia should decide the question of autonomy. The discussion ended without any definite decision.[1]

When the Austro-Hungarian Monarchy was approaching its inevitable end, the Archbishop of Esztergom, Ján Cardinal Černoch, (himself a Slovak, who had succumbed to Magyarization), called upon the clergy of his diocese, which included most of Slovakia, to do their utmost in order to keep the Slovaks from hastening the break-up of Hungary. Andrej Hlinka refused to comply with the Cardinal's demand and declared himself very decidedly in favor of Czechoslovakia. More than that, he put forward the suggestion that a department of the Church be organized to look after the interests of Slovak Catholics who were subordinated to a high

[1] Dr. Martin Grečo: Martinská deklarácia (The Martin Declaration), Bratislava, 1939, pp. 165-173.

clergy residing outside the Republic. As a result an execu-
tive committee was formed, consisting of twelve clergymen.
A little later, Hlinka further developed this initial vague idea
and on November 27, and 28, 1918, created a Council of
Priests in Ružomberok, with 100 members and an Executive
Committee of fifteen. Andrej Hlinka became the first chairman of the Executive Committee of the Council of Priests.
On this occasion it was also proposed that the Magyar Roman
Catholic Bishops in Slovakia be replaced by Slovaks and
that Andrej Hlinka be appointed Bishop of Nitra. The Council of Priests also resolved to publish a periodical under the
name of "Slovák," and proposed 27 Slovak Catholic candidates for the first Czechoslovak Parliament, the so-called
Revolutionary Parliament. In this manner, the Council of
Priests assumed the role of a political organization which
claimed the right to intervene not only in matters of religion,
but also with regard to general political questions.

Apart from political motives, there can be no doubt that
Hlinka's personal ambitions also influenced the origin of the
Council of Priests. This became evident from his subsequent
activities. Hlinka called on the new Minister Plenipotentiary
for Slovakia, Dr. Vavro Šrobár, in Žilina and presented to
him the proposals of the Council of Priests. Dr Šrobár then
committed a psychological blunder. Although he could not
appoint Hlinka as the Archbishop, he should have secured
the cooperation and support of the Council of Priests. It can
be said that Šrobár did not go far enough to win Hlinka.
Hlinka took this as a personal insult and as an affront to Slovak Catholics represented by the Council of Priests. After
this, his conflict with Dr. Šrobár acquired political color and
from then on Hlinka kept the issue as a political one. It must
be remembered that Dr. Šrobár was at that time the representative of the Czechoslovak State and its official policy of
a single united Czechoslovak Nation. Hlinka regarded the

policy as pregressive and anticlerical and not in the best interest of Slovakia. From then on he attacked it under the
slogan "For God and Nation," with a program of clericalism
and nationalism. Postwar disorganization and the resulting
inevitable difficulties and shortages, as well as the insecurity
created by the still unfinished struggle with the Magyars,
understandable mistakes, faulty decisions, and personal injustices provided Hlinka with sufficient day-to-day grievances
which he could exploit in his quarrel with Dr. Šrobár and in
his opposition to the new regime.

When he broke with Dr. Šrobár, Andrej Hlinka on December 19, 1918, announced the reestablishment of the Slovak
People's Party, which he had founded in 1905 but which
had never been fully constituted and had in fact disbanded
before the First World War. He became its Chairman. The
Council of Priests and its executive committee fused with the
new party. The periodical "Slovak" now became the official
daily of this party, which later assumed the name of Hlinka's
Slovak People's Party. The party's program was to fight for
Slovak autonomy and against centralism and liberalism. The
political attacks of the party and of its chairman, Hlinka,
who was never very scrupulous as to means, were aimed not
only at the Czechs, but also at those Slovaks who stood for
a progressive, Czechoslovak policy. The populists were against
the Czechs because they identified them with the new Czechoslovak national ideology and because they considered the
Czechs too progressive, especially insofar as the Czechs were
inclined also to blame Rome for the long oppression from
which they had just emerged. The Populists reproached those
Slovaks who opposed the idea of Slovak autonomy, for their
support of administrative centralism, their luke-warm attitude to the Catholic Church, the disproportionate number of
Czechs holding public and private jobs in Slovakia, their occasional neglect to give priority to the Slovak language in

Slovakia, and for their lack of reverence for Slovak National traditions, customs, and peculiarities of character. Prague, the new capital city of the Republic, was regarded by the members of the Slovak People's Party as the symbol of everything they considered bad in the State and the bulk of their propaganda and attacks were directed against it. At the same time Hlinka and his Populists conducted an equally ruthless fight against the non-autonomist Slovaks.

From the first the Slovak People's Party claimed the right to speak for all Slovakia, although it never represented the majority of the people. It never obtained more then 20 to 32% of the votes, including the votes cast for other small parties which joined them on a common ticket. The Populists also claimed to be the spokesmen of the Catholics of Slovakia, again only with partial justification. For one thing, the Catholic Church and a political party of Catholics are two very different things, not identical. Apart from that, statistics also deny such claims: according to the 1930 census there were 71.61% Roman Catholics and 6.42% Greco-Catholics in Slovakia, a total of 78.03% Catholics. There were 16.69% Protestants of different denominations, 4.11% Jews and the rest were of other religions. Even if one were to admit that all who voted for the Populists bloc were always Catholics—a presumption which would be clearly wrong since the Slovak National Party which always joined the Populist bloc in elections had an almost exlusively Protestant membership—the claim that they represented all the Catholics of Slovakia would still be unfounded. They could speak at best for 17 to 19% of the Catholics in Slovakia.

The Slovak Protestants must also be discussed here, not so much because of their numerical strength as because of their part in the struggle for national rights during the Hungarian regime and after liberation. From the time of the Reformation the importance of the Slovak Protestant leaders in the nation's life, in its cultural and political development, was out of all proportion to their numbers. The idea of Czecho-Slovak unity had the loyal support of the Slovak Protestants. It was therefore hardly surprising that the number of Slovak Protestants who achieved prominence in public life or in the administration after 1918 was substantially greater than their proportionate strength. Several of the non-Autonomist political parties in Slovakia were led by Protestants. This is not a denial of the immense national and cultural achievements of the Slovak Catholics, especially if one realizes that the Catholic Slovak intelligentsia, mostly priests and teachers, had been particularly exposed to the overwhelming pressure of Magyarization. Yet Hlinka and his Slovak Populists viewed the position of leadership of Slovak Protestants with violent disfavor, wrongfully identifying Protestants who held leading positions in political parties with the Protestant Churches. The Populist attacks on Protestant leaders undermined religious peace. The result was the creation of antagonism between Catholics and Protestants even to the point where the Catholics demanded a "numerus clausus". Great mischief was caused by the mixing of politics and religion and the confusion of secular interests with those of the Catholic Church; this developed into one of the most serious and very touchy problems of Slovak political life. Events after Munich and the consequences of World War II have given the problem a new facet, but have not made it any less acute.

While Dr. Vavro Šrobár was still Minister Plenipotentiary for Slovakia he turned the power of the state against the Slovak People's Party. As a result, an undesirable conflict arose between the state and the new party which injected the passions of the militant church and the fiery temperament of its leader, Hlinka, into the political arena. In 1919 the Slovak People's Party joined forces with the Czech Catholic Party, led by Msgr. Jan Šrámek, but the arrangement soon broke down because of certain excesses of the Populists. Andrej Hlinka, annoyed that the full powers of Dr. Šrobár in Slovakia were being limited gradually and encouraged by the fact that the Paris Peace Conference was discussing the autonomy of the Subcarpathian Ruthenians, began more emphatically to demand Slovak autonomy. Motivated by personal dissatisfaction, political opportunism, and egged on by dubious political advisers, Hlinka secretly left for Paris in September 1919, together with the ambitious František Jehlička, to demand Autonomy for Slovakia. The journey was undertaken without the knowledge of the Czechoslovak Government, the Slovak Members of the Czechoslovak Parliament, or the Executive Committee of his own party. He traveled on a faked Polish passport. The escapade ended in a fiasco and Jehlička never returned home preferring to stay abroad, in the pay of the Magyars, until his death. Though Hlinka returned, his trip created a scandal and a wave of resentment against him. Hlinka was first arrested but then released and the affair was settled as a political matter.[2] The incident was developed into the legend about Hlinka's martyrdom in Czechoslovakia and was used to justify the radical political course of the Populists.

When Parliament was discussing the new Czechoslovak Constitution, the six representatives of the Slovak People's Party declared, on February 19, 1920, that they would vote in favor of the Constitution, but that they would "in no way renounce their demand that Slovakia be autonomous, with its own diet, which ought to be assured in the future." In their opinion, Slovakia should be an administrative unit under a Minister Plenipotentiary aided by assistants who would form the Provincial Committee responsible to the Slovak Members of the Czechoslovak Parliament, who would at the same time

[2] Stephen Bonsal, in the book "Suitors and Supplicants," New York, 1946, pp. 156-159 makes the untrue statement that in Paris Hlinka's supporters presented a letter of recommendation by General M. R. Štefánik.

be Members of a Slovak Diet. The Slovak Populists came forward with this proposition once more when Parliament was discussing the setting up of a "County" (Župa) administration. The Czech and non-Populist Slovak Members of Parliament were opposed to Slovak Autonomy as suggested by the Slovak People's Party, because they still feared "the pressures of the recent past and because they had not yet acquired enough experience with the new administration." [3]

In 1919 Slovakia and the entire country suffered a serious loss. On May 4, on his way back home, the country's new Minister of Defense, Milan Rastislav Štefánik, who had been the Slovak leader in the Czechoslovak movement of liberation abroad during the war and who had acquired the rank of a General of the French Army, was killed in an air crash. The Populists exploited even this tragic event for their own political propaganda by spreading the rumor that Štefánik's plane had been deliberately shot down by Czech troops, acting upon orders of Štefánik's Czech political enemies.

The Slovak People's Party participated in the 1920 elections jointly with the Czech Catholics, with whom, however, they soon broke. The Party obtained 235,389 votes and 12 representatives in Parliament, amounting to 21% of the votes of Slovakia. After the elections they assumed a sharply aggressive attitude and persistently provoked disturbances and clashes with the police, which in turn caused counter-measures, trials, and political tension. It created a situation which raised the hopes of all enemies of the young Republic both at home and abroad. Elements disloyal and inimical to Czechoslovakia had found a congenial temporary or permanent political base in the Slovak People's Party. An example was the Slovak renegade, Vojtech Tuka, a former professor of law, who succeeded in gaining the confidence of Hlinka, whom he used

[3] František Bokes: Dejiny Slovákov a Slovenska (History of the Slovaks and of Slovakia), IV. Bratislava, 1946, pp. 369-370, 379-380.

for his own political purposes. V. Tuka introduced dangerous trends into the Slovak People's Party and established secret political contacts with Austria, Hungary, and even with Hitler's National Socialists. From 1923 to 1926 he was the secret publisher of the Vienna French language periodical "Correspondence Slovaque," devoted to propaganda inimical to Czechoslovakia. Tuka also became the chief ideologist who formulated the political demands of the Populists with the ability of an experienced jurist. Yet his radicalism provoked resentment even among many of the Populist leaders. Tuka spoke of Slovak Catholic youth as of "Christ's Guards" and of Slovakia as "Christ's Slovakia." [4] On August 3, 1922, the Slovak People's Party issued a memorandum proposed by Tuka, demanding an amendment to the Peace Treaty of Saint-Germain granting the right of self-determination to the Slovaks. The memorandum was delivered by Tuka to the Council of Ambassadors in Paris and Geneva. As soon as he had sufficiently established his position in the party, which he represented in Parliament, and in the party paper, "Slovak," as its Editor in Chief he proceeded to set up semi-military bands of party-guards, the "Rodobrana." The government could not tolerate this imitation of foreign totalitarian organizations and was compelled to forbid them for reasons of public security. The party-paper "Slovák" had written about these troopers: "The brilliant example of Italy lights up the road for us. It calls us to action. We Slovaks shall stand guard. Our gallant 'Rodobrana,' the Slovak Fascists, are fired by enthusiasm, their muscles are straining with self-assurance. They are animated by your phenomenal fascist firmness, resolution, and fearlessness. We are firmly convinced that by defending ourselves we are saving our fatherland, and rendering valuable services to all mankind." [5]

[4] Dr. Ján Brezovský, Cesta k samostatnosti (The Road to Freedom), Bratislava, 1941, p. 13.
[5] "Slovák," Bratislava, year VII, number 146.

On New Year's Day 1928, Tuka published a sensational article in the "Slovák" under the headline "In the Tenth Year of the Martin Declaration," alleging that it had contained a secret clause. The gist of his argument was stated as follows, "On October 31, 1928, extraordinary conditions, a *vacuum juris,* will exist in one half of the Czecho-Slovak Republic. On that critical day the ethical foundation of certain constitutional clauses will cease to exist, legal continuity will be interrupted, the temporary validity of certain laws will be terminated as a matter of principle." The article relied on allegations which were objectively untrue. In the ensuing great political trial over the alleged "secret clause" which took place on April 8 and 9, 1926, it was proved beyond doubt that the Declaration of the Slovak Nation of October 30, 1918, contained no secret clause. On October 5, 1929, Tuka faced trial for this article and for his subversive contacts with foreign powers and was sentenced to 15 years in jail. The man who was largely responsible for driving the Slovak People's Party toward radicalism disappeared for a while from the party and from Slovak political life.[6]

The intensification of the political struggle on the part of Andrej Hlinka and the Slovak People's Party was reflected in the results of the elections of November 15, 1925, when the Populists went into the general elections alone, without the Czech Catholics. They won 486,027 votes or a total of 32% of the Slovak voters giving them 23 of the 56 Slovak seats in Parliament. This was their greatest electoral success. After the election the party changed its attitude toward the Czechoslovak Government and joined forces with the government on January 15, 1927. The political deal which was their price for joining the government was the abolition of the "county" administrative system in Slovakia, which had

[6] Martin Grečo: Martinská Deklarácia (The Martin Declaration), Bratislava, 1939, pp. 174-185.

proved very satisfactory, and the establishment of a provincial administration for the Land of Slovakia. These changes meant establishing Slovakia as an administrative unit; the Populists claimed it was the first "spark of autonomy." Two Populists were given cabinet appointments in the Czechoslovak Government: Jozef Tiso and Marko Gažík, who was subsequently replaced by L'udovit Labaj. Tiso became Minister of Health and the others in turn Minister of Unification. After Tuka's trial the Populists once more walked out of the government and resumed their original line of opposition to the Government. In the general election which followed soon after, (October 27, 1929), they lost much of their previous gains. This time they obtained only 403,681 votes (28%) and 18 of the 56 Slovak seats in Parliament. This defeat was the direct result of their change in policy, of the ill feeling aroused by the Tuka affair and of strife inside the party. Such notable members as Ferdiš Juriga and Florián Tománek left the party, which had set up Tuka as a candidate for Parliament even after he had gone to jail. He failed to get elected.

The party, now substantially weakened, nevertheless continued to fight with the same methods. In fact the violence of its attacks increased, for a new generation of young members of the party, indoctrinated and led by Vojtech Tuka, was moving to the fore. They rallied around the review "Nástup," edited by two young lawyers, the brothers Ján and Ferdinand Ďurčanský. The group of young Populists came to be known as the "Nástupists." They were in sharp opposition to their own party, which had always claimed Slovak Autonomy within the framework of the Czechoslovak Republic, and their attacks upon the Republic now developed into a fight with no holds barred. Their political extremism gained followers both among the leaders of the Slovak People's Party and a large section of their members.

In the thirties radical trends of opposition were finding

a propitious atmosphere in Czechoslovakia. A deep economic depression with much unemployment had set in as the result of the general world depression. Grave political peril was threatening from abroad owing to Hitler's coming to power in the neighboring German Reich. The latter event brought about the creation of a new political party among the Sudeten-German minority in Czechoslovakia under the leadership of Konrad Henlein, operating entirely in accordance with secret orders from Berlin. The Slovak Populists were quick to exploit the situation and now they too began applying terror where democratic methods were judged unsuitable for their purposes. On May 12, 1932, by a surprise move, Andrej Hlinka forced his own candidates upon the annual assembly of the oldest Slovak cultural institution, the Matica, in which he had hitherto shown no interest whatever. His interference caused political influences to be introduced into the management of this institution, which, until then, had been independent of political parties and had served the entire nation. On June 25 and 26, 1932, at the Convention of Young Slovak Intelligentsia in Trenčianske Teplice the Populists managed to gain control of the meetings and to push through a resolution alleging, with complete disregard for facts, that "the entire younger generation of Slovaks is in favor of autonomy." On October 16, 1932, Andrej Hlinka proclaimed "national unity" with Martin Rázus, the leader of the other Slovak autonomist party, the Slovak National Party. Both parties together represented scarcely one third of the Slovak electorate and their union hardly meant a union of the nation. But the most drastic example of Hlinka's policy of surprises and intimidations was the Nitra incident. On August 13, 1933, the nation officially celebrated the 1,100 year's anniversary of the consecration of the first Christian Church in Slovakia. The Prime Minister of Czechoslovakia and a number of cabinet ministers as well as numerous foreign dignitaries were present when Hlinka,

leading a large column of his party followers, entered the
festival grounds, provoked a riot, and delivered a violent
tirade, which turned this great national celebration into a
party demonstration, all this in the presence of a large number
of Catholic archbishops, bishops, and high secular and church
delegates from all over the world. This provoked further
conflict in the country, vindictiveness, and political tension.
One of the Populists gestures of defiance was their ostentatious
abstention from voting on the occasion of the fourth reelection
of President Thomas G. Masaryk.

The last parliamentary elections before Munich and the
Second World War were held in the spring of 1935, amidst
internal political tension and under the threatening clouds
of Adolf Hitler's aggression. It was generally assumed that
the opposition and the radical political elements would win
the elections. Notwithstanding some very intensive campaigning of the opposition parties, only the Henlein Sudeten-
German party achieved any gains. It became the strongest
single party as to the number of votes and second in parliamentary seats. The Slovak Autonomists made no gains! The
Slovak People's Party had joined the Slovak National Party
as well as some other minor autonomist fractions in an
Autonomist Bloc for the elections, but they obtained only
489,641 votes of the 1,620,000 votes in Slovakia, a mere
30%. This gave the Autonomist Bloc, 20 of the 56 Slovak
seats in Parliament. One of these went to the chairman of the
Slovak National Party, Martin Rázus, and 19 to the Populists
—the same number they had after the 1929 elections. The
results proved that political radicalism had failed to attract
votes. The extremists commanded only about one fourth of
the Slovak electorate. This indicated their real strength and
sharply discounted their claim to speak for the entire Slovak
Nation.

Following the 1935 election, the Prime Minister of Czechoslovakia, the Slovak Milan Hodža, tried very hard to get the Slovak People's Party to join in forming a government, because that would have considerably strengthened the country in domestic matters and in its foreign relations. The Populists, however, refused all offers to share the responsibility for the country's future. They preferred to embark on a more radical course of action. Inside the party the Nastupist wing had gained the upper hand, reinforced by the political opportunists in the party who were tempted by the prospects of gains with the aid of the Germans, both inside the country and abroad.

The Slovak People's Party radicalism and totalitarian inclinations became especially clear at its seventh party convention in Piešťany on September 19, 1936. At this convention the party announced its opposition not only to the government's domestic but also to the Republic's foreign political orientation. The convention demanded that "Czechoslovakia join the anti-Communist front of nations which are guided by Christian principles." What they really meant was that Czechoslovakia should join forces with the right-wing authoritarian bloc consisting principally of Hitlerite Germany and Mussolini's Italy. They objected to the Czechoslovak-Soviet Treaty of Alliance, which Czechoslovakia had signed in 1935, to counter the ever increasing threat of Nazi aggression.

Even at this point, Hlinka's Slovak People's Party did not withdraw its allegiance to the Czechoslovak Republic, as is clear from statements made by its leaders. On February 25, 1933, Jozef Tiso, the party's deputy chairman declared: "Our autonomy does not mean any separatism" and on October 20, 1933, "We want to live in the (Czechoslovak) Republic and wish to regard this State as our own." On November 29, 1934, he again emphasized, "We do not feel that our Autonomism is aimed at establishing a dualistic form of State" and proclaimed as late as March 29, 1938, "Hlinka's Slovak People's Party stands for the indivisible unity of the Czechoslovak State and considers the Czechoslovak Republic as the state in which Slovak individuality can fully expand." No less unequivocal were the words of the Secretary-General of the Party, Martin Sokol, in the Prague Parliament on March 9, 1938, "Hlinka's People's Party stands firmly on the ground of this state, because this state is also the state of the Slovaks and whoever should raise his hand against the freedom and independence of the Czechoslovak State, would at the same time also be raising it against the freedom of the Slovak Nation." Many years later, after the catastrophe of the Second World War had passed over Slovakia, Jozef Tiso was still proclaiming, at his own trial before the National Tribunal in Bratislava, on March 17, 1947, that "nobody can doubt Hlinka's loyalty to the Czechoslovak Republic."

The other Autonomist party, the Slovak National Party, whose chairman was the notable poet and author, Martin Rázus, was also in opposition to the Czechoslovak Government and in favor of decentralization and autonomy for Slovakia, yet it never resorted to the unreasonable methods of the Populists. This party's significance lay not in its numbers, as it had never obtained more than 3 to 5% of the votes of Slovakia but rather in the fact that it was the oldest political party in Slovakia and a symbol of national resistance to Hungarian domination. What is more, its membership consisted predominantly of Slovak Protestants who were traditionally far closer to the Czechs than the Catholics. This party's loyalty to the Czechoslovak Republic was beyond doubt. The public speeches of Martin Rázus, his articles, as well as his entire literary work and political activities provide sufficient proof of this. Suffice it to quote briefly from two of his parliamentary speeches. On October 20, 1933, he said that, "By Autonomy we do not wish to break up this state. We stand behind it and will defend it," and on November 7,

1935, "we wish to maintain this Republic, we wish to maintain democracy in it." The alliance of the two Autonomist parties barely survived the 1935 elections. The Slovak National Party let it be known that the Populists had not kept faith with their pre-election promises, and that they were therefore forced to review their attitude towards them. After that, the Populists went their own way alone.

The critical year for the Czechoslovak Republic, 1938, was approaching. The great statesman, philosopher and European, President Thomas G. Masaryk, had died on September 14, 1937, and had been followed in office by the Foreign Minister Edvard Beneš, his collaborator for many years. The Slovak People's Party, strangely enough, voted for him as President. Ominous, dark clouds were gathering over Czechoslovakia, now openly threatened by Hitler from abroad and shaken by the ever increasing lawlessness of the Sudeten-German Party under Henlein inside the state. Armaments for the defense of the Republic became Czechoslovakia's first concern. At this grave moment the paper "Slovák" published a leading article on January 1, 1938, entitled, "Forward! On with the Attack in the New Year!" In it the Slovak People's Party announced a still sharper political course of action, which further aggravated internal conditions. Andrej Hlinka, by now aged, tired and seriously ill, no longer controlled events. He had become a symbol, instead of an active political leader, and his party now began forsaking his more reasonable principles and gradually embarking on a course inimical to Czechoslovakia, a course which was separatist and totalitarian.

A delegation of Henlein's Sudeten-German Party came to see Andrej Hlinka in Ružomberok on February 8, 1938. It consisted of three Sudeten-German members of the Czechoslovak Parliament, Karl Hermann Frank, Franz Karmasin and Ernst Kundt, and Secretary Kreisel. The purpose of the visit was to exchange views and to arrive at a political agreement regarding mutual political support between Sudeten-Germans and Populists.[7] This visit marked the crossroads at which the Slovak People's Party openly turned its back on the democratic past and began the fateful journey toward political subjugation to Hitler. The party now showed ever clearer signs of imitating the strategy and tactics which had been employed by the Germans against Czechoslovakia, ever since the 1935 elections. Many of the party's leaders and especially the young extremists now paid only lip service to Czechoslovakia. Their occasional professions of loyalty were but camouflage for their separatist activities. They accepted democratic institutions only as long as these happened to serve their purposes. Their real devotion was to totalitarian methods and hunger for exclusive power in the State became their supreme motivation.

Such were the overtones of the political mass-rally organized by the Slovak People's Party on June 5, 1938, in Bratislava, on the occasion of the twentieth anniversary of the Pittsburgh Agreement. A special delegation of the Slovak League in America came to the meeting, led by its chairman, Dr. Peter P. Hletko. They brought the original of the agreement with them. Fundamentally the radical Populists were no longer interested in having the principles of the Pittsburgh Agreement incorporated into the Constitution, although the rally did propose a draft law for the Autonomy of Slovakia. What the extremists in the party now wanted was to demonstrate the strength and dynamism of the party. Small wonder then, that the representative of the Henlein-Germans, Karmasin, occupied a position of honor all through the affair, at the side of Andrej Hlinka and Dr. Peter P. Hletko. It was Hlinka's last public appearance. He died soon after, on August 16, 1938. [8]

Hlinka's death coincided with the critical period of Hitler's

[7] Documents on German Foreign Policy, 1918-1945, D/II, Washington, 1949, pp. 124-125.
[8] Dr. L. G. Fagul'a: Andrej Hlinka, Bratislava, 1943, pp. 5-172.

pre-Munich aggressiveness, a period when not only the Republic, but the Slovak People's Party needed leaders of firm principles. Hlinka had been such a leader. With his departure, the party lost its founder and man of authority, the steady-handed, uncompromising helmsman. The Czechoslovak Republic also lost a great son, who even on his deathbed beseeched his collaborators to uphold Czechoslovakia. Few of his political successors heeded this advice. The party, deprived of its leader, became engulfed at once in a violent struggle for supremacy, which was conducted behind the scenes between Father Jozef Tiso and Karol Sidor, the first representing the clerical wing of the party, the latter its lay elements. At the same time the struggle continued as to political orientation. The old Populists, who remained faithful to Hlinka's principles, were in favor of Autonomy for Slovakia within the Czechoslovak Republic. Their opponents, consisting mainly of younger radicals, were soon to have their leader, Vojtech Tuka, released from prison before the expiration of his sentence. They stood for Slovak separatism, for political totalitarianism, and for close cooperation with Karmasin, Henlein and Adolf Hitler, though a few preferred a close collaboration with Poland. Polish foreign policy under Colonel Beck's regime had its own ambitions with Slovakia and relied upon the help of the Slovak Populists. The young radicals gravitating towards the Third Reich gained the upper hand. Munich and the events that followed helped them considerably.

Chapter Two

SEPARATISM

*Hitler's Plan to Destroy Czechoslovakia — The Sudeten-Germans —
Konrad Henlein — Collaboration Between Henlein's Followers and
the Slovak Separatists — Berlin Finances Henlein and the Separatists
— Political Instructions from Berlin — The Munich Crisis — Černák's
Ultimatum — The Seizure of Power in Slovakia by the Populists —
The Germans in Slovakia and Franz Karmasin — Trips Abroad —
Autonomism Replaced by Separatism — Conspiracy and Plots*

In "Mein Kampf" written years before his coming to power in
Germany, Adolf Hitler clearly explained his national socialist
ideology and his proposed domestic and foreign policies. What
he was aiming at was to undo the German defeat in the First
World War and to resume the policy of "Drang nach Osten."
His immediate objectives were three neighboring states East
of Germany: Poland, Czechoslovakia and Austria. He decided
to conquer them one by one, not by a single blow. To achieve
this, he was to fall first upon the weakest state, Austria, and
then upon Czechoslovakia. With this in mind he concluded a
treaty with Pilsudski's Poland in January, 1934, which blocked
any attempt at establishing a united front against German Nazi
aggression. Polish animosity against Czechoslovakia drew new
strength from the pact. Then the Soviet Union entered the
European political arena. It became a member of the League
of Nations and concluded a treaty of alliance with France on
May 2, 1935, and with Czechoslovakia on May 16 of the
same year. At the same time German policy was faced with

85

the dramatic alternative of either renouncing its plans for expansion and settling down in the "living space" allocated to Germany by the Treaty of Versailles, or else of risking war against both the West and the East. Hitler chose the second alternative. But first he went after limited objectives, Austria and Czechoslovakia, which he sought to subjugate without having to fight for them. On March 12, 1938, he occupied Austria by marching into Vienna without the loss of a single German soldier, having achieved this victory by intrigue and intimidation. It was the opening act of the Central European crisis. His next objective was Czechoslovakia.

Hitler knew that Czechoslovakia would be a tougher nut to crack. His pretext for intervention in Czechoslovakia's internal affairs was the so called Sudeten-German question, and by pressure and intimidation he tried to force Czechoslovakia to solve the problem according to his desires. In the campaign of intimidation he could rely on a powerful fifth column, consisting of the majority of Germans living in Czechoslovakia, of a part of the Magyars there, and of the extremist wing of the Slovak People's Party.[1] His conspiracy had been prepared even before the attack upon Austria. In June 1937 he had ordered the drawing up of military plans for an attack upon Czechoslovakia, known under the code name "Fall Green" and when he explained this plan to his military chiefs in the Berlin Reich-Chancellery on November 5, 1937, he brazenly declared that "the problem for Germany is how to gain the greatest possible booty at least cost, and where." As soon as Austria had been annexed to the Reich, Hitler returned to his plan of attack on Czechoslovakia. He discussed this with General Keitel on April 21, 1938. The "Fall Green" plan expressly stated that "The necessary conditions to justify such an action politically and in the eyes of

[1] Arnold Toynbee — Frank I. Ashton-Gwatkin: The World in March 1939, Oxford, 1952, p. 287.

international law must be created beforehand." On January 30, 1939, Hitler admitted in the Reichstag, that following the Czechoslovak mobilization which had been carried out in May 1938 in face of a threat of German attack, "on May 28, I ordered first: that preparation should be made for military action against this state by the second of October." Section 3/b of the plan explained the mode of procedure "Issue directions to national groups for support in the 'armed war' and influence neutrals to our way of thinking." [2]

Political preparations against Czechoslovakia proceeded simultaneously with German military preparations. The Sudeten-German Party (SDP) has been organized after the pattern of Hitler's National-Socialist German Workers' Party (NSDAP), with Konrad Henlein as its leader. In a speech in Vienna on March 4, 1941, Henlein admitted that "we were, of course, secretly in touch with the National Socialist revolution in Germany so that we might be a part of it. The struggle for Greater Germany was waged on Sudeten soil, too. This struggle could be waged only by those inspired by the spirit of National Socialism, persons who were true followers of our Führer, whatever their outward appearance." He then continued: "In the autumn of 1933 the leader of the NSDAP asked me to take over the political leadership of the Sudeten Germans." In the end Henlein acknowledged that he had decided in favor of "a struggle under camouflage and by methods which appeared quite legal to the outside world" for that was the only way "we could have fulfilled the political task of destroying Czechoslovakia, a bastion in the alliance against the German Reich." [3] These statements speak for themselves and require no comment.

On May 16, 1938, the German Minister in Prague, Ernst Eisenlohr, cabled the following dispatch to Berlin: "The line

[2] Trial of the Major War Criminals before the International Military Tribunal, Nuremberg, 1947 (further referred to as Trial of War Criminals), III/36-44.
[3] Opus cit. III/71

of German foreign policy, as it is transmitted by the German Legation, is exclusively decisive for policy and tactics of the Sudeten German Party. My directives will be complied with implicitly. Public speeches and the press will be coordinated uniformly with my approval. The editorial staff of *Zeit* (Time) is to be improved. Henlein will establish contact with me every week and will come to Prague at any time, if requested. I now hope to have the Sudeten German Party under firm control, as this is more than ever necessary for future developments in the interest of foreign policy. Please inform Ministries concerned and Mittelstelle (Central Office for Racial Germans) and request them to support this uniform direction of the Sudeten German Party." On the following day, March 17, 1938, Henlein wrote to the Reich's Foreign Minister von Ribbentrop: "We shall show our appreciation to the Führer by doubled effort in the service of the Greater German policy." Henlein, K. H. Frank, and other leading Germans from Czechoslovakia called on the Führer, Adolf Hitler, on March 28, 1938, and were given detailed instructions as to the manner of proceeding against the Czechoslovak Government. On the second day of that visit Ribbentrop advised Henlein to seek cooperation between the Sudeten German Party and "other minorities in Czechoslovakia, especially with the Slovaks." [4]

As indicated earlier, Henlein already had entered into contact with the Slovak People's Party and his emissaries had made an agreement with Andrej Hlinka on February 8, 1938. The Slovak People's Party confidential agent in Vienna, Rudolf Vávra, himself a Separatist, had arranged for two pronouncedly radical members of his party, Alexander Mach and Ferdinand Ďurčanský, to be in touch with the Viennese "Heimatsbund," organization of the Sudeten Germans. On March 29, 1938, Jozef Tiso voted in the Czechoslovak Parliament in

4 Opus cit. III/72-74

favor of Henlein's demands, in compliance with the secret agreement of February 8, 1938. On April 24, 1938, he agreed with the Germans to coordinate their anti-Czechoslovak propaganda. In the Summer of 1938, the Slovak People's Party appointed one of its Members of Parliament, Štefan Haššík, liaison officer with the Headquarters of the Sudeten German Party. Meanwhile, extremist Populists were in constant touch with the representative of the Henlein Party in Slovakia, Franz Karmasin, a paid Berlin agent. For his services Karmasin was receiving 30,000 Reichs Marks per month, and after April 1, 1940, 15,000 Marks. Since 1935 Henlein's Party had been receiving regular contributions from the Ministry of Foreign Affairs of the German Reich. These monthly contributions amounted to 15.000 Marks.[5] Not only the Germans were being paid by Berlin, but the young radical separatists of the Slovak People's Party were also receiving money from the Nazis. A memo of Günther Altenburg, chief of the Political Division IV-b of the Reich Ministry of Foreign Affairs, dated November 29, 1938, contains the following statement: "The Security Service (Sicherheitsdienst) maintains certain connections in Czechoslovakia which have proved useful in recent months. It has followed as a result of these connections that the Security Service has financed certain journeys of Slovak Ministers (for instance Ďurčanský), as well as journeys of other official Slovak persons who were to study state and Party institutions in the Reich." [6]

Thus the parties of Henlein and of Hlinka were guilty of treasonable and incriminating activities even before the Munich crisis. The Sudeten Germans and the Slovak Separatists were "useful," not to their own state but to a foreign power.

As October 2, 1938, the day designated in plan "Fall Green" for the attack upon Czechoslovakia drew nearer, the

---

[5] Opus cit. III/75, 147-148
[6] Documents on German Foreign Policy, D/IV, Washington, 1951, pp. 171-172

Germans had to keep increasing the pressure upon the Czechoslovak Government both from abroad and inside the country.
One of the moves under this plan was Henlein's announcement
of the notorious "Eight Points" in Karlovy Vary on April 24,
1938, which contained totally unacceptable demands for the
settlement of the Czechoslovak-Sudeten German problem.
These radical demands were made not for the benefit of the
Germans in Czechoslovakia but solely for the Third Reich.[7]
In May 1938, Germany concentrated troops along the Czechoslovak border and Czechoslovakia reacted by ordering a
partial mobilization on May 20. This is said to have enraged
Hitler to such an extent that he swore to destroy Czechoslovakia at all cost. The Henlein people continued to negotiate
with the Czechoslovak Government, allegedly in an effort to
settle the problem by agreement, but in reality the discussions
were no more than a maneuver to distract the attention of the
Czechoslovak and European leaders from the feverish preparations for a German attack on Czechoslovakia, according to
the original plan. In pursuance of this, Hitler instructed Henlein on September 1, 1938, to reject all proposals for a compromise which might be put forward by the Czechoslovak
Government and to demand nothing less than the ceding of
the so called Sudeten regions of Czechoslovakia to Germany.
The real crisis concerning the Sudeten Germans developed
after the incredibly aggressive speech Adolf Hitler made
against Czechoslovakia at the NSDAP Rally in Nuremberg
on September 12, 1938. This gave the Henleinists the green
light to stage a coup by force. They mobilized their Storm
Troopers and party-henchmen, and provoked incidents and
riots, yet their efforts failed. Berlin exerted immense political
and military pressure upon Czechoslovakia, and the danger
of a German-Czechoslovak war was very near at hand.

[7] S. Harrison Thomson: Czechoslovakia in European History, Princeton, N. J.,
1953, pp. 378 et seq.

France, bound by treaty to come to Czechoslovakia's aid in case of an unprovoked attack upon that country, gave clear indications that she was not going to fulfill her pledge. The Soviet Union, on the other hand, argued that her duty to come to the aid of Czechoslovakia was conditional upon France also fulfilling her obligations as an ally. Great Britain, speaking through her Prime Minister Sir Neville Chamberlain, left the world in no doubt that she was devoted to a policy of appeasing Hitler and saving temporarily the peace of Europe at the expense of Czechoslovakia. As a result, the British Prime Minister undertook several trips to see Hitler.

To insure his success Hitler intervened also in the domestic political affairs of Czechoslovakia. Apart from directing the Sudeten Germans, he had reactivated a liaison with the Slovak People's Party. On September 8, 1938, the representatives of Henlein's Sudeten German Party met with those of the Slovak People's Party, as well as with representatives of the united Magyar parties, and the Polish Committee of Understanding and agreed on a joint plan for the "reconstruction" of Czechoslovakia and a "settlement" of the nationality problems. On September 19, 1938, the Reich German Ministry of Foreign Affairs cabled the German Minister in Prague (See Document No. 6) requesting him to relay a message to the Sudeten German Member of Parliament, Ernst Kundt, that Henlein was to "get in touch with the Slovaks at once, and induce them to start their demand for autonomy tomorrow."[8]

How did the Slovak People's Party react to this suggestion by a foreign government at the moment when Czechoslovakia was facing the gravest crisis since the establishment of the Republic? Did the Party refuse the suggestion and redeem its national honor, or did it obey and thereby betray its own nation? The Slovak People's Party, which by then had lost its leader, Andrej Hlinka, chose the second alternative. The

---

[8] Trial of War Criminals, III/77.

German Legation in Prague notified the Reich Ministry of Foreign Affairs in Berlin on September 20, 1938, that Kundt had established contact with the Slovak People's Party even before the cable from Berlin instructed him to do so. (See Document No. 7). The result of this was that the Slovak People's Party proclaimed its own political demands on September 20 and these included: 1. Recognition of the Slovaks as a separate national entity; 2. Immediate and final settlement of the Slovak question in accordance with the Pittsburgh Agreement, and the most recent demands of the Slovak People's Party. On September 21 and 22, Jozef Tiso and the Secretary General of the Party, Martin Sokol, called on the Czechoslovak Prime Minister, Milan Hodža, in Prague and presented the demands for Slovak autonomy in such a manner that it was entirely impossible for the government and Parliament to accept them. The situation of the Republic had become so critical that an acceptance was out of question, and the Slovak Populists were, of course, well aware of this. The Party leaders, moreover, sent a letter to the President of the Republic, Edvard Beneš, on September 23 in which they energetically protested against the mobilization of the Czechoslovak Army which had been ordered to defend the State against the imminent armed German attack. There is a clear causal relation between these actions of the Slovak People's Party and the cable from Berlin of September 19, containing instructions from Hitler. By its conduct the Slovak People's Party decisively weakened the political and military ability of the Republic to resist the threat to its very existence.

Meanwhile the pre-Munich crisis had reached its climax. On September 29, 1938, Germany, Itály, Great Britain and France signed an agreement in Munich, purporting to settle the problem of the so called Sudeten Germans and of the Magyar minority in Czechoslovakia. (See Document No. 8). The Munich Agreement left Czechoslovakia with a truncated territory and at Hitler's mercy. Munich was Hitler's greatest triumph. . . [9] Czechoslovakia suffered a mortal blow and from now on it was but a question of time before Hitler would completely destroy the Republic. Czechoslovakia was broken up for the first time, and Czechs and Slovaks were split apart for the second time in their history. September 29, 1938, was to be a fateful day not only for the unfortunate Republic, but also for all Europe, and indeed all the world. By subduing Czechoslovakia, Hitler had outflanked Poland from the South and had advanced to the frontiers of Roumania. The balance of European power was seriously disturbed, and all the influence of France and the democratic West was squeezed out of Central Europe, where the Third Reich became temporary master.

In August 1939, Hitler signed his pact with the USSR and then invaded Poland—that same Poland which under the authoritarian regime of the "Colonels' Clique" had so eagerly helped to devour forsaken and betrayed Czechoslovakia— and ignited the flames of the Second World War which were to engulf Europe and bring his own downfall. Both West and East were to pay dearly for the Munich victory. Daladier's policy led to the military defeat of France in 1940. Chamberlain's policy left Great Britain isolated and forced to endure the terrible German air and sea attacks of 1940-1941. Moscow's collaboration with Hitler led first to its isolation and later to the German attack on the Soviet Union and to the occupation of large parts of its territory by the Nazis. It meant that the war was dragged out for several more years. This was the price the Western powers had to pay for having dealt with the threat to Czechoslovakia as if it were but a local German-Czechoslovak problem, and for not having united against Hitler's aggression in 1938. As though this were not enough, the most tragic political consequence of the Munich Agreement

[9] Sir Lewis Namier: In the Nazi Era, London, 1952, pp. 149-167.

was yet to come. The military defeat of the Third Reich submerged Central and Eastern Europe in the Soviet world. The Munich Agreement of the four European Great Powers became the hinge on which European political developments were to turn.

For Czechoslovakia, Munich was the beginning of the end, first of her territorial integrity, then of her democratic political system, and in the end, of her very liberty. The last parliamentary Government of Czechoslovakia, with Milan Hodža as Prime Minister, fell on September 22, 1938, and General Jan Syrový became the new Prime Minister. The Slovak People's Party did not participate in forming the new Government but one of their members, Matúš Černák, a young radical senior high school teacher was given a cabinet appointment. Scarcely had Černák been sworn in he immediately presented on October 3, 1938, an ultimatum to the Government and to President Beneš, demanding in the name of the Slovak People's Party that executive and administrative powers in Slovakia be immediately handed over to the Slovak People's Party. He threatened to resign in case of refusal. What Černák and the Slovak Populists now wanted was to grab all power in Slovakia by illegal and anti-democratic methods, since in reality they represented no more than one-fourth of the Slovak electorate. For this they had chosen the very moment when Czechoslovakia, harassed on all sides, had just been shorn of large areas for Germany's benefit, when Hungary was about to seize the Southern districts of Slovakia and all of Subcarpathian Ruthenia and when the Poles were about to occupy certain regions along the Northern frontiers. Czechoslovakia was in the throes of a tragic political and psychological depression. It was precisely this situation the Populists chose to exploit in their bid for total power. They correctly estimated that the Czechoslovak Government would not be able to resist the twofold threat to the very survival of the State, aggression by greedy neighbors and a serious internal crisis provoked by the disloyal Populists in Slovakia. When Černák's ultimatum was not accepted, he resigned on October 4, 1938, and this created a new government crisis which was followed, on October 5, by the resignation of the President of the Republic, Edvard Beneš.

The day after the tragic decision taken in Munich, the leaders of the Slovak People's Party decided to convoke the 60-member executive committee of their Party to meet in Žilina on October 6, 1938. This decision was timed to coincide with the resignation of Černák. Superficially the meeting was to appear a normal convention of the Executive Committee of the Party, but in reality it was to be the occasion for grabbing all executive power in Slovakia, a political coup. With complete disregard for democratic realities, the Executive Committee declared that the Slovak People's Party was the only true representative of Slovakia and demanded the exclusive power to control the fate of the Slovaks. Coincidently they demanded that the proposals for Slovak autonomy, which the Populists had so loudly proclaimed at their rally in Bratislava on June 5, 1938, be enacted as a constitutional amendment not later than October 28, 1938. If that were done, the constitutional position in Czechoslovakia would be settled forever. At the same time the Executive Committee of the Party decided to transfer the governmental and administrative powers in Slovakia to a Slovak Government at once, without waiting for appropriate legislative authorization. This government was to consist of a Prime Minister and four cabinet members and was to be formed by the acting leader of the Slovak People's Party, Jozef Tiso, as prime minister-designate. The other Czechoslovak and Slovak political parties had received advance information of what was being prepared by the Populists in Žilina and all of them with the exception of the Communists therefore sent representatives to Žilina to take appropriate measures. Some of these representatives, acting without authority of their own parties, individually jumped onto the Populist band-wagon, while others obeyed party instructions and endeavored to restrain the radicals and to prevent a catastrophe.

The situation was confused even in the Slovak People's Party itself. After Hlinka's death, two principal blocs struggled for leadership in the party and there were two candidates for leadership in each faction, of the Autonomists and of the Separatists. Jozef Tiso and Karol Sidor were competing for leadership in the Autonomist faction, while the Separatist wing was at first led by Ďurčanský, and a little later by Vojtech Tuka. On some issues the two groups were in sharp opposition to one another, such as on the question of whether Slovakia was to remain an autonomous part of the Czechoslovak Republic, as suggested by the Autonomists, or whether it should separate and form an independent state of its own. In other matters, however, both factions were in complete agreement. They thoroughly agreed that the Slovak People's Party should assume dictatorial powers in Slovakia and that democratic rights, liberties and institutions should be abolished. Step by step the Separatists were gaining the upper hand and eventually even the moderate and still democratically inclined functionaries succumbed to these radical tendencies. In the midst of so much uncertainty, nobody knew who would emerge as the head of the Populists after the Žilina meeting. The resolution carried on October 6, 1938, represented a compromise between the two wings of the party. In the matter of autonomy the more moderate group of Populists, the Autonomists, seemed to have won. As regards the political regime to be introduced in Slovakia, the radical Autonomists had carried the day. However, the victory of the more moderate Autonomists was to be of short duration, for soon after Žilina the Separatists moved into the driver's seat of the Slovak People's Party.

The Separatist group recognized that it lacked the strength to gain complete control of the Party, and through it, of Slovakia. Least of all could it rely on the support of the Slovak population. They could rely only on help from the Germans abroad and inside the country. At the time of the Munich crisis and immediately after it, the Separatists had not yet made up their mind who was to be the Protector of the independent Slovakia they were striving for, whether Germany or Poland. Some even looked toward Budapest. In any event they kept in close touch with Franz Karmasin as well as with the National Socialist Party in Germany, and high Populist party officials frequently traveled abroad to maintain contacts with their allies.

According to the 1930 census, there were 4.65% Germans living in Slovakia, and this percentage further decreased after the territorial changes following Munich. Under the constant pressure of Hitler's Germany, and especially as a result of the Munich events, this small German minority now became a state within the state. Their leader, Karmasin, who as a Sudeten German came from a part of Czechoslovakia other than Slovakia, was regarded as the real power behind the scene in the regime established by the Populists. No domestic or foreign policy matter was ever resolved without his approval, and his influence was felt in particular in the Populist demands for a separation of Slovakia from the Czech lands. The more subservient they became to the Third Reich, the more Karmasin dominated all their decisions. He became "Volksgruppenführer," that is Leader of the German Racial Group, a Secretary of State in the Slovak Government and a Member of the Slovak Diet. His principal role was to maintain contact between leading Populists and the Third Reich as well as the

NSDAP. He participated in most of the discussions held at that time between the representatives of the new Populist regime in Slovakia and German officials in the Reich. He also had the last word to say with regard to the policy toward Jews in Slovakia and the appointment of Germans to government and other public jobs. It was Karmasin who during the war saw to it that Germans from Slovakia served in the Army of the German Reich, not in that of Slovakia, and that they served in the German Armed SS and Security Corps. He used influence to integrate Slovak economy into the wartime industry of Germany. Karmasin and the group of people around him drew their organized support largely from the local German Party (DP), set up after the pattern of the NSDAP, from the uniformed Party Storm-Troops of Freiwillige Schutzstaffeln (FS), and the German Youth Organization, Deutsche Jugend (DJ). These organized bands had obtained the right to perform police duties without turning to the State police. The DP published two greatly expanded papers, the "Grenzbote" and the "Deutsche Stimmen," devoted to spreading German National-Socialist doctrines among Germans in Slovakia. What is more, Karmasin obtained financial support from the Slovak State for the DP, FS, and DJ. This numerically negligible minority in effect controlled a 90% majority of Slovaks up to Spring 1945 when almost all Germans emigrated ("evacuated") to Germany from Slovakia.

Everything that happened in Slovakia in those days shows how matters were made easy for the German Reich in Slovakia. This was frankly avowed by Viliam Ries-Javor, a Populist newspaperman: "In Germany, developments in Slovakia were followed with keen interest. When the Führer mentioned the Slovaks in his speech in the Berlin Sportpalast on September 26, 1938, he had the benefit of comprehensive information from Slovak and German sources. At that time the leaders of the Great German Reich were already counting on a separation of Czechs and Slovaks." [10] After Munich and after Žilina the Slovak Separatists, encouraged by those members of the Slovak People's Party who were still Autonomists, made a number of trips abroad, trips which were kept secret from the Czechoslovak Government, and indeed even from the Slovak Government. These were secret conspiratorial journeys of which the public knew little or nothing. The shroud of secrecy was lifted only by the publication of documents or memoirs in the free world after the end of the Second World War.

Following Hitler's tremendous success in Munich Field-Marshal Hermann Göring, the Prime Minister of Prussia and Chairman of the Reich's Parliament, held a secret conference in the Berlin Air Ministry on October 14, 1938, at which he declared that the Czech lands and Slovakia "would become German dominions" and that everything possible must be done toward that end. (see Document No. 9).[11] That is how the Third Reich and its Führer proposed to fulfill the obligations they had accepted at Munich to respect the sovereignty of the truncated Czechoslovak Republic. At about the same time, another meeting took place in Vienna, where Ferdinand Ďurčanský, Alexander Mach, and Franz Karmasin had gone to call on Arthur Seyss-Inquart. The object of the visit was to ask for German help for the separatist policy of the radical members of the Slovak People's Party. The three men left Vienna accompanied by Seyss-Inquart and proceeded to Berlin to see Hermann Göring. Ďurčanský read a "Declaration" to Göring (see Document No. 10) in which he expressed "gratitude to the Führer for the help he had given the Slovaks, enabling them to achieve autonomy." The Declaration further stated that "the Slovaks want full independence and the closest possible political, economic and military ties with

[10] Viliam Ries-Javor: Kontinent v prerode (Continent in Regeneration), Bratislava, 1943, p. 30.
[11] Trial of War Criminals, IV/69.

Germany"; that "an independent Slovakia will be proclaimed in the first Slovak Diet"; that "the Jewish question will be settled in the same manner as in Germany"; that "German influence in the Slovak Government appears desirable"; and that "a German will be appointed to the Cabinet as Minister." Göring replied to the Slovak Separatist delegates that "Slovak efforts to achieve independence are to be aided in a suitable manner" because "Czechia without Slovakia will then be entirely at our (i.e. German) mercy." Göring made no secret of his conviction that airfields in Slovakia would be of vital importance to the Luftwaffe in action against the East. [12] Soon after the return of Ďurčanský, Mach and Karmasin from Berlin, Jozef Tiso, the Prime Minister of Slovakia, created the office of Secretary of State for German Affairs in the Cabinet and gave the appointment to Karmasin on October 25, 1938.

On October 19, 1938, Jozef Tiso and Ferdinand Ďurčanský left for Munich to see Joachim von Ribbentrop, accompanied by a member of the Government of autonomous Subcarpathian Ruthenia, Edmund Bačinský. Tiso expressed his gratitude to Adolf Hitler for his speech of September 26, 1938, "which had brought the Czechoslovak problem to the notice of the world." In return, Ribbentrop assured Tiso that "Germany had great understanding for the Slovak problem"; that it "would welcome the greatest possible measure of independence"; and that "Germany was perfectly willing to cooperate politically and economically with Slovakia." They then discussed the ceding of certain regions in the South of Slovakia and of Subcarpathian Ruthenia to the Magyars. After this visit, that very day, Ribbentrop received Tiso and Ďurčanský "quite unofficially and privately in order to ask them what they thought of the development of their relations with Prague." Tiso argued that Slovakia now had autonomy "under

[12] Documents on German Foreign Policy, D/IV, Washington, 1951, pp. 82-83. Trial of War Criminals, III/148-149.

Prague" but Ďurčanský "seemed to be striving rather for the complete independence of Slovakia." Tiso added that he "thought that he would have to steer developments slowly and methodically." [13]

Simultaneously with Tiso's and Ďurčanský's trip to Germany, two more representatives of the Slovak People's Party went abroad for political discussions. Alexander Mach left for Zagreb in Yugoslavia to discuss matters with Croats who were in opposition to the Yugoslav Government and Karol Sidor proceeded to Warsaw for talks with the Polish Government. It is not yet known what Mach discussed in Zagreb but a detailed account of Sidor's negotiations with the Poles has been published, in the notes of the Polish Deputy-Minister of Foreign Affairs, Count Jean Szembek (see Document No. 11).[14] Sidor met Szembek twice. On October 19, 1938, he declared to Szembek that "responsible Slovak authorities will preserve a disinterested attitude in the matter of Subcarpathian Ruthenia"; that the tendency in Slovakia was "to establish a Slovak State, which would be entirely independent but would lean politically, militarily, and culturally upon Poland, and economically upon Germany and Hungary." According to Sidor the Slovaks "are yearning to be under some sort of a political and military protectorate of Poland." Another Pole who was present, Kobylanski, reminded Sidor that "the question of the independence of Slovakia had already been raised in the Warsaw City Hall on the occasion of the visit of American Slovaks to Poland." (The visit referred to had been made by a delegation of the Slovak League in America, consisting of its chairman Dr. Peter P. Hletko, and its members Jozef Hušek, Michal Sinčák, and Rev. Andrej Rolík who had brought the original of the Pittsburgh Agreement to Slovakia in May 1938.) On October 20, 1938, Szembek formally re-

---

[13] Documents on German Foreign Policy, D/IV, Washington, 1951, pp. 86-93.
[14] Comte Jean Szembek: Journal 1933-1939, Paris, 1952, pp. 359-362.

ceived Sidor and he supplied Szembek with detailed information about the plans of the Slovak People's Party to separate Slovakia from the Czech lands. Sidor explained that after the election of the new President of Czechoslovakia the first objective of the Slovak Separatists had been to change the Czechoslovak Constitution so as to legalize Slovak autonomy. The next step was to present the Czechs with unacceptable demands. The ultimate step would be the declaration of independence by the Slovak Diet. In view of this, the Slovak Government was busy organizing its own police forces and army. In the end Sidor confirmed that Slovak "emissaries who had recently been dispatched to European capitals had been sent by the Slovak Prime Minister Tiso and not by the Prague Government."

In the Memoirs of the Polish Foreign Minister Joseph Beck it is mentioned that Sidor also came to see him in Warsaw and that in the course of his visit "nous parvinmes á une entente trés satisfaisante" (we came to a very satisfactory understanding), but, according to Beck, Sidor chose to forget the agreement with him (Beck) after he returned to Bratislava.[15] It is no longer possible to ascertain whether that visit occurred on the same trip during which Sidor saw Szembek.

All these activities of the Slovak Separatist leaders, which went on secretly and behind the back of the Czechoslovak Government of which both Tiso and Ďurčanský were regular members, are clear evidence that the Slovak People's Party was only pretending to be loyal to the Czechoslovak Republic, as the Sudeten Germans had done before Munich. Actually they were doing everything in their power to destroy Czechoslovakia. Subsequent political moves of the Slovak People's Party followed the same line.

When the direct negotiations between Hungary and Czecho-

---

[15] Colonel Joseph Beck: Dernier Rapport, Politique Polonaise, 1926-1939, Bruxelles, 1951, p. 171.

slovakia which took place in Komárno in October, 1938, with a view to drawing a new frontier between the two countries as ordered by Munich failed to achieve an agreement, Jozef Tiso requested the German and Italian Governments to decide the matter. Berlin and Rome agreed to arbitrate. On November 2, 1938, Ribbentrop and Count Galeazzo Ciano announced the Vienna Arbitration Award according to which Slovakia was to cede to Hungary almost a third of her territory, including the most fertile parts, and the cities of Komárno, Nové Zámky, Šahy, Lučenec, Rimavská Sobota, Rožňava, and Košice. 859,885 inhabitants were lost, including 276,285 Slovaks! The Separatists had been so cock-sure that Germany would arbitrate favorably for Slovakia that Matúš Černák publicly announced that Košice, the second largest Slovak city, would never fall to Hungary. And Tiso had written to Ribbentrop on October 25, 1938, "I thus place the future of my people and of my country in the hands of the Reich Chancellor and of Your Excellency." [16]

Even after the Vienna disappointment the Slovak Separatists continued to conspire with the leaders of National-Socialist Germany. On November 11, 1938, Ferdinand Ďurčanský and Franz Karmasin again went to see Hermann Göring, accompanied by Edmund Veesenmayer of the Keppler Division of the Reich Ministry of Foreign Affairs. Göring told them that "at the moment the Slovak and the Ukrainian question could be dealt with only within the framework of the Czechoslovak State, but the goal was an independent Slovakia and an Autonomous Ukraine, oriented toward this independent Slovakia." Göring ended the discussion by assuring his visitors that "he certainly would not make concessions to a Czechoslovakia, but only to a Slovakia." [17]

Meanwhile Vojtech Tuka had reentered the political scene,

---

16 Documents on German Foreign Policy, D/IV, Washington, 1951, pp. 110-111.
17 Opus cit. pp. 142-143.

his jail sentence having been remitted. The moment he was free he surrounded himself with young Separatists, his former disciples at the time he was a Member of Parliament for the Slovak People's Party and editor in chief of the "Slovák." They included Ferdinand Ďurčanský, Alexander Mach, Karol Murgaš, Jozef Joštiak, and Ján Farkaš. Before the year 1938 came to an end Tuka had been twice to Germany to see Hermann Göring and the Secretary of State Wilhelm Keppler. The subject of their discussions was the destruction of Czechoslovakia and the creation of a Slovak State under German protection. In an interview he gave to the party paper "Slovák" on New Year's Day, 1939, Tuka declared that in his opinion "historic days" lay ahead of Slovakia. He was clearly referring to the events that were to take place in Czechoslovakia in March 1939.

While Czechoslovakia entered the new year of 1939 amidst grave anxieties for the future, the Slovak Separatists started out with great confidence, convinced that the day was at hand on which their dream of an independent Slovakia would come true. Consequently they did everything possible to incite anti-Czech feelings through their propaganda-organization, directed by Alexander Mach. In all this time they acted strictly in accordance with instructions received from Berlin.

On February 5, 1939, Alexander Mach announced at a rally of the Hlinka Guards at Rišňovce that the highest ideal of the Slovak people was "to have its independent state." Both Mach and Ďurčanský instructed their confidential agent in Vienna, Ľudovít Mutňanský, who was the announcer of the Slovak language broadcasts beamed to Slovakia by the Viennese German radio, to intensify the anti-Czech tone of the broadcasts, to argue that it was impossible for the Slovaks to continue to live in one state with the Czechs, and to emphasize the idea of a Slovak State. Mutňanský eagerly complied.

A further visit of Vojtech Tuka and Franz Karmasin to the

Reich Chancellery in Berlin, on February 12, 1939, was to be politically significant. They were received by Hitler himself. Tuka addressed Hitler as "Mein Führer!" and declared that he was speaking for the Slovak nation. He acknowledged that Hitler "had not only opened the Slovak question but had also been the first man to recognize the dignity of the Slovak Nation." He further declared that "the Slovak nation will gladly fight under the Führer's leadership for the protection of European civilization," and that "further unity with the Czechs has become impossible for the Slovaks, for psychological as well as economic reasons." Tuka ended his speech with the words: "I lay the destiny of my people in your hands, my Führer, my people await their complete liberation by you." (See Document No. 12).

After Tuka returned home, Jozef Tiso in the last days of February 1939, sent a delegation of Slovak economic and political experts to Berlin, led by Mikuláš Pružinský and Ferdinand Ďurčanský. They were to discuss with Hermann Göring the terms of economic cooperation between Germany and Slovakia, although under the Czechoslovak Constitution and under the Constitutional Amendment which had granted Slovakia autonomy, the conduct of foreign relations was expressly reserved to the Czechoslovak Government and Czechoslovak Ministry of Foreign Affairs. This delegation was greeted by Göring with the words "Now then, when are you going to be independent so we don't have to give you to the Magyars?" (Testimony of Jozef Tiso before the National Tribunal in Bratislava, on December 4, 1946). Göring promised to support Slovakia economically "only in the event of their separation from the Czechs." [18]

On February 21, 1939, Jozef Tiso declared in the Slovak Diet, "Here, on the floor of our own Diet, we are building

---

[18] Karol Sidor: Moje poznámky k historickým dňom (My Remarks on the Historic Days), (in manuscript form in 1939).

our Slovak State . . . It must never happen again that the Slovak Nation should run counter to its own state." He was a little more articulate when he stated on March 6, 1939, that one had to insist on building the Slovak State "by evolutionary methods" and that one was not to declare its constitution "right now." It is hard to say whether that was Tiso's real feeling or only a tactical maneuver. Two other leaders of the Separatist wing of the Slovak People's Party, Tuka and Ferdinand Ďurčanský, the latter of whom also happened to be a Member of Tiso's Government of Slovakia, held different views. These two wanted a Slovak State to be created at once under German protection with or without the approval of the Slovak Diet. With this in mind they went to Vienna at the end of February 1939 to see the Secretary of State in the German Ministry of Foreign Affairs, Wilhelm Keppler. They agreed with Keppler on a detailed technical plan for the establishment of Slovak independence and also on the terms of a treaty to be concluded between Germany and an independent Slovak State. They saw the German Reich Governor in Vienna, Arthur Seyss-Inquart, and the Austrian "Gauleiter," Josef Bürckel, with whom they agreed upon the physical support the Reich was to give "the operations for independence" of Slovakia. None of this had the support of the Slovak people or of the Slovak Diet, and it did not even express the will of the members of the Slovak People's Party. The alleged liberation of Slovakia, as agreed between Tuka, Ďurčanský, Keppler, Seyss-Inquart, and Bürckel was a conspiracy to be carried out by acts of terrorism against anyone who stood in the way of the conspirators. It was agreed in Vienna that trained terrorists would be sent from Germany into Slovakia to create confusion. This would give the Germans a pretext to intervene against Czechoslovakia. The plan was carried out and Slovakia "liberated herself" strictly according to the plan of the Nazis and the Slovak Separatists.

In Vienna Ďurčanský and Mach also agreed that Rudolf
Vávra would arrange for the Hlinka Guards, who had been
organized in Germany, to prepare to join the Nazi terrorists
in their attack on Slovakia. These same men met an un-
identified German emissary in Bratislava early in March 1939
who had come to enquire which Populist leader was to be
asked to go and see Hitler in Berlin for the purpose of discussing the formal proclamation of the Slovak State. At the
same time the chief of the Reich German Security Service,
Reinhold Heydrich, and the Chief of the Reich Criminal
Police, Nebe, ordered bombs made in the shape of small metal
cans to be used in the "liberation" of Slovakia. A member of
the German Secret Service (Sicherheitsdienst) by the name of
Alfred Helmut Neujoks brought these explosives to Petržalka,
a suburb of Bratislava on the opposite bank of the Danube,
which had been occupied by Germany after the Munich
Agreement, and there delivered them to Franz Karmasin,
Ferdinand Ďurčanský, Alexander Mach, Karol Murgaš, and
Jozef Kirschbaum. The explosives as well as weapons were
then smuggled over to Bratislava by members of the Rodobrana, the Hlinka Guards and the FS and cached there to
remain until such time when they were to be turned against the
Czechoslovak police force and used to produce the sort of
political and psychological atmosphere that would favor the
conspiracy.

A further step toward carrying out the plans made in
Vienna was the first visit to Bratislava of Seyss-Inquart and
his Secretary Hammerschmidt on March 7, 1939. The visitors
went to the private apartment of Karol Sidor, at that time
Deputy Prime Minister in the Czechoslovak Government,
where they also met Jozef Tiso to discuss the achievement of
Slovak independence in accordance with the ideas of the
Separatists and the Germans. At this point differences of
opinion arose. Seyss-Inquart insisted on immediate action,

whereas Tiso and Sidor argued: "We can achieve independence progressively and peacefully, by walking or running." Seyss-Inquart was not satisfied and insisted: "Running is not enough. You must leap." The attitude of Tiso and Sidor reflected a recent decision taken by the Slovak Government on March 6, 1939, together with the Chairman of the Slovak Diet, Martin Sokol, and two leading members of the Slovak People's Party, Jozef Buday, and Julius Stano. These three men represented the autonomist and democratic wing of the party. On that occasion the Government decided to "insist on building a Slovak State by evolution" as Tiso had announced on the same day in the Slovak Diet. The visit of Seyss-Inquart ended with the proposal that Hitler should invite Tiso to discuss the matter; Tiso then met Seyss-Inquart in Brück on the Leitha on March 8, 1939, to learn whether Hitler would receive him.

That is how the idea of a Slovak State was prepared at home and abroad! Such were the political and technical steps undertaken toward that end. There was no longer any Slovak autonomism. From now on there was only separatism, with a more radical and less radical wing. Both were only waiting for the right moment to act. They did not have to wait long.

When the Czechoslovak President, Emil Hácha, and the Prime Minister, Rudolf Beran, learned what the Slovak Separatists were planning to do with the direct aid of the Autonomous Government of Slovakia and of the Slovak People's Party, two meetings of the Czechoslovak Government were held, on March 1 and 9, 1939, in which violent recriminations were exchanged between the Czech and Slovak Members of the Cabinet. Finally the President of the Republic felt he had to take firm measures. On the night of March 9, President Hácha dismissed Tiso and his Government of Slovakia, declared an emergency in Slovakia, and entrusted the Czechoslovak Army with the maintenance of order. Scores of Populist politicians and members of the Hlinka Guards were arrested, but many escaped to Vienna.

The incident was well within the scope of the domestic affairs of the Czechoslovak Government, but Hitler had different ideas. He used the police action against the Tiso Government as a pretext for ruthless intervention in Czechoslovakia's domestic problems and for the final liquidation of the Republic. Before describing these dramatic events, let us look at the sort of political regime the Slovak People's Party had introduced in Slovakia after October 6, 1938. [19]

---

[19] Indictment of Jozef Tiso, Ferdinand Ďurčanský and Alexander Mach before the National Tribunal in Bratislava ("Čas" of December 3, 1946, pp. 2-3) and of Vojtech Tuka ("Čas", Bratislava, July 30, 1946, pp. 2-3) and cross examination of Jozef Tiso before the National Tribunal on December 4, 1946 ("Čas" of same date).

Chapter Three

TOTALITARIANISM

Totalitarian Autonomism — The First Slovak Government — The Liquidation of the Opposition — Suppression of Civil Liberties and Democratic Institutions — The HG and the HM — Antisemitism, Czecho-Phobia, Persecutions and Terror — Enactment of Autonomy — The End of the Period of Constitutional Lapse in Czechoslovakia — The Second Slovak Government — Elections to the Slovak Parliament — Strengthening the Authoritative Regime — The Third Slovak Government

As long as the Slovak People's Party adhered to the program of Autonomy for Slovakia, it stood on democratic ground, but the instant it renounced that program in favor of separatism, it also renounced democracy in favor of totalitarianism. Slovak separatism was not only anti-Czech; it was also anti-democratic. The Separatists within the Slovak People's Party began as a numerically insignificant fraction, yet they conquered the party. The Slovak People's Party represented a quarter of the Slovak electorate and yet came to dominate Slovakia. A minority imposed its will upon a majority. This is to be attributed to the totalitarian methods of the Separatists and later also to the totalitarian methods of the Autonomists. Not right, but power became the decisive factor. First the minority forced the majority to submit, then silenced it completely. After Munich, totalitarian autonomism in Slovakia tolerated no opposition. Freedom of the press, freedom of speech and of assembly were gradually abolished. In their place came government propaganda, a controlled press, compulsory organizations and a single political party with a Leader. Any expression of opinion at variance with the views of the regime, any peaceful association of citizens for the purpose of influencing public affairs, were branded as criminal offenses and punished by loss of jobs, of property and of liberty. Things got so bad that to be a Czech or a Jew was enough to expose a person to mass hatred and to organized persecution. The dictatorship of the Slovak People's Party was no longer interested in the opinions of the Slovak public. It relied entirely on the power of the state, especially on that of the police, of which the most ominous branch was the State Security Police—the regime's secret political police. Its power was strengthened by the party organization and the semi-military uniformed party corps, the Hlinka Guards and the Hlinka Youth (HG and HM). The Hlinka Guards were armed. They became the instrument of political terror.

The Slovak Populists declared that the coup perpetrated in Žilina on October 6, 1938, had been in agreement with the other political parties of Slovakia. It was no such thing. Quite the contrary, it was not an agreement, for it was forced upon the other political parties under duress by the Populist minority. A representative of the Slovak branch of the Republican (Agrarian) Party of those days, Ján Ursíny, testified about these events before the National Tribunal in Bratislava on January 13, 1947. He declared that on October 5, 1938, Jozef Tiso had told the representatives of the other Slovak parties present in Žilina that "an agreement with them would be possible only if they accepted their (the Populists) proposals" for Slovak Autonomy. When the representatives of the other parties showed reluctance to accept such conditions, Tiso gave them an ultimatum, "You will either accept our proposals or we shall negotiate no further." [1] Although it is true

---

[1] "Čas", Bratislava, January 15, 1947, p. 2.

that the representatives of those parties were forced to accept the Populists proposal for Slovak Autonomy, and to sign a joint declaration to that effect (see Document No.13), it is the circumstance of the event and not the joint declaration that was extorted from them which is relevant. Those circumstances indicated anything but an agreement freely concluded as became apparent on the very next day, October 6, when the first Slovak Government was formed.

According to Czechoslovak democratic parliamentary custom, the Slovak Populists had the right to ask that one of their representatives be entrusted with forming a government. They had, however, no right to a larger representation in the new government than that which corresponded to their actual political strength. Under no circumstances were they entitled to a majority of cabinet appointments. Nevertheless the Slovak Populists gave themselves three cabinet posts out of five. Jozef Tiso became Prime Minister and Minister of the Interior, Ferdinand Ďurčanský Minister of Justice, Social Welfare and Health, and Matúš Černák Minister of Education. The two remaining cabinet appointments went to representatives of the Republican (Agrarian) Party): Finance, Agriculture, Trade and Public Works to Pavel Teplanský, and Railroads and Post to Ján Lichner. None of the other parties received any cabinet posts at all, and complete control of the Slovak Government thus came into the hands of the Populists. Even before Tiso took the oath of office, he appointed the representative of the Slovak Separatists, Alexander Mach, chief of the Propaganda Office in Bratislava, which made him in effect the fourth Populist cabinet minister. This gave the Populists, including the Separatists, the authority to spread their anti-Czechoslovak, separatist, and totalitarian ideology. The first Slovak Government was neither constitutional, nor representative, nor was it a coalition government. It was a typical totalitarian government.

The establishment of an autonomous Slovak Government meant a turn for the worse. The uncertainty and confusion brought on by the cession of territories to neighboring states by the Munich Agreement were aggravated by increasing internal political disorder. There was no united leadership or joint authority in the Czechoslovak Government nor in the Slovak nation. The state lacked a head, the Czechoslovak Government was without political support, because the old democratic parties were facing dissolution and nobody knew what would come out of the two new Czech political parties which were being organized. And in Slovakia the powers of the Czechoslovak Government were being taken over by the Slovak Government, which was only slowly assuming its governmental functions. The Slovak Populists were not united. Leader of the party was Jozef Tiso, but Karol Sidor was the boss of the two revolutionary formations, the National Committees and the Hlinka Guards. Tiso and Sidor struggled for exclusive power in the party and in Slovak public life. Meanwhile the Chief of Propaganda, Alexander Mach, used the situation to make hay for his own separatist policies. All three, Tiso, Sidor, and Mach, nevertheless had one common political target: to attack the "Czechoslovaks," (meaning Czechs in general, and specifically Czechs living in Slovakia, as well as Slovaks favoring Czechoslovakia) and the Jews. As a result, totalitarian autonomism, represented by Tiso, Sidor, and the Separatists, embraced the program of separating Slovakia from the Czech lands, of liquidating political opposition and of getting rid of Czechs and Jews in Slovakia.

The Populist totalitarian regime decided to solve the problem of the other parties by various methods: by forcing the members of some to join the Slovak People's Party, by forcing others to suspend their activities, and by ordering the dissolution of those remaining. The first group consisted of the

Republican (Agrarian) Party, the Middle-Class Party, the Catholic Czechoslovak People's Party, the Czechoslovak National Socialists, the Fascist Party. The second category comprised the Social-Democratic (Labor) Party, and the third consisted of the Communists and of the other autonomist party, the Slovak National Party. The leaders of those parties which were forced to merge with the Slovak People's Party were classified as either cooperative, that is to say acceptable, or non-cooperative, that is objectionable. The cooperative ones were won over by promises and appointments, the non-cooperative ones were isolated and intimidated. The latter had placed before them the alternative of "joining" the Slovak People's Party or having their parties dissolved and their members persecuted. They chose the lesser evil and "voluntarily joined" the Populists on November 8, 1938. In view of this, the Slovak People's Party made a concession: It added the words "Party of Slovak National Unity" to its name. The Populists presented the Social-Democratic Party with the choice of either liquidating voluntarily, or of being liquidated by the regime. The party preferred voluntary liquidation, and suspended its activities on November 23, 1938. In his capacity of Minister of the Interior, Jozef Tiso ordered the dissolution of the Communist Party and of the Slovak National Party. The only difference between the two orders was that the decree ordering the dissolution of the Communist Party was enforced while the one concerning the Slovak National Party was revoked on November 27, 1938. Nevertheless the latter party was not permitted to continue its activities undisturbed and thus in effect also disappeared. The only surviving party was the Slovak People's Party (The Party of Slovak National Unity). One of the leading party functionaries of the Slovak People's Party had this comment to make: "It was correct for us to liquidate the political parties, because they showed a tendency to create their own legal orders and to tolerate such conduct in a state governed by law is always a dangerous thing and leads to anarchy." [2]

Political opposition was silenced by brutal interference with the freedom of the press. Tiso appointed government commissars to supervise every non-Populist periodical, whether it was political, trade-unionist, or devoted to some other interest, and these men had the power to censor texts, supervise personnel, and control finances. The purpose of these appointments was to create intolerable conditions for opposition papers. Newspapers which for twenty years had conducted a resolute fight against autonomism, separatism, and clericalism, all of a sudden began singing their praises. Within two months a large number of established publications ceased to exist.

While the regime was suppressing the opposition and the freedom of speech and of the press, it was also turning against associations, organizations, and institutions of every kind. On October 28, 1938, the Slovak Government issued a decree ordering the seizure of the property of all associations, organizations, and foundations the head offices of which were outside the territory of Slovakia. It also ordered the dissolution of all the traditional civic defense-organizations, in particular of Sokol and Orol, the oldest organizations which had in the past played an important part in the nation, Workers' Gymnastic Union, and the Farmers' Equestrian Guards (Sedliacka Jazda). The decree established the Hlinka Guards as the only defense-organization in Slovakia. By its terms, the Hlinka Guards "swears loyalty to the Slovak Government; it is the moral auxiliary organ of all government offices and is subordinated to the Slovak Government; it is under its direct orders and cooperates with the government's auxiliary body, the Central National Committee in Bratislava." [3]

2 "Slovák," Bratislava, January 18, 1940.
3 Úradné noviny (Official Gazette), Bratislava, Part I, No. 48, pp. 2-3.

The Hlinka Guards, and their affiliated Hlinka Youth, were created according to the pattern of the Italian Black Shirts, and the German SS. and SA. corps, including black uniforms and the fascist salute. Both the HG and HM were organized on military lines. They had principal-corps, regional-, district-, and local commanders, a general staff, an officers' and non-commissioned officers' corps, uniforms and insignia of rank. They were subject to military discipline and armed with light arms, such as pistols, rifles and daggers. The HG consisted of basic (defense) units, the Hlinka Transport Guards, the Hlinka University Guards, and the Hlinka Youth. The Hlinka Guards usurped the right to maintain order and security at the expense of the legitimate police corps; it also assumed the right to organize railroad traffic, propaganda, cultural, physical and pre-military training, for which it had neither facilities nor any other prerequisites. In brief, it became the instrument of political and racial incitement and persecution and the agent of chaos and anarchy. Conniving with the leaders of the regime, the Hlinka Guards fell upon Czech employees, evicted them from their homes, deported them to the Slovak-Moravian frontier, where they robbed them of valuables and then pushed them across the border. They behaved still worse toward the Jews. By force and usually at night, these thugs would drag them out of their homes, permitting them only 60 kilograms of personal luggage and no more than 500 Crowns in cash, shove them into trucks, and dump them into the territory, which had just been ceded to Hungary by the Vienna arbitration. The Hungarian Government, in turn, refused to accept these people and pushed them back into Slovakia. However, the Guardists had already taken possession of their businesses, workshops, houses, and apartments. From then on the Jews in Slovakia never knew a day of peace. Their lives, freedom, and property were perpetually threatened by the Guardists and their friends, the German "Ordners." Not even Jewish cemeteries were spared, graves were defiled, tombstones destroyed. Vindictiveness would not even spare the dead.

Karol Sidor became the first Commander in Chief of the Hlinka Guards. He in turn appointed Alexander Mach as his deputy on December 4, 1938, and Colonel Alexander Čunderlík Chief of Military Staff, Colonel Anton Pulanich Deputy Chief of Military Staff, Karol Murgaš Chief of the Political Staff, Matúš Černák Commander of the Hlinka Youth, Vojtech Tuka Honorary Commandant of the Rodobrana, Vladimír Moravčik Commander of the Storm Troops, Vladimír Černák Commander of the Defense Troops, Jozef Kirschbaum Commander of the University Hlinka Guards, Jozef Istvánčin Commander of the Hlinka Transport Guards, and Pavel Teplanský Commander of the Mounted Guards.[4] In those days Slovakia was swamped with Guardist uniforms and the Nazi salute. Even clergymen and some prelates, such as Canon Karol Körper, wore parts of the Guardist uniform and raised their right arms in the Nazi salute. When the Slovak Diet met for the first time on January 18, 1939, all Members of the Diet but for a few exceptions appeared dressed in the uniform of the Hlinka Guards.

When truncated Czechoslovakia recovered somewhat from the shock of the Munich blow, she turned her attention to constitutional problems. First she reorganized Czech-Slovak relations on a federative basis, and elected a new president of the Republic. On November 19, 1938, the Prague Parliament, "guided by the desire to reconcile the Slovak and Czech nation in the spirit of the Žilina agreement" voted "a constitutional amendment concerning the autonomy of the land of Slovakia." [5] Under that law "the Land of Slovakia is an autonomous part of the Czecho-Slovak Republic." Slovak was

4 Armáda v obrane a v práci, (The Army in Defense and in Work), published by the Ministry of National Defense, Bratislava, 1944, p. 11.

5 Collection of Laws and Decrees of the Czechoslovak Republic, No. 299/1938, p. 1161 and seq.

declared the official language of administration and in schools. Legislative, executive and judicial powers in the state were divided between the Czecho-Slovak Parliament, the Czecho-Slovak Government, and the courts on the one hand, and the Diet, government and courts of Slovakia, on the other. A position similar to that of Slovakia was also accorded to Subcarpathian Ruthenia, now called Transcarpathian Ukraine. The Secretary General of the Slovak People's Party, Martin Sokol, declared in the Prague Parliament during the debate on the autonomy of the Land of Slovakia, "May the law, which we are about to pass, forever remove the friction that has existed between Slovaks and Czechs and may it mark the beginning of a better future not only for Slovaks, but for the Czechs as well . . . If we want the new, truncated Czecho-Slovakia to be healthy and capable of life, we must build her not only with new methods, but in the spirit of mutual love, tolerance, and brotherly understanding." Not all leaders of the Slovak People's Party had such honest intentions.

After the passing of the law for Slovak Autonomy, a new President of the Republic was elected, Emil Hácha, the former President of the Supreme Administrative Tribunal of Czechoslovakia. He immediately appointed a new Czecho-Slovak Government with the chairman of the Republican (Agrarian) Party, Rudolf Beran, as Prime Minister, and a new Slovak Government with Jozef Tiso as its Prime Minister. The following persons became members of this second Slovak Government: Ferdinand Ďurčanský (Minister of Transport and Public Works), Miloš Vančo (Justice), Matúš Černák (Education), Pavel Teplanský (Economy). Tiso again held the posts of Minister of the Interior, Social Welfare, and Health besides being Prime Minister. Apart from that, Karol Sidor was appointed Deputy Prime Minister in the Czecho-Slovak Government. This terminated the state of constitutional uncertainty that had followed the abdication of President Edvard

Beneš and the *de facto* establishment of the autonomy of
Slovakia and of Subcarpathian Ruthenia. Unfortunately it did
not close the chapter of undemocratic development in Slovakia.

As soon as the Slovak People's Party had gained control
of governmental powers, its leaders concentrated on the
Slovak Diet. They could not gain control of the latter by legal
and democratic means; the Populists had lost much support
even among their old membership as a result of the despotic
methods the party had resorted to after Munich. The Populists
could not properly obtain control of the Slovak Diet, because
Article V of the constitutional amendment on Slovak Autonomy stipulated that the elections to the first Slovak Diet were
to be conducted under the democratic rules for elections of
the Czechoslovak Republic. Under this law, participation of
political parties was mandatory; the single party system was
unknown. It was an act of deceit and trickery when Tiso
signed and published the announcement of the forthcoming
elections in the Official Gazette of November 26, 1938. This
notice required political parties to file the list of their candidates for election with the chairman of the election committee
in Bratislava not later than by noon on the following day,
November 27. November 26 was a Saturday and the Official
Gazette which carried the announcement could not be delivered before Monday, November 28, whereas the deadline
for filing the lists of candidates was Sunday, the 27th. Clearly
none but the Populists had advance knowledge of this deadline and consequently only the Slovak People's Party filed
a joint list of candidates within the specified time. To make
matters even worse, the election notice also required that the
lists of candidates be signed by a certain number of voters.
Since the deadline expired before the notices could reach the
electorate, it was obviously impossible to obtain the signatures

in time.[5] This election fraud outraged the people of Slovakia; their feelings would surely have been reflected in the election results, had the regime not resorted to further violent interference with the elections.

Even the so-called joint list of candidates of the Slovak People's Party had been drawn up without the knowledge of some of the candidates. Miloš Vančo testified before the National Tribunal in Bratislava on February 10, 1947, that he learned that he had been listed as a candidate for election only when the lists were made public. The elections for the first Slovak Diet were set for December 18, 1938. There were no election-committees of representatives of the various political parties and therefore no means to insure the honesty of the elections. Apart from government officials, only representatives of the Slovak People's Party and of the Hlinka Guards were present in the voting places, except for some German and Magyar representatives in some of the areas with mixed populations. The voters were handed only one list of candidates. They had no choice but to vote for this list or not to vote at all. Uniformed Hlinka Guardists took the ballot slip from the hands of the voters and threw it into the ballot box. Nobody was encouraged to step behind the partition of the voting booth and the voting was, in effect, entirely public. A subsequent official publication of the Slovak Ministry of National Defense[7] praised this conduct of the Guardists as a "beneficial activity in the pre-election period." Nobody but the Populists were permitted to count the votes. It was all characteristic of totalitarian elections. The joint list of candidates of the Slovak People's Party obtained 99% of all votes!

---

[6] Number 49: Notice of the Government of the Land of Slovakia in Bratislava, November 26, 1938, No. 844/1938 (Official Gazette, Bratislava, Part I., No. 58, p. 1).

[7] Armáda v obrane a v práci (The Army in Defense and in Work), Bratislava, 1944, p. 12.

Of course it obtained all seats in the Slovak Diet. The candidates were exactly what one would expect under the circumstances. Sixty-three representatives were elected. Of these 48 were Populists (76%), 12 were non-Populist Slovaks (19%), two were Germans (3%) and one Magyar (1%). Fifty-eight (92%) of the 63 representatives were Catholics, 12 of whom (nearly 20%) were actually Catholic priests and only five were Protestants, that is less than 8%. This Diet did not represent Slovakia. It had received no mandate from the people but only from a totalitarian party.

The government ordered town and district councils to be dissolved, and removed the elected mayors, replacing them by government commissars. This eliminated any direct influence of the people upon communal affairs. In the same way the regime also interfered with business and other corporations. It removed directors and replaced them with temporary administrators. This was a convenient method of rewarding party-henchmen and of punishing opponents. Mass purges were carried out among government and private employees. The regime fired, transferred, down-graded, and retired Czech, Jewish, and non-Populist Slovak employees, in complete disregard of public interest or acquired rights.

Laws were observed only as they were in the interest of the regime. If the law stood in the way, the regime overrode it or changed it. Principles of justice and traditions were no longer of any avail. Power alone ruled supreme. The end justified the means.

Official propaganda by now was entirely in the hands of the authoritarian regime. All papers and publications, and the radio were now slanted as dictated by political objectives. Within a few weeks after Munich, Slovakia had changed beyond recognition. Hand-in-hand with separatism, totalitarianism was forging ahead. The spirit of German National Socialism had infiltrated democratic Slovakia. In the period from

October 1938 until March 1939, the regime had established its power so firmly that it even brazenly conducted a foreign and domestic policy of its own, in complete disregard of the Czecho-Slovak Government. Some improvement might have been effected by the last Autonomous Slovak Government, headed by Karol Sidor, had it not been engulfed in the turmoil of the events of March. These events also put an end to Slovak Autonomy. They did not, however, put an end to the totalitarian regime of the Slovak People's Party.

PART III

THE SLOVAK STATE

Chapter One

THE PROTECTORATE

The Prague-Bratislava Conflict — Ďurčanský in Vienna — German Intervention in Bratislava — Sidor's Refusal — German Acts of Terror — Tiso Visits Hitler — The Slovak Diet Proclaims Slovak Independence — The First Government of the Slovak State — Protest of the Legionnaires and of the Slovak League in America — Occupation of Bohemia, Moravia and Western Slovakia by the Germans — The Disappearance of Czechoslovakia — Hácha and Chvalkovský in Berlin — The Bohemian-Moravian Protectorate — The German-Slovak Treaty of Protection — The Slovak State as a German Protectorate — Hungarian Aggression Against Czechoslovakia — Protests of the Great Powers in Berlin

The conflict between President Emil Hácha and the Czecho-Slovak Government on one side and the Slovak Autonomous Government under Tiso on the other, which had culminated in the dismissal of Tiso's Government, was settled within two days. President Hácha, accepting the recommendations of the Slovak People's Party, appointed a new government. Karol Sidor became Prime Minister. The conflict between Prague and Bratislava was not settled, however, to the satisfaction of Adolf Hitler and his followers among the Slovak Separatists. Hitler turned the matter into a conflict between Prague and Berlin, an opportunity for which he had long been waiting. On November 23, 1939, he brazenly admitted to the German military leaders, "It was clear to me from the first moment that I could not be satisfied with the Sudeten German territory. That was only a partial solution. The decision to march into

Bohemia was made." [1] Two documents of the High Command of the German Army, one dated October 21, 1938, and signed by Hitler, and the other dated December 17, 1938, and signed by Keitl, entitled "Liquidation of the Remnants of Czechoslovakia," clearly specify the actual preparations, not only the intent. The invasion of Czechoslovakia was to be prepared in such a manner that "to the outside world, too, it must clearly appear that it is merely an action of pacification, and not a warlike undertaking." [2] The following statements make clear how valuable a prize Czechoslovakia really was. Ribbentrop declared on February 12, 1939, that "we were not interested in a speedy conclusion of the work of the German-Czech Frontier Delimitation Committee," created under the Munich Agreement.[3] Göring said on July 27, 1939: "Air bases in Slovakia are of great importance for the German Air Force for use against the East," and added: "In view of Czechoslovakia's economic capacity, Germany has gained great economic advantages from the transfer." Hitler declared in Munich on November 7, 1943, that "the bloodless solution of the Czech conflict in the autumn of 1938 and spring of 1939 and the annexation of Slovakia rounded off the territory of Greater Germany in such a way that it now became possible to consider the Polish problem on the basis of more or less favorable strategic premises." [4]

Karol Sidor's acceptance of the post of Prime Minister of Slovakia caused great disappointment in Berlin, and provoked such violent resentment on the part of Ferdinand Ďurčanský, the Separatist, that he fled to Vienna. German propaganda renewed its broadsides against the Czechoslovak Republic, blasting it for alleged persecution of the Germans still in the

1 Trial of War Criminals, III/112.
2 Documents on German Foreign Policy, 1918-1945, D/IV. Washington, 1951, pp. 185-6, Trial of War Criminals, III/87-89.
3 Documents on German Foreign Policy, etc. D/IV, p. 208.
4 Trial of War Criminals, III/169-171.

Republic, as well as for its stand against Tiso's Government and the Slovak Separatists. Ďurčanský joined forces with the Germans, attacked Sidor, and took the lead in the campaign for the secession of Slovakia from the Czech Lands.

While the leaders of the Slovak People's Party were discussing the appointment of a new Slovak Government with the representatives of the Czecho-Slovak Government, armed Guardists and German "Ordners" were fighting Czechoslovak troops in Bratislava. The German "Ordners" occupied the government building on March 11, 1939. Couriers were hurrying back and forth with orders from Nazi headquarters and from Ďurčanský in Vienna, and taking back reports from Karmasin's people and some of the Separatists in Bratislava. The German agent Carbus and a representative of the Deutsche Partei went to Sidor and demanded that he proclaim the secession of Slovakia over the radio. They informed him that Germany would immediately provide two army divisions to support Slovakia. Sidor refused. Another Separatist working for the Germans, Karol Murgaš, approached Sidor with the same suggestion. Pressure to accept the German demands was exerted upon Sidor also by Jozef Kirschbaum and Tibor Wodráška. Kirschbaum insisted that Sidor sign at least a written statement that he was in favor of an independent Slovakia. Kirschbaum wanted to take that statement back to Ďurčanský, who was waiting in Petržalka, on the German side of the Danube. Sidor continued to refuse. Thereupon Ďurčanský called him on the telephone and demanded that he announce over the radio that a Slovak State had been created. These men were carrying out the instructions of the Vienna headquarters of the Nazi Party.

When all these German-Separatist attempts failed, a group of German emissaries, led by the Secretary of State, Wilhelm Keppler, arrived secretly in Bratislava at 4 o'clock in the morning of March 12, 1939. The group included the Reichs

Governor in Vienna, Seyss-Inquart, the Gauleiter of Austria, Joseph Bürckel, and the "Führer of the German Ethnic Group" (Volksgruppenführer) Karmasin. These men went to the government building where Karol Sidor and the other members of his cabinet were waiting for them. Keppler informed Sidor that Adolf Hitler was getting numerous requests from Slovakia for an independent Slovak State. He demanded that Sidor state his views since he, Keppler, had come "upon orders of the Führer to ascertain the real state of affairs." Sidor flatly refused and a stormy discussion ensued. Bürckel called Sidor aside and showed him a telegram which Ďurčanský as "Minister of Foreign Affairs of Slovakia" had sent to Hitler. Ďurčanský informed Hitler that an independent Slovak State had been proclaimed and that a Slovak Government had been formed; furthermore he requested that "this state and its government be placed under the protection of the German Reich." Sidor declared that he had no knowledge whatsoever of the alleged statements in Ďurčanský's message. Bürckel retorted by announcing to Sidor that "the Führer had already recognized him as Prime Minister." Then he reproached Sidor for having "just accepted the office of the Prime Minister from the hands of the Czechs." After that he shouted at him that "the Führer must not be embarrassed, the Führer can not be deceived." Sidor tried to explain that he had neither embarrassed nor deceived the Führer. After these dramatic discussions, the German delegation, greatly annoyed, left Bratislava and returned to Vienna, but the Germans did not give up the fight.

The German Army was preparing feverishly for the occupation of Bratislava. Great quantities of arms had been smuggled there from Germany for the planned armed invasion on the pretext of suppressing terrorism. The acts of terrorism had been planned long ago by the Germans, the German minority in Slovakia, and the Separatist Slovaks. Apart from that, strong pressure was being exerted upon Sidor, in the hope of creating the appearance of legitimacy by involving his office in the planned proclamation of the independent Slovak State. A strong propaganda campaign was launched against Sidor over the Vienna radio in which even some of Sidor's friends and collaborators in the Hlinka Guards, such as Ďurčanský, Murgaš, Mutňansky, and Vávra took part. When Sidor still refused to submit, the Germans tried to assassinate him, but the plot was discovered and foiled. A charge of 26 pounds of high explosives had been placed in the yard of his house. German agents then placed a time bomb in the building of the Jesuit Monastery in Bratislava, which went off in the evening of March 13, 1939. The explosion caused much damage and consternation.[5] Great tension prevailed in Bratislava and all of Slovakia. Aggressive propaganda, general insecurity, acts of terrorism, fear of occupation by the Germans and their Separatist henchmen, all were part of the German plan deliberately to destroy Czechoslovakia.

On March 13, 1939, Jozef Tiso received an official invitation from Adolf Hitler to visit Berlin at once. The invitation was first brought to him by two Germans, escorted by Ján Dafčík, the Corps Commandant of the Hlinka Youth, and later confirmed by the German Consul-General in Bratislava, Ernst von Drüffel. Tiso asked the leaders of the Slovak People's Party for advice and at a joint meeting of the Party leadership and the Slovak Government it was decided to accept the invitation. Accompanied by Štefan Danihel, a Member of Parliament, and Franz Karmasin, Jozef Tiso immediately left for Berlin. In Vienna they were joined by Ferdinand Ďurčanský and Secretary of State Wilhelm Keppler.

That same evening, March 13, 1939, Tiso arrived by air

---

[5] Karol Sidor: Moje poznámky k historickým dňom, (My Remarks on the Historic Days), 1939 (manuscript).

in Berlin and was received by the Minister of Foreign Affairs
Joachim von Ribbentrop. Ribbentrop expressed his amaze-
ment that the Slovaks showed no enthusiasm for an independent Slovak State. He hinted that the Slovaks better be careful
not to miss the opportunity for independence. Tiso was then
received by Hitler, in the presence of Ribbentrop, Reichs
Minister Otto Meissner, Secretaries of State Wilhelm Keppler
and Otto Dietrich, and General Wilhelm Keitel. In a long
monologue Hitler held forth to Tiso about German "living-
space" and about the difficulties the Germans were having
with the Czechs, such as the acts of violence in Jihlava and
Brno. (No such acts of violence had occurred.) He then turned
to the subject of Slovakia. He informed Tiso that he was
disappointed with the attitude of the Slovaks. Furthermore,
he told him that he was about to turn on the Czechs, that it
would be unfortunate for the Slovaks if they were still with
the Czechs. It was not necessary for him to emphasize what
the Poles and the Magyars wanted from Slovakia. The Slovaks
had to decide as soon as possible whether or not they wished
to conduct their affairs themselves. He had no demands upon
Slovakia, but would not tolerate internal instability there. He
had invited Tiso in order that Tiso might hear his decision.
It was now a matter of hours only, not of days. Should
Slovakia wish to be independent, he would support and guarantee her independence. But if Slovakia were to refuse to
sever her ties with Prague "he would leave the destiny of
Slovakia to the mercy of events for which he was no longer
responsible. In that case he would only intercede on behalf
of German interests, and these did not extend east of the
Carpathians." Hitler then turned to Ribbentrop and asked
him whether he had anything to add. Ribbentrop emphatically
repeated that "in this case a decision was a question of hours,
not of days." He showed the Führer a message he had just
received which reported Hungarian troop movements on the

Slovak frontiers. Hitler read the message, showed it to Tiso "and expressed the hope that Slovakia would soon decide clearly for herself." [6] Tiso was taken aback by all this, and asked for a short time for reflection. He first put a call through to Bratislava asking Sidor to call a session of the Slovak Diet for the following morning, March 14, 1939, at 10 A.M. He then called again on Ribbentrop in the Ministry of Foreign Affairs. Ribbentrop now surprised Tiso with the text of a proclamation of Slovak independence, demanded that he sign it, and announce the creation of an independent Slovak State at once, from Berlin. Tiso explained that only the Slovak Diet and not he was authorized to make such a decision. He told Ribbentrop that he had arranged for the Diet to be called. Ribbentrop took notice of this, but gave Tiso an ultimatum: should he, Ribbentrop, fail to receive a report by 1 P.M. on the following day, that the Slovak Diet had voted the secession of Slovakia, Germany would act accordingly. Tiso promised Ribbentrop an answer within this time limit and immediately flew back to Bratislava, where he arrived during the night of March 13. While Tiso was on his way home, Sidor prevailed on the President of Czecho-Slovakia, Emil Hácha, to convoke formally the Slovak Diet in accordance with the constitutional amendment concerning Slovak Autonomy. Hácha at once sent a letter to Bratislava requesting the Diet to convene. The letter was co-signed by the Prime Minister of the Central Czecho-Slovak Government, Rudolf Beran, but neither the President nor Beran knew that the Slovak Diet was to pronounce Czechoslovakia's death sentence. [7]

On March 14, at 9 A.M., the last Slovak Autonomous Government held its last meeting with the leaders of the Slovak People's Party. Tiso gave a report of his meeting with

[6] Trial of War Criminals, III/156-157.
[7] Testimony of Jozef Tiso before the National Tribunal in Bratislava, on Dec. 5, 1946 ("Čas", Bratislava, December 7, 1946). See also Otto Meissner: Staatssekretär unter Ebert-Hindenburg-Hitler, Hamburg, 1950, pp. 474-475.

the leaders of the German Reich in Berlin. The government
and the leadership of the Party unanimously decided to present
a motion to the Slovak Diet demanding "secession from the
Czechs and a proclamation of independence of the Slovak
State." Tiso and Ďurčanský informed Sidor that Adolf Hitler
refused to recognize Sidor's Slovak Government and that he
would only recognize the previous Slovak Government of
Tiso, because Hitler regarded Sidor as a "soldier of Prague."

The Slovak Diet met as ordered in what was to be a secret
session. The first man to speak was Karol Sidor. He explained
the circumstances under which he had accepted the appointment as Prime Minister of the Slovak Autonomous Government and then declared that "in view of the international
situation he and his government are no longer in a position
to carry out what they had undertaken to do" and that he
therefore was "resigning with his entire government." He had
notified the constitutional authorities in Prague of this decision
and thereby terminated his government's brief tenure of office.
Tiso then took the floor and reported on his visit with Hitler
and Ribbentrop. After these speeches the Slovak Diet unanimously passed a law, the first article of which read, "The Land
of Slovakia declares itself to be an independent and self-
governing Slovak State. The Diet of the Land of Slovakia
will be transformed into a legislative Diet of the Slovak State."
After a short recess discussions were resumed on the formation of a Government of the new Slovak State. There was
disagreement regarding candidates but in the end a government was formed composed of the following persons: Prime
Minister Jozef Tiso, Minister Without Portfolio Vojtech
Tuka, Minister of Foreign Affairs Ferdinand Ďurčanský,
Minister of the Interior Karol Sidor, Minister of Transport
Julius Stano, Minister of Education Jozef Sivák, Minister of
National Defense General Ferdinand Čatloš, Minister of Fi-
nance Mikuláš Pružinský, Minister of Justice Gejza Fritz,

Minister of Economy Gejza Medrický. With the exception of General Čatloš, who belonged to no political party, all the members of the government were Populists. It was a government of a single party and a party which represented only a minority.

The disagreement over appointments to the Cabinet centered on Sidor, who refused to accept a position in view of the fact that he did not have Hitler's confidence. He declared, "The important thing today is that those who will be cabinet ministers should enjoy the confidence of the Reichs Chancellor A. Hitler, and, according to what has been reported by Tiso and Ďurčanský, I do not enjoy that confidence . . . I am withdrawing and will resume the duties of a head of a ministerial department when Berlin will deem it desirable."[8] This shows that the necessary condition for holding a post in the Slovak Government was not the confidence of the Slovak people, not even that of the Slovak People's Party, but exclusively the confidence of Adolf Hitler! The Slovak Government felt responsible not to the Slovak People but to Berlin.

When the session was resumed, the Diet approved the proposed Slovak Government, and its members immediately took the oath of office. With that the session of the Diet came to an end. It was possible to inform the German Minister of Foreign Affairs even before the deadline at 1 P.M. that the Slovak Diet had obeyed Hitler's orders: that it had carried out the formal secession of Slovakia from the Czech Lands of the Republic; that it had severed the ties between the Slovak people and the Czechs and reduced the common Czechoslovak State to ruins. For the third time in their history the Slovaks had been forced to separate from the Czechs. This second partition of Czechoslovakia was the inevitable con-

8 Karol Sidor: Moje poznámky k historickým dňom (My Remarks on the Historic Days) (manuscript of 1939).

sequence of the first partition at Munich under the Four Power Agreement. Adolf Hitler got what he had wanted from the start, the destruction of Czechoslovakia. The fate of the Czech nation thus became no more than an isuue of domestic policy of the German Reich.

On the evening of March 14, 1939, the German Legation in Prague requested President Emil Hácha and the Minister of Foreign Affairs, František Chvalkovský, to proceed at once to Berlin to hear Hitler's sentence regarding the Czech Lands. Hitler received Hácha and Chvalkovský during the night of March 14, and told them that "it was only a matter of hours until Germany would interfere in the Czech Lands." In Hitler's words, "at 6 o'clock in the morning the German Army would invade Czechoslovakia from all sides and the German Air Force would occupy the Czech airfields." With unheard of brutality Hitler pressed the aged and ailing President Hácha, who suffered a physical collapse during the night, to sign a document by which he placed the Czech Lands under German protection. The document stated that "the President of the Czechoslovak State entrusts with entire confidence the destiny of the Czech people and the Czech country to the hands of the Führer of the German Reich." Czechoslovakia became the victim of the "international banditry" of Hitler's Germany. On March 15, 1939, the German Army began the occupation of Bohemia and Moravia, which Hitler incorporated into his Reich as a "Protectorate." [9] That which had really been decided in September 1938, could not be prevented in March 1939. Kamil Krofta, who was Foreign Minister of Czechoslovakia in 1938, had clearly forseen the future when, on September 30, he told the British Minister Basil Newton, the French Minister Victor Leopold de Lacroix, and the Italian Minister Francesco Fransoni: "We have been forced into this

[9] Trial of War Criminals, III/158-165.

situation; now everything is at an end; today is our turn, tomorrow will be the turn of others." [10] Others were to follow. Now that Hitler had destroyed Czechoslovakia the road to Poland lay open to him.

On that fateful March 14, 1939, began a new chapter of Slovak political history under the protective wing of Adolf Hitler's Great German Reich. The Slovak Nation received the report of Tiso's visit to Hitler and of the decision of the Slovak Diet with a deep sense of grief, anger and shame. The Slovaks felt cheated, betrayed, sold down the river. They regarded the conduct of Tiso, Sidor and of the Diet as the result of gross terror on the part of a foreign power. Tiso himself acknowledged this before the National Tribunal in Bratislava on March 17, 1947, when he said, "Without the pressure exercised by Hitler, the Slovak Diet would never have voted in favor of the independence of Slovakia." The people of Slovakia could not however find any excuse for those Populists, in particular of the Separatist faction, who had, directly or indirectly, but deliberately, helped to create the situation which permitted Germany to obtain the Munich Agreement and then completely to destroy the Czechoslovak Republic.

The leaders of the new regime received numerous written and oral threats and protests from individual Slovak patriots, associations and organizations. Two of these were characteristic, the protests of the Slovak Legionnaires and the Slovak League in America. Twelve prominent Slovak Legionnaires who had fought during the First World War for the Czechoslovak Republic (including the authors Jozef Gregor-Tajovský and Janko Jesenský, General Rudolf Viest, Lieut. Colonel August Malár, and Anton Granatier) met in Bratislava on March 14, 1939, with Janko Jesenský in the chair and drew up a formal protest against the destruction of the Czechoslovak Republic and the proclamation of the Slovak State. They

10 Documents on German Policy, D/IV, pp. 4-5.

all signed this protest and sent it to the Diet of Slovakia. It declared that "Slovak patriots had fought and died together
with the Czechs for the liberty of the Slovak Nation" and that
"it had been the Czechs who had helped the Slovaks in the
worst moments of their history." The Legionnaires admon-
ished the Members of the Diet "not to tarnish the national
honor of the Slovaks and the memory of our fallen comrades,
first among whom was General M. R. Štefánik" and to remember that these "Legionnaires were speaking from the hearts of
the great majority of the Slovak People." (Document No. 14.)
The Chairman of the Slovak League of America, Jozef Hušek
of Palmyra, Pennsylvania, cabled Prime Minister Karol Sidor
on March 12, 1939, "Advise strong stand against secession.
Slovak League is for federation with Czechs on equal basis."
The cable was sent off in agreement with another leader of
the Slovak League in America, Dr. Peter P. Hletko.[11] The
Legionnaires stood on the platform of Czechoslovak national
and political unity. The Slovak League in America, on the
other hand, was in favor of Slovak Autonomy under the terms
of the Pittsburgh Agreement. At the critical hour of Czechoslovakia and of Slovakia these two opposing camps stood on
common ground—in favor of saving the Czechoslovak Republic. Only the extremists in the Slovak People's Party had
forsaken this aim. Even Karol Sidor found it difficult in the
end to come to a decision. Not that he was opposed to
separatism, but because the Separatist program had been
taken over by the Germans and ruthlessly exploited by them.
On May 30, 1939, Ján Ferenčík, the Mayor of the city of
Ružomberok, confirmed this fundamental attitude on the part
of Sidor. He declared, "In November 1938 the representatives
of Ružomberok declared in Černová that the limits of autonomy were not enough for us and that the dream of Andrej
Hlinka of an independent Slovakia was to be fulfilled. The

[11] Karol Sidor: Dve Cesty (Two Roads), Montreal, 1951, p. 23.

Ministers Karol Sidor and Ďurčanský were present at the meeting and were assigned the task of requesting the Führer of the German Nation, Adolf Hitler, to guarantee the independence of the Slovak State. Minutes of the meeting were drawn up and these also bore the signature of Karol Sidor." [12]

There is no record of a Communist protest.

With the destruction of Czechoslovakia and the setting up of a Slovak State, Sidor's star also began to wane. On the day the Slovak State was proclaimed, Sidor had to resign from the influential function of Commander in Chief of the Hlinka Guards, and Alexander Mach was appointed in his stead. On the following day, March 15, 1939, Sidor also resigned from his post as Minister of the Interior. He was eventually appointed Minister of Slovakia to the Vatican, where he spent the entire period of the Second World War. He was thus completely removed from politics because he did not enjoy the confidence of Adolf Hitler. Representatives of the Separatists faction now assumed control, men whom Berlin viewed with favor, such as Vojtech Tuka, Ferdinand Ďurčanský, and their followers. Tiso's political influence continued to grow at home. Although Berlin continued to recognize him, the Germans preferred Tuka.

While the Slovak Separatists were busy proclaiming Slovakia an independent and self-governing state, Hitler regarded it as territory annexed by Germany. March 14 therefore could scarcely remain the last phase of development in Slovak-German relations. Berlin now applied the same tactics to the Slovak Government as it had previously employed in its dealings with Czechoslovakia. It resorted to treachery, threats, and violence.

On the very day of declaration of Slovak independence, units of the German Army penetrated into Western Slovakia without notifying the Slovak Government of the action, began

12 "Slovák," Bratislava, June 2, 1939.

to disarm Slovak garrisons and to occupy Slovak towns, military objectives and airfields. Vast quantities of valuable equipment of the Czechoslovak Army had been stored in places along the Váh (Waag) Valley. These stores were simply plundered by the Germans and removed to Germany. They included arms, motor fuel, airplanes, automobiles, and trucks worth more than $700,000,000. In every community the German Army posted notices saying that it was taking over all powers including those of civil administration.[13] The Hlinka Guards were ordered to assist the German troops. The Chief of the German General Staff, General von Brauchitsch, sent a memorandum to Hitler on March 25, 1939, saying: "Colonel-General Keitel shall inform the Slovak Government via Foreign Office that it will not be allowed to keep or garrison armed Slovak units (Hlinka Guards) on this side of the border formed by the river Waag. They shall be transferred to the new Slovak territory. Hlinka Guards should be disarmed." [14] The Germans also occupied the two modern ammunition and armament factories in Dubnica nad Váhom and Považská Bystrica in Slovakia. Later they evacuated part of the territory they had occupied in Slovakia, but remained in occupation of the region beyond the Small Carpathian range until the end of World War II. They never returned the equipment they had carried away and never paid a penny for it.

The day after the proclamation of the Slovak State, Franz Karmasin, accompanied by a man called Hermann, called on Prime Minister Jozef Tiso and informed him that Germans in Slovakia felt their lives and property were being threatened by the Hungarians and because they were unable to obtain adequate protection from the Slovak authorities, they "are compelled to ask the German Reich for protection." This was so absurd and unfounded an allegation that Tiso at first

13 "Slovák", Bratislava, March 19, 1939.
14 Trial of War Criminals, III/167.

refused to take it seriously. Very soon, however, the Minister
of Foreign Affairs, Ďurčanský, appeared and suggested that
Tiso make a formal request to Adolf Hitler for protection of
the Slovak State and that he be prepared to sign a German-
Slovak Treaty of Protection, which had already been "agreed
upon." [15] He was referring to an agreement Ďurčanský himself
had made in February 1939, that is before the Slovak State
came into existence. The Secretary of State in the Reichs
German Ministry of Foreign Affairs, Baron Ernst von Weizsäcker, declared to the Hungarian Minis.ter Döme Sztójay on
March 15, 1939, that "the final fate of Slovakia was not yet
settled. Orientation toward Germany, however, seemed to
me the best solution." [16] Further developments were to show
what Weizsäcker meant by "orientation toward Germany."

Without discussing it with the government and without
the approval of the Diet, Tiso accepted Ďurčanský's suggestion
and immediately sent a cable to Hitler. (See Document No.
15.) Tiso stated that he was turning to Hitler "with complete
confidence"; that "the Slovak State is placing itself under
your protection and is asking you for such protection." Hitler
replied to Tiso on March 16 that he was assuming "the
protection of the Slovak State." (See Document No 16.) When
Hitler passed through Vienna on his way back from Prague,
Tiso, Ferdinand Ďurčanský, Tuka and Mach called on him
on March 18, 1939, and the first three men signed a Treaty
of Protection (see Document No. 17) which had been drawn
up without prior discussion with the Slovak Government. The
treaty stated that "The Slovak State is placing itself under the
protection of the German Reich" which "assumes the protection of the political independence of the Slovak State and its
territorial integrity." In view of this, Germany reserved the
right "for the German Armed Forces to maintain military

---

[15] Testimony of Jozef Tiso before the National Tribunal in Bratislava on
August 2, 1946, ("Čas", Bratislava, August 3, 1946).
[16] Documents on German Foreign Policy, D/IV, pp. 276-277.

installations at any time and to man these with such forces as they will deem necessary in the zone bordered in the West by the Slovak State frontier and in the East by the eastern slopes of the Small Carpathian range and the eastern slopes of the Javorníky." The Slovak Government undertook to provide the "required land and space" and to allow "supplies for the German units to be brought in free of duty and to permit deliveries from the Reich without duty." In the above zone "the German Armed Forces exercise sovereign military rights." German employees in that zone "are subject to German jurisdiction." The Slovak Government also accepted the obligation to "organize armed forces in close cooperation with the German Government." The treaty which was to be valid for 25 years was signed by the Slovaks on March 18 in Vienna and by the Germans on March 23, 1939, in Berlin. Although Clause 5 stipulated that the treaty was to operate from the day it was signed, it was not published in the Slovak official code until September 23, 1940.[17] The original text of Article 3 had been more favorable to Slovakia. It stipulated that the Slovak Government was to organize armed forces in close agreement with the German Armed Forces "in order to safeguard the Slovak State against any outside attack." Before signing, Ribbentrop crossed out the words "Um die Verteidigung des Slowakishen Staates gegen etwaige äussere Angriffe zu erleichtern" ("in order to safeguard the Slovak State against any outside attack") which made the treaty obligation to organize the Slovak Army in close cooperation with that of Germany a general and unconditional duty to be carried out even if Slovakia was not threatened by external aggression.

The German-Slovak Treaty of Protection put an end to any independent Slovak foreign and defense policy and subordinated Slovakia to the German Reich in these fields. Even before the signing of the treaty the Third Reich had

<hr>

[17] Code of Slovakia, Bratislava, year 1940, part 47, pp. 363-364.

already interfered with the sovereignty and territorial integrity
of the Slovak State. A part of Slovakia was occupied by the
Germans from the moment of proclamation of the Slovak
State until its disappearance. Slovakia had been an independent
state, at least in theory, only from March 14 to March 18
or 23, 1939. With the signing of the Treaty of Protection, it
became a German Protectorate, only less rigid than the
Protectorate of Bohemia and Moravia. The Populist regime
in Slovakia retained no more than a delusion of independence
and sovereignty but its propaganda continued to boast of independence
to the people at home and abroad. Toward Slovakia,
the Germans behaved like a strict governess. They not
only controlled her foreign and defense policy but also gave
orders in the domestic field, especially with regard to economic
and financial matters. Hitler even decided who was and who
was not to be a member of the Slovak Government; he sent
a military mission to Bratislava to control the Slovak Army;
he placed "advisers" (Berater) in Slovak Government departments.
What the Reich Germans were unable to accomplish,
was taken care of by the local, so called Carpathian Germans
and Franz Karmasin. During the existence of the Slovak
State, the Germans conducted themselves in Slovakia as if
they were in annexed territory.

Besides Sudeten Germans and Slovak Separatists, Hungary
under Horthy was another eager ally who helped Hitler to
destroy Czechoslovakia and keep Slovakia in bondage. A
Hungarian Government delegation visited Hitler between
August 21 and 26, 1938. It consisted of the Regent himself,
Admiral Miklós Horthy, of the Prime Minister Béla Imrédy,
the Minister of Foreign Affairs Kálmán Kánya, and the
Minister of War Jenő Rátz. The purpose of the visit was
to discuss the partition of Czechoslovakia and the share of the
loot Hungary was to receive. Hitler made sure of Hungarian
participation in his plans by stating that "whoever wanted to

join the meal would have to participate in the cooking as well." Although the Magyars demanded parts of Czechoslovak territory, they had little appetite for joining any military action. Nevertheless they agreed to render Hitler military assistance in carrying out the plan of "Fall Green." [18] Hitler's diplomatic victory at Munich obviated the need for "Fall Green" or for Hungarian help.

The question of German-Magyar cooperation came once more to the fore in March 1939, when Hitler called on Horthy to participate in the partition of the remnants of Czechoslovakia. Horthy agreed with enthusiasm. In his letter of March 13, 1939, (see Document No. 18) he replied to Hitler: "I can hardly tell you how happy I am. Although Hungarian recruits have been in the army only five weeks, they would fall upon Czechoslovakia with eager enthusiasm. The appropriate dispositions have already been made." As regards timing, the Hungarian invasion would occur "on Thursday, the 16th of this month," when "a frontier incident will take place which will be followed by the big blow on Saturday." Horthy concluded this cynical letter with the words, "I shall never forget this proof of friendship, and your Excellency may rely on my unshakeable gratitude at all times."

Horthy's "big blow" did not fall. Hitler liquidated the remnants of Czechoslovakia without having to fight and there was no need for assistance from Horthy. But Horthy participated in the second partition of Czechoslovakia. He received the remainder of Subcarpathian Ruthenia which he simply annexed to Hungary. Even this was not enough for him. Without the slightest reason, Hungarian units penetrated into Slovakia on March 23, 1939, in spite of the fact that the Slovak State was already in existence, and that the German-Slovak Treaty of Protection was in effect. The Hungarians

[18] Trial of War Criminals, III/51-54. Documents on German Foreign Policy, D/IV, pp. 651-654.

invaded the districts of Sobrance and Michalovce and bombed the airfield of Spišská Nová Ves, which lay deep inside Slovak territory, causing many casualties and great material damage.[19] The incident ended in an armistice on March 24, 1939, and an agreement between Slovakia and Hungary on April 4, 1939, under which Slovakia lost the entire district of Sobrance. Hitler could not have failed to be aware of the Hungarian plan to attack Slovakia. He encited the Slovaks against the Czechs and the Magyars against both. He forced independence upon Slovakia and assumed the protection of the Slovak State. Yet, when the Magyars attacked Slovakia, he gave neither military nor diplomatic assistance.

All of a sudden the world realized not only the important role Czechoslovakia had played in maintaining the balance of power in Europe, but also the acute danger of German aggression to the peace of Europe and of the world. On March 17, 1939, the United States issued a declaration condemning Hitler's aggression against Czechoslovakia. The Declaration (see Document No. 19) states that "the people of the United States have maintained specially close and friendly relations" with Czechoslovakia. On the same day the British Government also lodged a formal protest with the German Government, because of "the flagrant breach of the spirit and the letter of the Munich Agreement" and refused to recognize the new situation in Czechoslovakia as legal. On March 18, 1939, the Soviet Government also protested in Berlin.

---

[19] Armáda v obrane a práci, (The Army in Defense and in Work), Bratislava 1944, pp. 15-25.

Chapter Two

UNDER THE SWASTIKA

Disillusionment and Uncertainty — Terror — The Concentration Camp in Ilava — The Headquarters of State Security — The State Under the "Leader"-Principle — The Constitution of the Slovak State — Privileged Position of HG, HM, FS and DJ — Controlled Press — Slovak National Socialism — Tuka's Program — Cultural Workers — Manifesto of August 31, 1940 — Spiritual and Political Tyranny

As soon as the Slovak State had been proclaimed a feeling of helplessness and of complete dependence on the unreliable and unpredictable German protectors was aggravated by the disillusionment which now set in even among a large group of eager Separatists. From the West the German protectors were invading Slovakia, from the East the Hungarians. Karmasin's Deutsche Partei gave the Bratislava police a 15-minute ultimatum to release the four Reichs-German criminals caught in the act of detonating the time bomb in front of the Jesuit Monastery, guilty also of attempting to assassinate Sidor and of other acts of terrorism. The police capitulated and Sidor resigned from the post of Minister of Interior. Vojtech Tuka was appointed in his stead.[1] Tuka's right hand in the government was Ferdinand Ďurčanský. The third strong man was Alexander Mach, Chief of the Propaganda Office and now also Commander-in-Chief of the Hlinka Guards. These three represented the pro-Nazi and totalitarian wing of the regime.

[1] Karol Sidor: Moje poznámky k historickým dňom, (My Remarks on the Historic Days), 1939 (in manuscript).

142

Jozef Tiso, with the other members of the government and with Jozef Kirschbaum, newly appointed Secretary General of the Slovak People's Party, constituted the more moderate wing. Behind the scenes both factions were fighting each other for power and for German favor. Both were, however, united in their efforts to muzzle their former opponents, especially those who stood for a Czechoslovak political orientation, to get rid of Czechs and Jews, and to strengthen the regime.

Slovakia was at the mercy of the Hlinka Guards and the German Ordners. The advent of Slovak independence led to a wave of uncontrolled terror, persecution, and looting. The Guardists and the Ordners assaulted people of democratic and anti-Separatist views, as well as Czechs and Jews; by day and by night, they picked them in the streets and in their homes, threw them into jail, and beat and robbed them. The former publishing offices of the party's daily, the *"Slovák,"* on Radlinský Street in Bratislava, acquired a morbid notoriety in this respect. This was where the Guardists conducted their most brutal interrogations. People, beaten up and bleeding from their wounds, were thrown into dirty, stifling underground coal-cellars. Personal and political accounts from the past were so settled.

When prisons were no longer adequate, the Slovak Government issued an order on March 24, 1939, "concerning the imprisonment of the enemies of the Slovak State." (See Document No. 20). This order authorized the Minister of Interior to "arrange for the jailing of persons whose past and present activities give reason to fear that they would continue to obstruct the building of the Slovak State." The Minister of the Interior was further authorized to create "a camp for the detention of such persons in which prisoners would be compelled to perform physical labor." [2] Vojtech Tuka lost no time in transforming the old state prison in Ilava into a "security

---

[2] Code of Slovakia, Bratislava, 1939, Order No. 32, part 8, p. 32.

camp," the first concentration camp in Slovak history. The Ilava prison thus became the home of Slovak democrats—of authors, priests, teachers, newspapermen and statesmen, as well as of simple farmers, workmen and students. The first inmates of this camp, brought there on March 30, 1939, were: Anton Štefánek, Ján Ursíny, František Zimák, Ján Pocisk, Ferdinand Benda, Karol Hušek, Ján Paulíny-Tóth, Jozef Rudinský, Pavel Fábry, Andrej Djuračka, František Třešnák, Hana Styková, Vinco Mihaluś and Jozef Lettrich, three Members of Parliament, two Senators, three journalists, the Chairman of the Slovak National Party, and an actress from the Slovak National Theater. Others soon followed. In the few years of existence of the Slovak State more than 3,000 persons were to pass through the gates of the Ilava concentration camp. Some remained a few days, some for months, and others for several years. They were all sent to Ilava without trial, without judgment, without indictment, merely upon a denunciation and by administrative order of the Ministry of Interior. Tuka, on April 15, 1939, made the following characteristic statement, "Those who spread alarming rumors and false reports are obstructing our way. We have made arrangements to handle all of them in Ilava. Many of them are there now and many others will follow them there. It is your duty to denounce these instigators to the police and the Hlinka Guards, and the Slovak Government will take care of them." [3]

Following the German example, the Ministry of Interior set up two other institutions: the Headquarters of State Security (the ÚŠB) and the labor camps. Both were created without legal authority, by simple administrative order. Both rendered signal services in subjecting people to terrible persecution. The Headquarters of State Security became the chief place for interrogating and torturing political opponents. The ÚŠB arrested, imprisoned, persecuted people they did not like.

[3] *"Slovák"*, Bratislava, April 17, 1939.

Some of them were eventually tried, others were sent to Ilava, still others to the labor camps, whether they were guilty of anything or not. The Guardists and Ordners helped the ÚŠB with arrests and investigations. Shock-troops of the HG received special training for this in Germany. Another curious institution emerged in the Slovak State. There was a Police-Attaché, a man named Alfred Goltz, at the German Legation in Bratislava—an agent of the Nazi Gestapo and Sichercheitsdienst. He wielded tremendous powers for he could order the arrest of persons and even their transfer to Germany. Three thousand five hundred ninety-five people were put into jail for political crimes during the existence of the Slovak State. Several thousands more suffered terrible hardship in the labor camps, where they were made to perform very heavy labor in the forests, quarries, on the roads etc. No one had the right to appeal against imprisonment or commitment to a labor camp by ÚŠB. They had no rights and were given no redress, being completely at the mercy of the regime. If released, they were subjected to disagreeable limitations of personal freedom. They were forbidden to enter public places; they were not allowed to have radios; they could not leave their community without special passes; they had to submit their correspondence to the security offices for censorship. The ÚŠB, Ilava, the labor camps, criminal courts, prisons, police, Guardists and Ordners became both the means of terror, symbols of the Slovak regime.

The Slovak Government persecuted its adversaries by other means as well: by firing them from jobs, by making it impossible for them to earn a living, and by confiscating their property. Although these measures were primarily applied to Czechs and Jews, they were also used against a large number of Slovaks. The government decree No. 73/1939 of the Code of Slovakia, "Concerning political profiteers," ordered the confiscation of property of those persons who had acquired their wealth by political means. This decree was nothing but another instrument of vengeance against political opponents.

Whatever has been said of the totalitarian regime introduced by the Slovak People's Party in the period of Slovak Autonomy (October 6, 1938 up to March 14, 1939), was all the more true under the Slovak State. There was no political life at all in the democratic sense of the expression. The Slovak People's Party with 280,000 members in 1943 was the only political party permitted. However, it was no longer a domestic party but a mere imitation of the Nazi NSDAP organization. It, too, was built on the Führer-principle, and all power was vested in the "Leader." Party organs and members were mere advisory elements. The organization was controlled by a system of secretariats and a party bureaucracy, subordinated to the head of the party and to the Secretary General. Jozef Tiso was Prime Minister and as of autumn 1939 he was President of the Slovak State, Chief of the Slovak People's Party and Supreme Commander of the Hlinka Guards. The position in the state of the Slovak People's Party was guaranteed by the Constitution and by a special law. Article 58 of the Constitution of the Slovak State provided that "the Slovak Nation shall participate in government through Hlinka's Slovak People's Party." Law No. 215 of the Code of Slovakia, passed on October 22, 1942, established the Leader-principle in the party. Under this law, the "Leader" stands at the head of the party and "guides the policy of the party." In the course of the Diet debate prior to passing this law, Aladár Kočiš declared that the party "being an organization of selected individuals of the Slovak Nation, is the supreme representative and authorized agent of all expressions of will" of the nation. The party "with the magnanimous help of the Führer of the Great-German Reich, Adolf Hitler, has given back to the nation the state it had a thousand years ago." According to Kočiš the "Leader" had "the supreme right to speak for and to make decisions on behalf of the Party and thereby also on behalf of the nation." "Derived from the Leader's authority is the similar authority and the similar position within their appropriate spheres of the chiefs of regional, district and local organizations, who are directly subordinated to the Leader, and who are responsible to him." Kočiš argued in the Diet that "this is the only system which can guarantee a unified political trend all down the line and an elastic performance of duties, which constitutes the creed of an authoritative system and of an authoritative state." In the political field, the party "likewise operates entirely, one hundred percent, on the authoritative principle. Both the power to decide and full responsibility for decision are entrusted to the single individual." Consequently, a broader party leadership, as we have known it, "is now being changed to an advisory body of the Leader, which will be called the Central Committee." This system "will eliminate entirely the danger of undermining the nation by barren liberalistic-democratic policies." [4]

On July 21, 1939, the Slovak Diet passed the Constitutional Law of the Republic of Slovakia. According to this, the Slovak State was a republic, with an elected President at its head. Bratislava was the capital city. Legislative powers were vested in a Diet consisting of 80 members, elected for five years by universal, direct, equal, and secret voting. The government was given the power to issue "orders with the validity of laws" in cases which could bear no delay. Another body, somewhat similar to an upper Chamber of Parliament, the Council of State, was given the power to impeach the President and Members of the Government, to draw up the list of candidates for election to the Diet and to introduce bills. The Council of State was to consist of six members appointed by the President, ten chosen by the Slovak People's Party, and of one

[4] A. Kočiš: Cesta k Slobode (Road to Liberty) Bratislava, 1944, pp. 120-128.

member each for the minority nationalities and the social
Estates. The Prime Minister and the Speaker of the Diet were
ex officio members of the Council. Members of the Council
were to serve terms of three years. The Constitution accepted
the corporative system of state organization. The population
was grouped into six social Estates, divided between employers
and employees. Apart from that, the Constitution also recognized local units of government. It imposed duties on the
citizens (military service, labor service, the duty to pay taxes,
to provide for the education and schooling of children) and
assured them civil rights and liberties. The rights and liberties,
however, remained mere paper promises which the regime
completely ignored. The Constitution forbade organized interference with work (strikes). Special rights were guaranteed to
the churches and to national minority groups. The Constitution had an odd stipulation. By this provision all laws would
automatically become ineffective after 25 years, and any laws
passed before March 14, 1939, would cease to be operative
after the end of January 1950, unless the Government extended their validity for another 25 years.[5] The Constitution
was never really respected unless it served the ends of the
regime.

Little by little, the legislative powers of the Slovak Diet were
pared down until it was left with practically no power of control at all. The decisive element in the state was the government (cabinet). By means of government decrees, by orders
and by statutory decrees, it usurped all legislative powers.
Next to the government, the most powerful influence was the
President, Tiso. All other agencies of government, with the
sole exception of the HG and the FS, degenerated into mere
executive instruments of the government and the President.

Political opposition was denounced as anti-state activity
and thus was punishable as a serious offense. There was no

[5] No. 185/1939 of the Code of Slovakia.

freedom of assembly and no freedom of the press. Only those associations were tolerated which served the objectives of the regime or which the government specifically permitted. All other associations and all other political or non-political organizations were dissolved and their property confiscated by the state.[6] Workers' unions in factories and mines were dis-banded. In their place, the authorities established workers' councils. [7] Only the Hlinka Guards and the Freiwillige Schutz-staffel of the Germans enjoyed any privileges.

A government order of September 5, 1939, decreed compulsory membership of all males between 6 and 18 years of age in the Hlinka Youth and of men between 18 and 60 years in the Hlinka Guards.[8] This order provoked sharp resentment among the people. The Society of Protestant Clergymen submitted a memorandum of protest to the President, the Government and the Diet on November 21, 1939, demanding that the requirement of compulsory membership in the HG and HY be changed to voluntary. The government had to give way to public resentment and issued a new statutory decree on December 21, 1939. The Decree stipulated that "the Hlinka Guards are a corps organized according to military principles within the framework of Hlinka's Slovak People's Party" whose duty is "to provide pre-military training, submit appropriate reports and proposals to those authorities whom it may concern, and to assist the authorities in defending the state as well as in maintaining public order and public security." The Hlinka Guards were organized in Youth Corps (the Hlinka Youth) and Guard Corps. Members of the Guard Corps, specially chosen for specific duties, constituted the Rodobrana. The Guardists had the right to wear a uniform and to bear and use arms under the same rules as the police. They enjoyed the protection provided by law for

---

[6] Government Decree No. 125/1939, Code of Slovakia.
[7] Government Decree No. 142/1939, Code of Slovakia.
[8] Statutory Decree No. 220/1939, Code of Slovakia.

the police corps. Their expenditure came from budgetary
funds. Any employer who failed to permit a Guardist to attend
his Guard duties was found guilty of a misdemeanor and
subjected to a fine up to 5,000 Crowns and imprisonment up
to one month.[9] Identical rules applied to the Freiwillige
Schutzstaffel and its component part, the Deutsche Jugend
(DJ), which were organized in the same way. Its privileges
were assured by the Statutory Decree of December 21, 1939.[10]
By a law of July 4, 1940, the Chairman of the Slovak People's
Party was made the Commander-in-Chief of the Hlinka
Guards and the Party's Deputy-Chairmen were made his Dep-
uty Commanders.[11]

Apart from party newspapers, only one paper was permitted
to make its appearance, the *"Národnie Noviny,"* the oldest
Slovak paper, which had been the party-paper of the Slovak
National Party. There were no other political periodicals. Cultural publications and those of the churches were rigidly
controlled and were not permitted to print anything not in
complete accord with the official doctrines of the regime. Not
a word could be uttered that did not square with the party
line. A former member of the Slovak Autonomous Government and a Member of the Slovak Diet, Miloš Vančo, gave
the following testimony before the National Tribunal in Bratislava on February 10, 1947: "The *'Národnie Noviny'* and
the church periodicals *'Cirkevné Listy'* and *'Evanjelický Posol
zpod Tatier'* had to pass the censorship of the District Office,
the State police and the District Attorney, and every edition
had to be submitted to the Ministry of Interior which again
censored it. We were often instructed that such and such an
article was to appear and that one of us, either Fedor Jesenský
or I, was to sign it as the author. We used to draw matches
and the one who drew the burnt match then signed the article

9 Statutory Decree No 310/1939, Code of Slovakia.
10 Statutory Decree No. 311/1939, Code of Slovakia.
11 Law No. 166/1940, Code of Slovakia.

as his own. We quipped about that, saying it was symbolic of what was in store for the author, whose reputation in the eyes of the nation would go up in flames." These three newspapers were opposed to the Slovak totalitarian regime. Nevertheless, if they wanted to continue to make their appearance, they had to submit to ruthless censorship and to publish articles supplied by the regime under the names of their own publishers and editors, no matter how offensive to their traditions and conscience.

The Propaganda Office became the exclusive source of information about events at home and abroad. It supplied papers, the radio, and other publications with articles which were but monotonous repetitions of such slogans as Germany's leadership of the European continent, Hitler's genius, the unalterable alliance of Slovakia with Germany, the freedom and independence of the Slovak State, the wisdom of Tiso's leadership, the glorious exploits of the Slovak Army on the battlefront, the need to rid the state of Jews, Czechs, Czechoslovaks, and so forth. Alexander Mach, and after him Tido Gašpar, were the Chief of the Propaganda Office. Another no less zealous propagandist of the regime was Konštantín Čulen, whose output in numbers of articles and radio-harangues surpassed even the performance of the other two.

The ideology of the Slovak People's Party underwent a significant change. From a conservative, nationalist, and clerical party with democratic traditions, it developed into one dedicated to the doctrine of totalitarian separatism. After the proclamation of the Slovak State, the party found itself on the horns of a preposterous dilemma: it tried to find a compromise between the principles proclaimed by the Papal Encyclicals and by German National Socialism. It tried to square the circle. The end product was a confused corporate doctrine, solemnized by the constitution of the state. Following the outbreak of the Second World War a regroupment took place within the party. One part of the Populists, grouped around Tuka, favored the adoption of an undiluted German national socialist order in Slovakia; the other, led by Tiso, was more inclined to preserve Populist traditionalism, nationalism, and clericalism. The conflict between the two trends was, however, soon resolved by Hitler's interference in this domestic problem of Slovakia. In the course of a visit by Tiso with Hitler in Salzburg, toward the end of July 1940, Hitler simply ordered that all key positions be given to Tuka's adherents. These, in turn, introduced a new political ideology in Slovakia, which they called Slovak national socialism. The fundamental idea of this imported ideology was the mythical unity of a racially pure Slovak Nation, organized by the Slovak People's Party and led by the Leader Jozef Tiso. Slovak national socialism professed the creed of a "common destiny" of Slovakia and the German Reich, and of a common destiny of Slovaks and the German and Hungarian racial minorities in Slovakia. As a result, it sternly denounced any intermixing of Slovak blood with that of Czechs and Jews. This doctrine fully endorsed solving the Jewish problem according to the Nuremberg laws of Germany. In the realm of politics, the new creed opposed democratic institutions and embraced authoritarianism, with the slogan—"One nation, one party, one Leader." Slovak national socialists agitated with equal fervor against a liberal economic system which it denounced as a "plutocracy" and demanded that it be replaced by a national socialist and Christian economic structure. Tuka became the ideologist of Slovak national socialism. In faithful imitation of the 25 points of German National Socialism proclaimed by Hitler in Munich on February 24, 1924, he, in turn, proclaimed a 14 Point-Program of Slovak national socialism at a course for commanders of the Hlinka Guards in Trenčianske Teplice, on January 21, 1941. Willy-nilly, Tiso and his faction joined the ranks of Slovak national socialists, and the Slovak People's Party thus also came to accept this program as its own. From 1940 on, all official pronouncements, speeches, articles, and radio-comments proclaimed the ideas of national socialism. From then on, worshiping and adulating of Hitler became the order of the day. Rev. Ján Ferenčik, who had succeeded Hlinka as Roman Catholic priest in Ružomberok, proclaimed on March 13, 1940, in the Slovak Diet, that he regarded Hitler as "the extraordinary tool of Divine Providence." In May 1940, Msgr. Alexander Messik-Vajda explained to his audience in Sliač, that "90% of the Catholic clergy in Slovakia are enthusiastic disciples of Hitler who are praying for his victory." On May 25, 1940, Alexander Mach declared in Nitra that "Hitler was the finger of God pointing the way and showing what had to be done." Vojtech Tuka wrote the following in the paper *"Gardista"* on January 1, 1942, "I need only point to repeated pronouncements of Hitler himself in which he incessantly invokes Providence and God's help and in which he religiously emphasizes that he is nothing but a tool in the hands of just Providence." Following the unsuccessful attempt upon Hitler's life, Alexander Mach wrote the German Minister, Hans Elard Ludin, on July 21, 1944, "Not only Germany needs the Führer, but the other nations of Europe also need him." Konštantín Čulen wrote in the *"Slovák"* on February 21, 1940, "They write of Germany as an undemocratic country, yet for sure few democracies in the world have done as much for the little man as has Germany in the last few years where a word with deeper intrinsic meaning has been substituted for the word democracy —the word friendship . . . May we be inspired to move forward by the example of German discipline, order, manly courage to overcome obstacles, and purposeful work." According to the *"Slovák"* of November 21, 1939, Franz Karmasin declared that "the Germans in Slovakia are doing what the Führer (Adolf Hitler) commands them to do."

Other cultural workers behaved in the same manner while serving the regime. For instance the author Tido J. Gašpar said that he had fought "for the radical elimination of all remnants of the old system of exploitation carried over from the liberalist constitution of capitalism" because "so long as there was a liberalist-capitalist system in the world, we were slaves" and then he added: "As soon as the National Socialist forces began to demolish and remove that system, we were freed." According to Gašpar "national socialism is a system which will inject a new spirit into the new European order" and therefore "we must fulfil and systematically carry out the program of Slovak national socialism."[12]

Two young ideologists of the party made an attempt to analyse and to justify the confused notions of Slovak national socialism. Stanislav Mečiar wrote a book entitled *Slovak National Socialism* and Štefan Polakovič wrote two books, *The Foundations of the Slovak State* and *Tiso's Struggle*. Mečiar explained that "national socialism is in complete harmony with Slovak national traditions," that "it is impossible to accept the doctrine that all people are alike" that "Jews are not equal to Slovaks"; that "one cannot create such conditions as to make it possible for Slovaks and Jews to live together"; that "the essential elements of the nation, indeed the nation itself is (determined by) race and blood"; that "the national socialist system repudiates the old democratic forms of Parliament"; that "we have accepted an authoritative system"; that "a Slovak priest ought not let himself be misled by allegations that the Church in Germany is in conflict with national socialism"; that "rigid decrees, such as not even Germany has applied, had been introduced by us to prevent all sorts of machinations between Jews and the so-called White Jews" (i.e. people who were helping persecuted Jews); that

---

[12] Tido J. Gašpar: Za dobro celku, (For the Commonwealth), Bratislava, 1942, pp. 45, 50, 54, 86.

"not until the last Jew has left Slovakia will we be able to say that the Jewish problem has been solved"; and that "it is our fervent hope that we shall soon see the day when there will be no more Jews in Slovakia, nor in all of Europe." Another ideologist, Viliam Ries-Javor, had this to say: "National socialism and fascism, two positive and constructive principles of state, recognize the authoritarian form of government as opposed to the false principles of democracy by which the people are allegedly the source of all power, and place a Leader at the head of the state. All power and all responsibility are vested in the Leader. After destroying outdated parliamentarism, the Leader is directly answerable to the nation which placed him at its head. The entire legislative and administrative process has been simplified." [13]

Tiso himself, when inaugurating the new railroad line from Prešov to Strážske, declared on September 5, 1943, that loyalty and devotion to Hitler and the German Reich are products of Slovak patriotism. On the same day Tuka told the Cabinet that "Slovakia reaffirms her will to fulfil all her duties under the Slovak-German Treaty." The periodical *"Gardista"* appealed to the public on September 3, 1943, to "remain sincerely and faithfully at the side of Germany." The Editor in Chief of the *"Gardista"* was the author Milo Urban. Besides Gašpar, Urban, Mečiar and Polakovič, two poets, Andrej Žarnov (whose real name is Dr. František Šubík) and Valentín Beniak also performed valuable services to the national socialist ideology and to the totalitarian policy of the Slovak People's Party. They sponsored a convention of cultural workers in Tatranská Lomnica on August 31, 1940. The meeting passed a resolution which was also signed by the following: František Hrušovský, Stanislav Mečiar, Juraj Čečetka, Jozef Ambruš, Frico Motoška, Ján Smrek, Vladimír Rolko, Henrik

[13] Viliam Ries-Javor: Kontinent v prerode (Continent in Regeneration), Bratislava, 1943, p. 78.

Bartek and Jozef Cincík. This resolution (see Document No. 21) proclaimed that Slovak national socialism is "the continuation and further development of Slovak national forces in the spirit of our traditions." National socialism is, it is claimed, the system "which best complies with the needs of Slovak life." Through it "Slovak life is extricating itself from the liberalist-capitalist sphere." In view of this, the assembled cultural workers "emphatically demand that this system, which best assures Slovak statehood, be systematically, uncompromisingly and immediately put into effect by the responsible authorities in all fields of national existence."

Opposed to these Slovak authors were the men of letters who stood firm for spiritual freedom and who led the resistance against the enslavers and their stooges. Foremost among them was the fearless poet, a former Legionnaire of the First World War, Janko Jesenský. His fighting poems, aimed at the torrent of national socialism, at the puppets and idols of the day, helped to maintain the faith and hope of the Slovak people in the final victory of the Czechoslovak cause. The two Protestant bishops, Vladimír Čobrda and Samuel Š. Osuský, issued a pastoral letter on May 20, 1942, in which they took a stand against "the changing, nationally immature, and unproven philosophic political and social ideologies" of the Slovak State.

The political tyranny of the Slovak State was aggravated by the spiritual tyranny of national socialism. From time immemorial Slovakia had as her emblem the episcopal cross as a symbol of Christianity and Western civilization. Now the Hlinka Guards adopted the cross and wore it on arm-bands and insignia, after the pattern of the German swastika. It was an abuse of the cross, an abuse all the more painful as the cross covered up the anti-Christian, basically pagan spirit of Hitler's National Socialism, symbolized by the swastika.

IN GERMANY'S GRIP

Vassals of the Third Reich — Černák as Minister in Berlin — German Attack on Poland — Slovakia a Base for the Attack — Participation of the Slovak State in the War Against Poland — Friendly Relations between Bratislava and Moscow — Visit with Hitler in Salzburg — Changes in the Slovak Government — The Fall of Ďurčanský — The Joining of Slovakia in the Tripartite Pact — Slovakia at War with the USSR, USA and Great Britain — German Economic Exploitation of Slovakia — Occupation of All of Slovakia by the German Army

The ideology, diplomacy and politics of the Slovak State made it well suited for the role of a German vassal. The establishment of political totalitarianism of German pattern, the signing of the Slovak-German Treaty of Protection, and the adoption of German National Socialist doctrines had well prepared Slovakia for the performance of any assignment given to it by Berlin. All this was of vital importance for the Reich in view of Slovakia's significant strategic position, its great natural wealth and its means of communication. These became even more vital after Germany had started the Second World War. The Bratislava regime was absolutely dependent upon the Third Reich. Consequently it faithfully fulfilled the role of a German satellite and made great and incessant efforts to convince the people of Slovakia that Germany's interests were identical with the interests of Slovakia, that service to the Germans was also service to Slovakia. The entire collaborationist policy of the leaders of the Slovak State was based

157

on this spurious argument, which they tried to make more palatable by proclaiming that Hitler had a personal, nay, a emotional interest in the Slovaks and that Slovakia owed a debt of gratitude to Germany for her liberation. Official propaganda rammed Hitler down the throats of the Slovak people as their liberator and as the protector of a joint German-Slovak future. Hitler's 50th birthday was celebrated with much official ostentation in Slovakia. In Michalovce, e.g., local Hlinka Guard Commanders ordered the hanging out of Slovak and swastika flags from April 19 to 21, 1939.[1] On June 4, 1939, J. Kirschbaum, at a meeting in Devinská Nová Ves, publicly denounced those who, in protest, had put secret leaflets in circulation, protesting this. Kirschbaum asked his audience, "Tell me where do you see that German slavery which the cowardly authors of the leaflet would have you believe? Every worthy Slovak man and woman knows that the Slovak Nation never had such opportunities for living according to its own inclinations as it has today. For that we must thank the Great German Nation."

The Slovak Legation in Berlin was the most significant diplomatic mission of the Slovak State. The Minister of Slovakia, accredited to Adolf Hitler in Berlin, had to enjoy the unlimited confidence of both the Bratislava and the Berlin regimes, being the liaison between the Chief of the Slovak State and the Führer of the Third Reich. The importance of the Legation in Berlin was further increased by the circumstance that the foreign and military policy of Slovakia, in accordance with the Treaty of Protection, was made, in effect, in Berlin and not in Bratislava.

Matúš Černák was the man chosen for this post. The Slovak Minister in Berlin was the Commander of the Hlinka Youth and a Member of the Slovak Diet; earlier he had been a member of Slovak and Czechoslovak Cabinets. Černák was

[1] *"Slovák"*, Bratislava, May 2, 1939.

fully aware of the importance of his position. When leaving for Berlin, on April 13, 1939, he declared, "Upon Germany has fallen the burden of organizing a new Central Europe and in this task we, too, wish to assume our share at the side of Germany." At the first audience granted to him by Hitler on April 19, 1939, he emphasized that "the Slovak State was created in a time characterized by an upsurge of nationalist thinking in Europe, under the powerful influence of German National Socialism" and that "the Slovak State is a link in the chain of this development." [2] German National Socialists welcomed Černák among themselves with open arms. On July 10, 1939, he was the guest of honor of the Reich-leader of the Hitler Youth, Baldur von Schirach, in Greibsee-Senftenberg, in Magdeburg and in Halle. On February 13, 1940, he was the guest of Reich-Marshal Hermann Göring in Karinhalle. Every diplomatic or military act of the Slovak State during the Second World War was linked with Černák's five years of activity in Berlin, in particular Slovak participation in the wars against Poland and the USSR, Slovakia's accession to the Tripartite Pact and the declaration of war against the Western Powers. As the principal speaker at the anniversary celebration of the establishment of the Slovak State, Černák declared in Berlin on March 14, 1944, that "it was not the exalted democracies of the West but Germany which had helped Slovakia to come into her own." The Slovak Minister concluded his speech by pledging his country to continue as an ardent and faithful comrade-in-arms of Germany in the fight for a better Europe, which would be liberated from materialism.

Slovakia was of outstanding value to Hitler in his attack on Poland, as he was now able from it to threaten the entire southern border of Poland. The Polish Army, deprived of a natural line of defense, was at the mercy of the Germans.

[2] *"Slovák"*, Bratislava, April 20, 1939.

The German Army Command had made the necessary preparation in Slovakia, long before the attack. German military
advisers had been placed in the Ministry of National Defense
in Bratislava as early as April 1939. Their task was to adapt
the training of Slovak troops to that of the German Army and
prepare the passage of German forces through Slovakia into
Poland. During the summer of 1939, highways, bridges, and
railroad sidings were adapted to German requirements and
specifications. The German Army accumulated six railroad
cars of 1000 pound aircraft bombs and 50,000 gallons of
aircraft fuel in Spišská Nová Ves. In August 1939 German
armored, mountain, and infantry units moved through Slovakia and took up positions along the Slovak-Polish border,
in readiness for the attack. At the end of August, the Slovak
Government placed the airfields in Spišská Nová Ves, Vinné
and elsewhere at the disposal of the German Air Forces as
bases for bombing attacks upon Poland. General mobilization
of the Slovak Army and of the Hlinka Guards was ordered
on August 28, 1939, in anticipation of an attack on Poland.
The Minister of National Defense, General Ferdinand Čatloš,
issued an order of the day on September 1, 1939, stating—"A
new historic test of the Slovak Nation, of the Slovak Army
has arisen. Our interests have linked us with the German
Army and have established a state of war between us and
Poland. Fighting has begun on this day!" [3] Slovakia had diplomatic relations with Poland. Poland had neither declared
war upon nor attacked Slovakia. Yet, upon orders of the
Slovak Government and in pursuance of instructions from
Berlin, the Slovak forces attacked Poland on September 1,
1939, and occupied the communities that had been taken
from Slovakia and ceded to Poland in 1919. Military operations were confined to Polish territory along the Slovak-Polish

[3] *"Slovák"*, Bratislava, September 3, 1939.

frontier.[4] When the military campaign against Poland came
to an end, Hitler sent a telegram to Jozef Tiso on September
25, 1939, thanking him "for the resolute stand and tested
brotherhood in arms" and assuring him that "the German
Nation and its government fully appreciated this attitude and
will fully reciprocate the feelings of which it bears evidence."
In October 1939, Hitler made two gestures of appreciation
to the Slovak State. He permitted annexation to Slovakia of
the communities in the regions of Spiš and Orava, which had
been ceded to Poland in 1919, and awarded the Grand Cross
of the Order of the German Eagle to Tiso on the occasion of
his election as President of the Slovak State.[5]

After the military invasion of Poland was completed, Tiso,
on October 1, 1939, formulated the policy of the state, at a
convention of the Slovak People's Party in Trenčín. He declared, "We chose a German orientation. And we shall continue along this path, because we believe in this orientation
. . . I assured Hitler that he would never be disappointed in
the Slovak State." True to the spirit of this orientation, Tiso's
regime had succeeded in antagonizing two Slav nations within
six months, the Czechs and the Poles. He did not stop there.
Slovakia also became a German base for attack against the
Balkans and the East. During the winter of 1940/41 and in
spring 1941 Slovakia placed all her means of communication
at the disposal of the Germans for moving troops, arms and
ammunition needed in the attacks upon Greece, Yugoslavia
and the Soviet Union. Official Slovak policy was antagonistic
to Yugoslavia and Russia because these countries were anti-
German in their attitude. The Slovak State maintained friendly relations only with two other Slav nations, the Croatians
and the Bulgarians. This was because the war-time Croatian

[4] Armáda v obrane a práci (The Army in Defense and in Work) Bratislava,
1944, pp. 26-32.
[5] *"Slovák"*, Bratislava, October 3, 1939.

puppet-state under Ante Pavelić and Bulgaria under Czar Boris were satellites of the Third Reich no less than Slovakia. Relations of the Slovak State with the Soviet Union faithfully followed Germany's policy. At first it proclaimed a sharply anti-Soviet and anti-Communist attitude. On March 22, 1939, an anti-Bolshevik exhibition was opened in Bratislava. The propaganda of the Slovak State denounced communism as an anti-Christian doctrine and Bolshevism as a threat to European peace. After the Nazi-Soviet Pact was signed, the pact which cleared the decks for the start of the Second World War, the Slovak State completely reversed itself. Minister Matúš Černák called on the Soviet Ambassador in Berlin in September 1939. The Slovak Press Agency issued an official bulletin about this visit, which stated that "upon instructions of the Council of People's Commissars of the USSR and of its chairman, Comissar for Foreign Affairs Molotov, the Soviet Ambassador in Berlin (Alexander) Shkarcev today notified the Slovak Minister Černák of the decision that the USSR was extending recognition de jure and de facto to the Slovak State and that it wished to enter into diplomatic relations with it." [6] Meanwhile Slovak propaganda was making frantic efforts to explain to the people of Slovakia that Russians were also Slavs, that Nazi-Soviet friendship was the best safeguard of European stability, that the Soviet regime was a domestic matter, of concern only to the Russians etc.

On November 18, 1939, the *"Slovák"* reported that a Slovak Legation was being set up in Moscow, that Fraňo Tiso had been appointed first Slovak Minister to the USSR and had already taken up duties there. At that time, there still existed a Czechoslovak Legation in Moscow, with Zdeněk Fierlinger as Minister. The fact that the Soviet Government had continued to recognize the Czechoslovak Legation in

6 *"Slovák"*, Bratislava, September 16, 1939.

Moscow even after the German invasion of Czechoslovakia, had been interpreted as an indication that Czechoslovakia would be restored after the end of the war; this hope had contributed toward maintaining the spirit of resistance of Czechs and Slovaks against the German oppressors. It was also entirely natural that the Soviet Union should continue to recognize Czechoslovakia even after the German occupation, in view of the fact that Czechoslovakia had a Treaty of Alliance with only two Powers, France and the Soviet Union. Now, the Soviet Government treacherously broke the Czechoslovak-Soviet Treaty of Alliance, withdrew recognition from Czechoslovakia, broke off diplomatic relations with the Republic and instead, recognized the Slovak State and entered into diplomatic relations with Bratislava. Minister Fierlinger was formally notified on December 14, 1939, that the Soviet Government "can no longer recognize his diplomatic character." The new Soviet Minister in Bratislava, Georgi Maximovich Pushkin, arrived in Bratislava on February 3, 1940. On February 14, 1940, he told President Jozef Tiso in his first address that "the nations of the Soviet Union had taken great satisfaction in the establishment of diplomatic relations between the Soviet Union and the Slovak Republic," a fact which "in view of the war in Europe is of significance beyond the interests of our two nations." Tiso was no less generous in expressing his warm feelings to the representative of Moscow. In his reply to Pushkin he emphasized that he welcomed "with sincere joy Pushkin's appointment to Bratislava" and that "the Slovak Nation welcomes the arrival of the representative of the Soviet Union." [7] The Soviet Legation in Bratislava set to work with a conspicuously large staff, whose duties could hardly have been limited to diplomatic activities.

Slovak-Soviet relations began to develop with much cordiality. When the Slovak Prime Minister Vojtech Tuka was

[7] *"Slovák"*, Bratislava, February 15, 1940.

inaugurated as President of the University of Slovakia, on January 14, 1940, the Soviet Government sent a special delegation to Bratislava to participate at the ceremony. The Soviet delegation was led by the Chairman of the Committee for Universities, Professor Kaftanov, and the delegation included Professors Novikov, Deynek, Vilensky, and Egolin. The Soviet delegation loudly proclaimed friendship between the Soviet Union and the Slovak State. Kaftanov predicted a great future to the Slovak State as a result of the collaboration of "the two most powerful nations (Germany and Russia) who have resolved to reorganize the shape of Europe." [8] Bratislava paid back Moscow's compliment by sending a delegation, led by the Minister of Education and Enlightenment, Jozef Sivák, to Moscow, to participate in the celebrations at Moscow University and of May-Day, 1940. This delegation included Professors Dr. Michal Šeliga, Dr. Jozef Fundárek, Dr. Emanuel Filo and Dr. Ján Stanislav. Political propaganda in Slovakia saw in this sufficient proof that "the Slovak State exists and will continue to exist, for such is the will of Germany and the will of Russia. We are on good terms with both these mighty empires, now working together in friendly cooperation in all matters. It is at the same time interesting to note that whilst Jewish owls of doom in our country are trying to frighten us with stories about Bolshevism, genuine Russian patriotism in opposition to internationalism is awakening in Russia." This change occurred, to quote these speakers, "as a result of Russian-German cooperation.[9]

Neither the Nazi-Soviet cooperation nor Moscow's friendship toward Slovakia were very durable. As soon as Hitler invaded the Soviet Union in June 1941, Slovak troops were again marching along with the German Army. Without even declaring war, the Slovak State attacked the Soviet Union.

[8] *"Slovák"*, Bratislava, January 16, 1940.
[9] Juraj Gajdoš-Breza: Dni obrody (Days of Regeneration), Prešov, 1940, pp. 136-137.

That was the end of Slovak-Soviet cooperation and friendship.

In 1940, the Bratislava regime was again in the throes of an acute political crisis, caused by a struggle for power inside the Slovak People's Party and the Government between the followers of Tiso and those of Tuka. One of Tuka's adherents, Alexander Mach, resigned his position as Commander-in-Chief of the Hlinka Guards, on February 21, 1940. Tiso accepted the resignation on May 21, 1940, and appointed one of his own men, František Galan, to command the Guards. Both in Slovakia and Germany this change was considered to be indicative of a strengthening of the influence of Tiso at the expense of Tuka's radical pro-German tendencies. At that time, Ferdinand Ďurčanský also attempted to conduct a more independent Slovak foreign policy, especially with regard to Soviet Russia. Germany was vigilantly watching these developments and there can be little doubt that Tuka's people were intriguing against Tiso in Germany. Berlin once more ruthlessly interfered in Slovak domestic matters. The German Minister left Bratislava and Berlin thereby gave the Slovaks to understand that it would not tolerate political changes in Slovakia without its prior consent. The German Minister returned in July and informed Tiso that Adolf Hitler wished to meet with Tiso, Tuka and Mach in Salzburg. The ommission of Ferdinand Ďurčanský was significant, as he had previously been *persona grata* in Berlin. Nevertheless, Tiso took Ďurčanský along with him. When Ribbentrop met Tiso in Salzburg, on July 29, 1940, Ribbentrop requested Tiso to dismiss Ďurčanský as Minister of Foreign Affairs and to appoint Tuka in his stead. Alexander Mach was to be made Minister of Interior. When Tiso showed signs of disagreement, Ribbentrop threatened that Hitler would not receive him unless he accepted Ribbentrop's demands for a change in the Slovak Government. Tiso could not resist this pressure and accepted, promising Ribbentrop that he would effect the required changes as soon as he returned to Bratislava. After the visit with Ribbentrop, Hitler received Tiso, Tuka and Mach. The reception was cool. Hitler told Tiso that if "the Slovaks, as Slavs, wished to go along with the Russians, he would have no objections, but they would then have to bear the consequences." Ribbentrop informed Hitler in Tiso's presence that he had already "straightened out" the matter of the changes in the Slovak Government. Neither Ribbentrop nor Hitler received Ďurčanský. Meanwhile Ďurčanský was waiting in embarrassed isolation in Salzburg the sentence that would be pronounced on his political career by those same representatives of the Third Reich to whom he had rendered such signal services, especially in 1938-1939.[10]

The Salzburg visit was of far-reaching importance for the internal and foreign policy of the Slovak State. Back from Salzburg, Tiso made the required changes in the Government. Tuka became Minister of Foreign Affairs. Alexander Mach was appointed Minister of Interior and Commander-in-Chief of the Hlinka Guards. Ferdinand Ďurčanský was dismissed from the government and from political activities, thus sharing the earlier fate of his political rival, Karol Sidor. Tuka's people, entirely subservient to Germany, now came to the fore and Tiso's more moderate followers were pushed aside. Salzburg meant the victory of Germanophile tendencies even in those fields where a semblance of independent political attitudes had been precariously maintained. German National Socialism became the political ideology of the regime in Slovakia. Slovakia became still more subservient to the Third Reich.

After the fall of France, Hitler, failing to subdue Britain, resolved to attack the Soviet Union. On September 27, 1940, he signed the Tripartite Pact with Italy and Japan by which

---

[10] Testimony of Jozef Tiso before the National Tribunal in Bratislava. (*"Čas"*, Bratislava, August 3, 1946).

these three powers divided Europe and Asia into spheres of interest. Article 1 of the Pact states that "Japan recognizes and will respect German and Italian leadership in establishing a new order in Europe." In return, Germany and Italy, according to Article 2 "recognize and will respect the leadership of Japan in establishing a new order in the Great East-Asian area." The Powers of the Berlin-Rome-Tokio Axis "agreed to coordinate their efforts on the above basis" and accepted "the obligation mutually to support one another with all political, economic and military means." (Article 3.) The Tripartite Pact changed the course of the Second World War. Germany obtained pledges from her satellites that they would go along with her military operations which were being prepared against the East and the West. Following the preliminary discussions by Minister Matúš Černák, Prime Minister and Minister of Foreign Affairs Vojtech Tuka signed an agreement in Berlin, on November 24, 1940, with the assistance of Matúš Černák, whereby the Slovak State acceded to the Tripartite Pact. The Protocol concerning this accession was published in the Code of Slovakia as No. 32/1941. The initiative for this had been taken by Tuka. The participation of the Slovak State in the war against the Soviet Union and the United States was the logical consequence. The Slovak Diet gave its approval to the Protocol of Accession to the Tripartite Pact on February 6, 1941.

In accordance with the stipulations of the German-Slovak Treaty of Protection and of the Tripartite Pact, the Slovak Army was made ready for action. In March 1941 the Slovak Government negotiated an agreement with Germany concerning the anti-aircraft defense, the construction of railroad sidings and the adaptation of railroad stations to accommodate German military transports in preparation for the attack upon the USSR. When Hitler attacked the Soviet Union on June 22, 1941, the Slovak Government ordered Slovak troops to take part in the attack along with the German Army, although it had never declared war nor obtained the approval of the Slovak Diet, as required by the Constitution. That is how the Slovak State became involved in the war with the Soviet Union. On June 24, 1941, Jozef Tiso sent Hitler a cable declaring that "Slovakia, with gun in hand, is joining in the decisive fight." Tiso further assured Hitler of "the loyalty and alliance of the Slovak Nation and its government, as well as its unshakeable faith in victory." (See Document No. 22.) On the same day Hitler cabled back to Tiso, thanking him for "the statement that Slovakia had entered the decisive fight for the future of Europe at the side of Germany and for the assurance of its faithful alliance." (See Document No. 23.) In the first phase of the German-Soviet War, the Slovak State sent 50,689 armed troops against the USSR. In the second phase of the war, but 16,303 effectives were fighting against the USSR. Slovak citizens belonging to the German racial group, supported by the German Government, had obtained permission from the Slovak Government on July 21, 1940, to serve in the German Army. Slovak participation in the war against the USSR cost Slovakia a great many casualties and exceptionally large economic sacrifices. Participation was determined exclusively by German imperialistic ambitions, to which the regime of Slovakia was so eagerly subservient. The outcome was that the battle-front swept across Slovak territory in 1944-45, causing immeasurable suffering and damage.

The Slovak State also made common cause with Germany in its attitude toward Great Britain and the United States, although it was not immediately given an opportunity to fight the armies of the Western Powers. When Bratislava declared war on Great Britain and the United States, it again failed to comply with the procedures prescribed by the Constitution and international law. Doubts have been voiced as to whether the Slovak State had been in a state of war with those powers at all. Such doubts are, however, dispelled by the facts of the matter. Between September 3, 1939, the date when Great Britain entered the war with Germany, and December 11, 1941, when Germany declared war upon the United States, Slovakia had been involved only in psychological, not military warfare with Great Britain. A change took place after the Japanese attack on Pearl Harbor. At the request of Berlin, the Slovak Ministry of Foreign Affairs sent a note to the Chancellery of Jozef Tiso on December 13, 1941, attached to which was the text of an announcement of a declaration of war on the United States and Great Britain. The note mentioned that Tiso had approved the declaration of war by telephone from Javorina. The Chancellery of the President of the Republic replied to the Ministry of Foreign Affairs on the same day that it was returning the proclamation of the declaration of war, signed by Tiso. The Constitutional provision was again ignored. A report of the state of war between Slovakia and the United States as well as Great Britain was published on December 13, 1941, in the paper *"Slovenská politika."* The President of the United States, Franklin D. Roosevelt, already on December 12, 1941 learned that the Slovak Government had declared war on the United States and informed the Secretary of State, Cordell Hull, in a memorandum that same day (Document No. 24) that the United States "should pay no attention to any declarations of war by puppet Governments" (of Germany, such as the Slovak, Hungarian, Rumanian, and Bulgarian Governments).[11]

From then on the Slovak State behaved toward America and Britain as toward enemy countries. When Anglo-American aircraft appeared over Slovakia, the state-controlled radio always announced the arrival of "enemy war-planes." The British and American authorities themselves considered Slovakia as an enemy region subject to their bombing attacks.

11 The Memoirs of Cordell Hull, Volume II, New York, 1948, p. 1175.

Anglo-American planes bombed Bratislava on June 16, and December 9, 1944, Dubnica nad Váhom at the end of June 1944, Dubová on August 26, 1944, as well as other Slovak cities. In the autumn of 1943, the Slovak Government withdrew its so-called security division from the Soviet front, reequipped it as a technical division and moved it, in October 1943, against the American and British armies in Italy, where it built bridges and fortifications. Under the command of Ján Veselý, its operations eventually covered most of Italy.[12] When the Anglo-American forces landed in France, Tido J. Gašpar proclaimed: "All our thoughts and hearts observe this grandiose (German) fight with admiration and we believe that the shady alliance for the annihilation of Europe will be conquered. The Slovaks, fighting for the future of free Slovakia, will continue faithfully on the path pointed out by the Leader and President, because this is the path of honor, truth, and victory and we shall not be misled by the foreign enemy tempter."[13] Prime Minister Vojtech Tuka reacted as follows to the reports of the invasion by the American and British forces: "The attempt at invasion is the climax of the Anglo-American crime to surrender Europe to the Bolshevik hordes. The hearts of all true Europeans are with the German soldiers and their allies in the West and in the East" (*Deutsche Zeitung in Norwegen*, June 7, 1944). Minister of the Interior, Alexander Mach, upon hearing of the landing of these armies in France, had this to say in the School of the Hlinka Guards in Zvolen: "In this fight the heart of the Slovak Nation is on the side of the German soldier and of all those who defend Europe."

Even the Slovak League in America, while defending the Slovak State and its policy, has had to admit that "Slovakia got

[12] *"Slovák"*, Bratislava, January 21, 1945.
[13] *"Slovák"*, June 13, 1944.

into the war against the United States." [14] Slovak troops were
dispatched to battle with such bombastic phrases as "our
confession of faith" in "the Führer of national socialist Europe
—Adolf Hitler," in "the victory of the German armies on all
battlefronts" and the victory of "the German soldier over
world Jewry, capitalism and communism," in "the birth of a
New Europe" and so forth, which appear in a book by Eduard
Pyšný, published by the Bratislava Ministry of National Defense. [15]

Apart from direct participation in the fighting during the
Second World War, Slovakia also provided valuable economic
and material aid to Germany. After the Salzburg conference,
the Germans got hold of by far the greater part of Slovak
exports, for which they either paid nothing, because the price
paid for Slovak goods was put into clearing-accounts and
never cleared, or else paid for with luxury-goods or useless
products (cameras, field-glasses, etc.). The Germans exploited
Slovak natural resources, such as lumber and ores. The Slovak
railroads, the great armament works in Dubnica nad Váhom,
Povážska Bystrica, and Stará Turá, the oil refineries in Bratislava and Dubová, chemical and other industries essential to
the war effort, were almost exclusively geared to serve the
Germans. The most blatant instance of German exploitation
occurred when on March 29, 1941, Germany forced Slovakia
to hand over the large Slovak foundries in Podbrezová, with
all branch factories, to the German Hermann Göring Works
trust, free of charge. The value of these assets was 70,000,000
Crowns. The Governor of the National Bank of Slovakia,
Imrich Karvaš, complained at the general assembly of the
bank that "the officials responsible for our monetary policy

[14] Míkuláš Šprinc in the book: Slovenská Liga v Amerike štyridsať'ročná (Forty
years of the Slovak League in America) Scranton, Pa., 1947, p. 72.
[15] Lieut. Eduard Pyšný: Oceľ a myšlienka, (Steel and Idea), Bratislava, 1941,
p. 15.

are confronted with the gigantic problem of financing the losses suffered in the Slovak-German balance of payments which have attained 3 billion Crowns." [16] Of this sum, the Slovak National Bank should have received 1,680 million Crowns, the Slovak Government 690 millions and the rest should have been paid to individual exporters. The public debt of the Slovak State, which resulted from Slovak economic policy during the war years and especially from the non-productive relations with Germany, had reached the total of 8,600 million Crowns (about $150,000,000) by June 1944.

In its efforts to help German war production, the Slovak Government ordered the general mobilization for labor of Slovak citizens. As many as 100,000 to 140,000 Slovak workers were shipped to Germany to work in armament and other industries. The wages earned by these workers were credited the German-Slovak clearing account. The Slovak Government paid allowances from its own funds to the dependents of the workers. The resulting losses to Slovakia ran into billions.[17] In the summer of 1943 the Slovak Government made an offer to Berlin to send 10,500 men of the labor units of the Slovak Army to help defend the German Reich against air attacks. The agreement to do this could not be fulfilled, however, because the Slovak soldiers, who had been concentrated for this purpose in the military centers of Trnava and Senica, revolted and refused to put on German uniforms and be shipped to Germany. In August 1943 another Slovak-German agreement was signed concerning the manufacture of aircraft for the German forces in Slovakia. In March 1944 the Slovak Government sent a military mission, headed by Colonel Pilfousek, to Budapest to discuss with the Hungarian General Staff the defense of mountain passes in the Car-

16 *"Slovák"*, Bratislava, February 29, 1944.
17 Indictment of J. Tiso and V. Tuka before the National Tribunal in Bratislava, *("Čas"*, Bratislava, July 30, 1946, and December 3, 1946).

pathians against the advancing Soviet Armies. In June 1944 an agreement was signed in Budapest for the fortification of the Vihorlat foothills in Eastern Slovakia.

Throughout its entire existence the Slovak State was hanging onto the coattails of Germany's war policies. Tido J. Gašpar summed this up in the following words, "The Slovak Nation, unafraid of the risks involved, was the first to decide, without reservations and resolutely, to march into battle at the side of Germany." [18]

As long as Hitler's star was ascending, as long as he kept occupying one country after another and winning the war, the Slovak Quislings followed him voluntarily and eagerly. When Hitler's luck began to wane, when he was beginning to lose battles and vast areas of conquered territory, his Slovak allies continued to follow him from sheer necessity. They had no alternative. As the situation deteriorated, the last vestiges of Slovakia's paper-independence were wiped out and Slovakia became more and more a mere German province. By the end of August 1944 Tiso could no longer feel any reluctance about calling in German forces to help him maintain order in Slovakia against his own army, the partisans, and Slovak citizens who refused obedience to the Slovak Government, revolted against it, and threatened the very existence of the Slovak State. In this manner the head of the Slovak State handed back the last remnants of Slovak sovereignty to that alien power from which he had accepted that sovereignty in 1939. What followed was merely the final liquidation of the Slovak State.

---

[18] Tido J. Gašpar: *Za dobro celku* (For the Commonwealth), Bratislava, 1942, p. 98.

Chapter Four

ANTI-SEMITISM

The Jews in Slovakia — Origins of Antisemitism — An Element of Totalitarian Separatism — Anti-Jewish Regulations of 1939 — The Jewish Code — Deportations — Aryanization and Jewish Exemptions — The Resistance of the Christian Churches — Protest by the Vatican — The Final Act of the Calvary of the Jews after the Partial Suppression of the Uprising

The Jews represented an insignificant minority in Slovakia. According to the 1930 population census 136,737 persons (4.11%) claimed to be of the Jewish faith and 72,527 (2.18%) regarded themselves as having Jewish nationality. Following the cessions of territory after 1938, this figure decreased by about one fifth. Jewish economic influence was, however, disproportionately greater. Since 1918, Jews in Slovakia had also taken active part in Slovak national and cultural life. There were Slovak Jews even among the founding members of the Matica Slovenská in 1863. Although there was in Slovakia, as in any other Central or East-European country, a certain amount of feeling against the Jews, produced by religious and social prejudices whose origins reach back to the Middle Ages, the modern variety of racial hatred and anti-Semitism nevertheless remained entirely alien to the Slovak people. Dynamic anti-Semitism, with its racial, political, and social-economic motivation, which split society into two antagonistic fractions, the Aryan and the Semitic-Jewish, made its appearance in Slovakia with totalitarian

Separatism. This, in turn, was the outgrowth of a radical Slovak nationalism, linked with the expansionist ambitions of Hitlerite national socialism. Both Separatism and anti-Semitism were confined to a relatively small circle of political fanatics and extremists. They became dangerous only as a result of the circumstance that they managed to capture all power in Slovakia after Munich and thereby came into a position where they could force their ideology and will upon the Slovak people. Under the democratic regime, Separatism as well as anti-Semitism had been condemned. The totalitarian Separatists were well aware of this and consequently first proceeded to destroy democratic institutions, after which they were able to realize their Separatist and anti-Jewish objectives. Anti-Semitism moved ahead in indivisible unity with Separatism. The landmarks along the road of political development of Separatism are also the landmarks in the growth of anti-Semitism. The significant dates are October 6, 1938, when the dictatorship of the Slovak People's Party was established, March 14, 1939, when Slovakia was forced into independence, June 22, 1941, when the Slovak State entered the war against Soviet Russia, and August 29, 1944, when the Slovak National Uprising began.

The Executive Committee of the Slovak People's Party, in which the younger radicals were most prominent, declared in its Žilina Manifesto, On October 6, 1938, that they were on the side of "those fighting against the Marxist-Jewish ideology of disorganization and violence." This was the beginning of anti-Semitism in Slovakia. The Slovak Autonomous Government, in which the Populists had the majority, not only failed to prevent the organized persecution by the Hlinka Guards and the German Ordners of the Jews in Slovakia, but in effect shielded these unlawful acts of violence. The Hlinka Guards launched a crusade against the Jews under the slogan "With Sidor and against the Jews!" The Guardists and German

Ordners attacked, arrested or beat up innocent Jews in the streets. They forced their way into their dwellings or places of business, carried away whatever they wanted, and organized boycotts of Jewish enterprises. Jews were not allowed to appear in cafés, theaters, or at public meetings. They were thrown out of trains and other public conveyances. The Guards and the FS posted conspicuous and indecent notices on Jewish shops, warning Christians they had no business to enter. The Jews could not invoke the protection of courts, officials or police. The Propaganda Office, which was a government agency, assumed the lead in this anti-Jewish hysteria. Anti-Semitism was made a matter of official policy, allegedly justified by the need to protect the national interests from Jewry, which it declared enemy No. 1 of the Slovak people. In the spirit of this ideology, the lower echelon government offices gradually eliminated all Jews from public service and private businesses, revoked their licenses and imposed business administrators upon them, called Temporary or National Administrators. A minute fraction of the Jews sought escape in exile abroad, while the great majority looked toward the future with fear. Ferdinand Ďurčanský, a member of the Slovak Autonomous Government, had promised to Field-Marshal Hermann Göring as early as October 1938, in Berlin that "the Jewish question (in Slovakia) will be settled in the same way as in Germany."

As democracy and the Czechoslovak Republic were slowly extinguished, the hopes of the Jews in Slovakia for a turn for the better also waned. When Czechoslovakia was destroyed and the Slovak State proclaimed on March 14, 1939, the Jews lost all hope that was still left to them. Simultaneously with the establishment of the Slovak State, the darkest phase of the history of Jews of Slovakia began. On top of all that had already been done between October 6, 1938, and March 14, 1939, legislation enacting racial discrimination was now passed. The Nuremberg laws were extended to Slovakia.

Government Decree No. 63/1939 of the Slovak Code defined Jews so as to include all persons who had been converted from the Jewish faith to Christianity after October 30, 1918, or who had at least one Jewish parent, or had either married a Jew or were living in illegal union with a Jew subsequent to April 20, 1939. The decree also established a *numerus clausus* for certain professions. A further Govern-ment Decree, No. 74/1939 Slovak Code, excluded Jews from public offices and similar services. Government Decree No. 145/1939 of the Code forbade Jews to operate pharmacies and established a numerus clausus as to Jewish employees in pharmacies. Government Decree No. 184/1939 of the Code limited the numbers of Jews admitted to the practice of medi-cine. Decrees No. 150/1939 and 230/1939 of the Code regulated the conditions of military service of Jews, No. 193/1939 limited the right of Jewish lawyers to collect their fees, Nos. 147/1939 and 197/1939 ordered the confiscation of farm land owned by Jews. Although the Constitution of the Slovak State stipulated in Article 81 that "all inhabitants will enjoy the protection of life, liberty, and property, regard-less of differences of origin, nationality, religion or occupa-tion" and Article 85 declared that "the freedom of religion, of speech, of scientific research and of the arts are guaran-teed," the Jews of Slovakia were nevertheless deprived, un-constitutionally and illegally, of their most basic human rights —liberty, property, religious freedom, and, in the end, their lives.

A further sharpening of the anti-Jewish trend resulted from the Statutory Decree No. 130/1940 of May 29, 1940, which ordered that "Jews and gypsies shall perform labor for the benefit of the state, in lieu of military duties." Decree No. 255/1940 of the Slovak Code ordered "all Jews to be ex-cluded from studies of whatsoever nature in all schools and educational institutes except elementary schools." This was one of those barbarian orders which now resulted from the Slovak national socialism, which had been introduced following the visit of Jozef Tiso to Hitler in Salzburg, and his complete capitulation to the latter's demands there on July 29, 1940. The policy of the Slovak Government toward the Jews was now determined by the programatic declaration of Slovak national socialism made by Prime Minister and Minister of Foreign Affairs, Vojtech Tuka, at a course for commandants of the Hlinka Guards held in Trenčianske Teplice on January 21, 1941, as well as by the participation of Slovakia in the Nazi-Soviet War.

On June 15, 1941, the Ministry of Interior issued an order forbidding Jews to enter places of public recreation and parks, stores and markets, before 10 A.M., to be in the streets and public places after 9 P.M., to visit with Aryan families or for Aryans to enter Jewish homes. Breaches of this order were punishable with imprisonment up to six months.

All the earlier humiliating and inhuman anti-Jewish legislation was codified in the notorious "Order (of the Slovak Government) of September 9, 1941, concerning the legal position of Jews," No. 198/1941 of the Slovak Code, which was referred to as the "Jewish Code." Very few codes of law of civilized nations can boast of any document which derides all rules of humanity, decency, and culture, as brazenly as this "Code." In many respects this Slovak version of anti-Jewish legislation went beyond even the anti-Jewish statutes, known as the Nuremberg Laws of the Third Reich. From the racial point of view the Jewish Code defined a Jew still more rigidly than hitherto. It applied equally to persons of mixed blood and of Jewish associations. The Code ordered the compulsory registration and visible marking of Jews by a large yellow Star of David, which had to be worn on the chest. It ordered limitations upon marriages with Jews and

sexual intercourse with Jews. It deprived Jews of the right
to vote and to hold public office. It decreed the ineligibility
of Jews for government employment, for the professions of
public notaries, lawyers, civil engineers, medicine, veterinary
surgery and pharmacy. It ordered all Jews between the ages
of 16 and 60 to perform forced labor according to the orders
of the Ministry of the Interior, made them perpetually subject
to searches of the person and homes, limited the secrecy of
written communication to them, deprived them of the right to
form associations or to assemble, and limited their exercise
of religious worship and education. The Code forbade the
ritual slaughter of animals, restricted the education and employment of Jews, restricted the right of Jews to counsel and
forbade Jews to petition or enquire at government offices.
These laws restricted the rights of Jews to acquire tangible
property, cash or securities. Jews were forbidden "to possess
the pictures, statues, and busts of national leaders" as well
as "emblems of the state, and flags." Jews were not allowed
to have "cameras, field glasses or records of national tunes."
The Code cancelled tenancy agreements and leases, excluded
Jews from public life, ordered the dismissal of all Jews from
public office, prohibited appeals by Jews to the Supreme
Administrative Tribunal, and denied the right to make claims
for relief in the state courts. In short the Code outlawed the
Jews.

Decree No. 199/1941 of the Slovak Code imposed a capital
levy upon Jewish property which profited 213,056,387.45
Crowns. The value of the Jewish jewels confiscated was
24, 887,120.50 Crowns at the end of 1942.

The Slovak Government created two agencies to deal with
Jewish matters. One was the Central Office of Economy
(Ústredný hospodársky úrad—ÚHÚ) which was to control
transfers of Jewish property, especially in the framework of
the so-called "Aryanization." The head of this office was

Augustín Morávek. The other agency was the Jewish Central Office (Ústredňa Židov—ÚŽ) which was to protect Jewish interests. Both these agencies were subordinated to the Ministry of the Interior, at the head of which stood the radical Slovak National Socialist and Commander-in-Chief of the Hlinka Guards, Alexander Mach. The Ministry of Interior had a special division, the fourteenth, chief of which was Anton Vašek, who was also the Chief of the Propaganda Section of Hlinka Guards. This division handled everything that concerned the property and freedom, the life and death of Jews in Slovakia, and was in particular responsible for delivering them into labor camps or deportation trains. The German Government sent a representative, its Berater, to work with this division. He was SS-Haupsturmführer Dieter Wisliczeny, who was active in Bratislava from 1940 to 1943.

The question of the Jews in Slovakia was being settled according to German instructions. Of this Wisliczeny gave testimony before the International Military Tribunal in Nuremberg on January 3, 1946. He testified that "until 1940 the general policy was to settle the Jewish question in Germany by means of planned emigration. The second phase, after that date, was the concentration of all Jews in ghettos in Poland and in other territories occupied by Germany in the East. This period lasted approximately until the beginning of 1942. The third period was the so-called "final solution" of the Jewish question, that is, the planned extermination and destruction of the Jewish race; this period lasted until October 1944, when Himmler gave the order to stop their destruction." [1]

With no regard to the needs of the Slovak State, and in complete disregard of Christian, moral, or humanitarian principles and laws, the representatives of the Slovak totalitarian regime embarked upon the last phase of "solving" the

[1] Trial of War Criminals, IV/356-358.

Jewish question, which was the liquidation of Jews. President Tiso declared that "the new social and business order can be established only when we shall have completely uprooted the Jews from our national life." V. Tuka, A. Mach, T. J. Gašpar, A. Vašek, and a large number of newspapermen, radio commentators, and official propagandists were calling with a single voice for the final and definite solution of the Jewish problem. Stanislav Mečiar boasted that "the notion of Jew has now been defined in our country in the same manner as in national socialist Germany, that is to say according to the Nuremberg laws." Mečiar commented with evident glee that "Jews have no political rights whatever." He expressed the firm hope that "we shall soon reach the day when there will be no more Jews in Slovakia, nor in any part of Europe." [2] According to another propagandist, Juraj Gajdoš-Breza, "the Jew is our great enemy. He disrupts, destroys, demoralizes . . . Jewry therefore presents not only a social problem but also a moral one." [3]

Although the Jews had already passed through three years of terrible suffering, humiliation, perpetual fear and insecurity, the most terrible year, 1942, the year of mass arrests, of deportations, lay still ahead. That was the "third period" according to Wisliczeny.

The stage was set for this mass tragedy by establishing camps into which the Jews were concentrated in Bratislava, Sered, Nováky, Žilina and Poprad. The Ministry of Interior ordered the rounding up of all Jews, except those who had been granted the so-called Presidential Exemption—young people and old, the healthy and the sick, men, women, even newly-born babies. The Jews all knew well in advance that from these camps of concentration they would be shipped abroad, and horror and terrible frustration now gripped them, as well as most of the people of Slovakia. Jews tried to save

2 Stanislav Mečiar: *Slovenský národný socializmus* (Slovak National Socialism) Bratislava, 1942, pp. 116-120.
3 Juraj Gajdoš-Breza: *Dni obrody* (Days of Regeneration) Prešov, 1940, p. 66.

themselves by running away, and by hiding. The Hlinka Guards and the German Ordners staged manhunts for them, by day and by night, in their homes and in the streets, in the synagogues and in the open country, arrested them and hauled them away to concentration camps. There were heartrending scenes, when children were taken from their parents, or parents from their children, and when the Guardists, breaking in upon Jews in the middle of the night, dragged them out of their beds. For the voyage into the unknown the Jews were permitted to take only 40 lbs of clothes or food. Everything else they had to leave behind.[4] In this manner, 1,969 Jews were concentrated in the camp in Bratislava-Patronka, 17,351 in Sered, 2,000 in Nováky, 26,384 in Žilina and 6,858 in Poprad. In the camps, the Jews were forced to perform physical labor without compensation under the supervision of ruthless and frequently inhuman Guardists. On April 10, 1942, Vojtech Tuka made an agreement in Bratislava with the Plenipotentiary of the Reichs-Führer of the SS and Chief of the Police Heinrich Himmler, acting as the agent of Marshal Hermann Göring, who had received direct orders from Hitler to solve the problem of Jews in Europe. Under this agreement, Slovak Jews were to be deported to the vicinity of the Polish city of Lublin as persons placed into the custody (Schutzbefohlene) of the German Reich. Jews who had been baptized were to be moved separately from those who had not. The German Government promised that it would "take care of the Jews as humanely as possible" (see Document No. 25). The Minister of Interior, Alexander Mach, declared at a meeting of regional inspectors, district commanders, and commanders of the Hlinka Guard Shock Troops in Štola on April 26, 1942, that "one will forever remember the day of March 25, 1942, when the evacuation of Jews from Slovakia began," because "the supreme law of the land is: deport all

---

[4] Louis Mandel: *The Tragedy of Slovak Jewry in Slovakia*, New York (?), p. 72.

Jews." [5] A perusal of figures indicates that the deportation of
Jews had started in effect even before the formal agreement
with Germany. Nevertheless, on May 15, 1942, the Slovak
Diet passed a Constitutional Law (No. 68/1942 Slovak Code)
allowing "that Jews be deported from the territory of the
Slovak Republic" and stating that "the expellees are to be
deprived of citizenship" and their "property confiscated by the
state." The Slovak Government undertook to pay the German
Government the sum of 500 Marks for each Jew deported
from Slovakia. When the deportations started, the Slovak
Government paid the Germans the sum of 100,000,000
Crowns, which amounted to some 9,000,000 German Marks
and was the price for the deportation of 18,000 Jews.

After these preparations, the Slovak Government started
the deportations proper. The unfortunate Jews were herded
into unheated, unfurnished cattle-cars and, under strict guard
of Hlinka Guardists, German Ordners and State Security
Police, were shipped out of the country. For a considerable
time nobody knew where the Jews had been taken. Eventually
news began to trickle through which showed that the allegations of the official propaganda of the Slovak Government
were entirely untrue. The propaganda had been alleging that
the Jews were living in Jewish reservations, where they had
their own local government and families were kept together,
that the Germans were taking good care of their safety and
protection, etc. In reality the Jews had been taken to the worst
kind of German concentration camps, such as Oswiećim,
Majdanek, Mauthausen, and Buchenwald. As regards figures,
Wisliczeny testified in Nuremberg on the occasion mentioned
earlier that "in the spring of 1942 about 17,000 Jews were
taken from Slovakia to Poland as workers . . . The Slovak
Government further asked whether the families of those workers might not be taken to Poland . . . As a result of this . . .

5 *"Gardista", Žilina*, April 28, 1942.

about 35,000 Jews were taken from Slovakia into Poland."
When the Slovak Government subsequently asked for permission to send a delegation to investigate the conditions
under which the Jews deported from Slovakia were living in
Poland, according to Wisliczeny, this was refused by Adolf
Eichmann, because "most of these Jews were no longer alive."
This testimony has been entirely corroborated by factual evidence. Altogether 68,000 Jews were deported from Slovakia
in 1942. Nearly all of them were exterminated by the Germans, either in mass-executions or in gas-chambers. That is
how the Slovak Government settled the Jewish problem with
the aid of the Germans. The German Government was "taking
care of the Jews as humanely" as only Germans were capable
of doing. With the connivance of its satellite Slovak Government, the German Government simply murdered the Slovak
Jews in cold blood. It was one of the major crimes against
humanity committed during the Slovak regime.

During these persecutions the Jews tried every device to
escape deportation and certain death. Some tried to escape
to Hungary where, in 1942, conditions were still tolerable
for Jews. Others hid with Slovak families. The Slovak people
were not only showing sincere sympathy with these persecuted
Jews but were trying to help them in every way to endure this
terrible life. The people helped in the hiding of Jews, provided
them with material aid, and tried to intervene in their behalf.
The Slovak Government denounced this as treason. The official propaganda labelled those who helped Jews "White
Jews," and "White Jews" were subjected to annoyance and
persecution. Yet, such acts of Christian charity saved the lives
of thousands of Jews. Those critical days exhibited not only
the generous hearts of the Slovak people, but also their tolerance of Jews, when unspoilt by the contagious disease of anti-
Semitism. The official "care for the Jews" was of a very
different quality. Article 255 of the Jewish Code gave the

President of the Slovak State the right to grant Jews exemptions from the restrictions of the Jewish Code and to allow some of them to stay in Slovakia in the interest of the national economy. These presidential exemptions might have been a great blessing for the persecuted Jews, had it not been for the prevailing corruption, the abuses of the Hlinka Guards and of the Germans and much malfeasance. A number of scandals broke out in connection with the presidential exemptions, scandals that involved individual members of the Guards, local functionaries, officials and members of the higher hierarchy of the Slovak People's Party and the Hlinka Guards. Substantial funds flowed into the pockets of high civil servants of the regime who profited from this situation for their own corrupt purposes. The head of the Fourteenth Division of the Ministry of Interior, Anton Vašek, was indicted before the National Tribunal after the war for, amongst other things, having accepted bribes amounting to 2,000,000 Crowns between 1942 and 1944 for releasing Jews from concentration camps and having taken additional 1,000,000 Crowns from the Central Office for Jews in Bratislava. Vašek agreed to release one R. Reis from a concentration camp in 1943, after the latter had agreed to purchase 500 copies of Vašek's book *Anti-Jewish Laws in Slovakia* for the price of some 20,000 Crowns.[6] Similar corruption ruled supreme in matters relating to the transfer of Jewish property to non-Jews, in the so-called process of Aryanization. Jewish property in Slovakia represented values running into billions of crowns, consisting of real estate, established and smoothly operating businesses and industrial enterprises, stocks and equipment. These assets, insofar as they were not confiscated outright by the State, became the happy hunting grounds of corrupt political hench-

[6] Indictments of Jozef Tiso and Confederates (*"Čas"*, Bratislava December 3, 1946) against Anton Vašek, (*"Čas"* Bratislava, June 26, 1946) and against Vojtech Tuka (*"Čas"*, Bratislava, July 30, 1946) before the National Tribunal in Bratislava.

men. The Aryanizers drew twofold benefits, first when they
were given Jewish properties at ridiculously low prices and
under extremely favorable terms of payment, and second when
they proceeded to exploit the former Jewish owners as their
employees.

The churches attempted to help the persecuted Jews. The
Council of Slovak Roman Catholic Bishops assumed a favorable attitude toward the Slovak State from the very moment
of its proclamation and had issued a Pastoral Letter on October 24, 1939, which read, "We welcome the Slovak Republic—we are praying for it every day and are dedicating it to
the protection of the Holy Trinity of the eternal God, with
Whom we beg the patron-saint of Slovakia, Mary of the Seven
Sorrows, to intercede, as well as the Holy patrons Cyril and
Methodius, Andrej and Beňadik and the blessed Martyrs of
Košice." Now, however, the Bishops turned against the official
anti-Semitic policy of the Government, especially against the
arrest and deportation of persons of the Christian faith who
were of Jewish ancestry. The Bishops Ján Vojtaššák and
Andrej Škrábik presented President Tiso and Prime Minister
Tuka with a memorandum, drawn up on October 7, 1941,
which states: "The Slovak Catholic Bishops, in the fulfillment
of their duties, are raising their voices in protest on behalf of
those Catholic families and individuals who are being affected
by the provisions of the Decree concerning the legal position
of Jews." In their Memorandum the Bishops made it clear
that they were "dealing with the Decree exclusively from the
ecclesiastical point of view, because it affected a few thousand
persons of our own faith." The heads of the Lutheran Church
repeatedly protested with much vigor to the Slovak Government against anti-Semitism as such for being in conflict with
humanitarian principles and Christian morality. They demanded that an end be made to the concentration and deportation of Jews, regardless of whether they were baptized

in a Christian faith or not. The Association of Protestant
Clergymen had protested as early as November 21, 1939, in
a memorandum submitted to the President, Jozef Tiso, to the
Government and to the Slovak Diet, proclaiming that "we,
as Lutheran clergymen, can never condone such actions as
the illegal extortion of money from Jews, the removal of
innocent people into concentration camps." The Slovak Government and the new leaders of the Slovak State payed
precious little heed to these protests. They went ahead with
their program of deportations exactly as it suited the Third
Reich. They also ignored the protests of the Vatican.

The Vatican repeatedly and energetically intervened with
the Bratislava Government against the application of the
Jewish Code. According to a Note from the Vatican dated
November 12, 1941, the Jewish Code "enacts a detailed racial
legislation, which includes a number of rules that are clearly
contrary to Catholic principles." When the Vatican failed to
receive a reply to this note, it pressed for a reply from the
Slovak Government in a new Note of March 14, 1942, stating
expressly, "These people (some 80,000 and it is alleged that
some 135,000) are supposed to be deported to Galicia and
to the Lublin region and such deportation was to be carried
out separately for men, for women and for children. The
Secretariat of State (of the Vatican) would like to believe that
such reports are unfounded in fact, being unable to presume
that in a state, which purports to be governed by Catholic
principles, such grave measures could be put into effect,
measures which would be so painful for so many families."
On May 8, 1942, at a time when the deportation of Jews
had already begun, the Bratislava Ministry of Foreign Affairs
instructed the Slovak Minister with the Vatican, Karol Sidor,
to supply the Vatican with untrue information regarding the
fate of the deported Jews. Sidor was to assure the Holy See
that "the Jews from Slovakia are to be settled in several places

in the district of Lublin, where they will remain permanently
. . . where they will be able to live among themselves and
support themselves by their own efforts . . . Families will
remain together . . . The alarm was caused by the circumstance that able-bodied Jews and Jewesses had first to be
sent there to prepare shelter for others, especially the women,
the old, the ailing, and the children. The sending off of the
other members of the families has already started, and Jewish
families will thus soon be reunited. The position of these Jews
from the standpoint of international and constitutional law
will be that of protegés (*Schutzbefohlene*) of the German
Reich. Baptized Jews will be settled separately in another
region, according to the assurances of the Third Reich . . .
We have been notified officially that the German Government
will look after the Jews as humanely as at all possible. This
has been confirmed by the official report of an expert of the
Ministry of Interior, who saw in August last year what the
Jewish city looked like (Sosnowitz, Oppel) which has its own
administration, a number of town-elders and its own police." [7]

In March 1944, Anton Vašek stated that there had been
100,000 Jews in Slovakia. By deportations between March
and October 1942, by legitimate and clandestine emigration,
and by confinement to labor camps and labor centers, the
number of Jews had decreased to 12,000, of whom one half
was integrated into Slovak economic life and the other half
constituted members of their families.[8] In reality the figures
were a little higher.

The final blow aimed at the Jews who had still managed to
survive all earlier persecutions was motivated purely by the
desire for revenge by the Germans and the defeated Slovak
Government after the partial liquidation of the Slovak National Uprising. The Jews participated in the fighting against the

[7] Karol Sidor: *Šesť rokov pri Vatikáne*, (Six years at the Vatican) Scranton,
Pa., 1947, pp. 119-148.
[8] *Berliner Börsen-Zeitung*, March 21, 1944.

German troops and the Slovak puppet Government, for to them the Czechoslovak Republic represented liberation. Of course their numbers were not great. Yet whether or not Jews had anything to do with the uprising, whether or not their participation was significant, the Slovak Government in Bratislava and the Germans made the uprising a pretext for completing the Calvary of the Jews of Slovakia. The Prime Minister of the Slovak State, Štefan Tiso, declared in the course of a statement of governmental policy before the Diet on October 4, 1944, "We shall bring to book all the Slovaks who betrayed us, and we shall not hesitate to eliminate forever from our national life the Czech and Jewish elements which took part in the bloody attack against the state and the nation." The daily *Slovák,* edited by Jozef Paučo, printed an article on November 3, 1944, dealing with the participation of Jews in the uprising, which stated, "While wielding temporary power they behaved like wild beasts, and like beasts they ended their own lives; however, they did not all do so, but even for those who remained alive there is no room in a world of renewed order, and they will not escape their well-deserved punishment, should they not already have committed suicide before then." Anton Vašek, who had meanwhile been appointed Chief Clerk of Bratislava, ordered all Jews in Bratislava to meet on November 20 at 8 A.M. in the courtyard of the City Hall for evacuation to the labor camp in Sered. The order applied to "all Jews, irrespective of citizenship, profession, age or sex, including Jews to whom exemptions had been granted by Slovak or German authorities or enterprises, also Jews of mixed marriages who have no children, or whose children are above 18. Those who fail to comply with the order will be placed in a penal camp." [9]

In that vindictive mood, the German SS-Units, the Gestapo, the Ordners, Hlinka Guards and such remnants of the security

[9] *"Slovák",* Bratislava, November 19, 1944.

organs as had remained faithful to the regime began the rounding up, arrest and final liquidation of Jews. Any Jew caught in the area in which the uprising had taken place was ruthlessly shot, without questioning. Nobody bothered to investigate whether or not they had injured the interests of the Germans or their Slovak satellites or had participated in any action. It was enough that a person was a Jew and that he was found in former insurgent territory summarily to execute him. The corpses of hundreds of Jews executed in this manner were found in a number of mass-graves left behind by the Germans and Hlinka Guards. Jews found elsewhere were thrown into concentration camps, whence they were sent to German concentration camps, especially to the ill-famed ghetto of Terezín, Bohemia. The vast majority of these unfortunates perished by starvation, disease or outright execution. Only a negligible fraction returned to their homes after the liberation.

By December 9, 1944, the Commandant of the German Gestapo in Bratislava *(Befehlshaber des Sicherheits und des SD-Sicherheitsdienstes)* could send a secret report to his Berlin Headquarters informing it that 9,653 Jews had been caught among the insurgents, of whom 2,257 had "received the special treatment" *(Sonderbehandlung)*—had been murdered. These terrible figures speak for themselves. The long years of the war had been one interminable, dreadful nightmare for the Jews. For them the bright light of a better future did not begin to dawn until the Czechoslovak Republic returned to life once more.

The disappearance of the Slovak State closed the terrible chapter of crimes against humanity which had been committed behind the façade of totalitarian anti-Semitism. The responsibility for the lives of tens of thousands of Slovak citizens of Jewish faith rests jointly and severally upon the Germans of the Reich, the Germans of Slovakia and upon their henchmen, the Slovak Separatists. Many of them were tried after the war, sentenced, a few to death. Yet no punishment in the world could give back the lives of innocent people they exterminated nor could it wipe out this blot from the history of Slovakia. The crime committed against the Jews by the leaders of the Slovak State is all the more heinous, because they committed it of their own initiative, of their own free will. The Jewish question was not dealt with in such a manner in any other state under German control, except Germany itself. During the six years of existence of the Slovak State, three-fourths of the Jews of Slovakia perished. Of 180 rabbis, six only remained alive. That is the balance-sheet of the regime which pretended to govern in the spirit of the Christian commandment, "Thou shalt love thy neighbor."

PART IV

THE STRUGGLE FOR FREEDOM

Chapter One

THE RESISTANCE AGAINST GERMAN DOMINATION

The Ideological Background — Resistance to Totalitarian Separatism — The Second Czechoslovak Liberation Movement Abroad — Paris, London, USA and USSR — The Second Czechoslovak Liberation Movement in Slovakia — Unified Leadership — The Christmas Agreement — Preparations for Armed Uprising — August 29, 1944 — Revolution in Slovakia — The Declaration of the Slovak National Council — Renewal of Czechoslovak State Sovereignty — Allied Attitude — Two Months of Fighting of the First Czechoslovak Army and another Six Months of Partisan Combat — Reprisals Against the Insurgents — Liquidation of the Slovak State and Its Regime — Liberation of Czechoslovakia

No despotism can silence a nation's natural yearning for liberty. The Czechs, Slovaks, and Subcarpathian Ruthenians had achieved national liberties and political independence in the Czechoslovak Republic. They never accepted the situation created by force under the Four-Power Agreement of Munich, and still less did they reconcile themselves to the German occupation of Bohemia and Moravia, to the creation of a German Protectorate of Bohemia-Moravia, to the existence of a satellite State of Slovakia and to the Magyar occupation of Subcarpathian Ruthenia. The great majority of the Slovak people disapproved of Slovak separatism, of the authoritarian regime of the Slovak People's Party, of the Slovak Government's pro-Nazi policy and its inhuman anti-Semitism. They disagreed with Slovak participation in the war against Poland and the Soviet Union, and with the declaration of war upon the Western Allies. The majority of Slovaks remained faithful to Czechoslovakia and Western democratic ideals. All through the Second World War, the Slovaks never went along with the government, with the totalitarian Slovak People's Party, or the Germans. Their sympathies were with the enemies of Hitler. They regarded the Western democracies as their traditional friends and allies and were looking to them for help in liberation from German domination. True, confidence in the West was to some extent shaken by the participation of two of the major Western democracies in the Munich Agreement, but their subsequent declaration of war upon Hitlerite Germany redeemed these powers in the eyes of the people. The Second Czechoslovak Liberation Movement at Home was thus entirely devoted to these principles. The Slovaks played an even more significant part than in the First Liberation Movement during World War I.

The Resistance at Home began as far back as the Fall of 1938 after the establishment of the dictatorship of the Slovak People's Party on October 6, 1938, while the Czechoslovak liberation movement abroad began after the destruction of the Czechoslovak Republic, on March 15, 1939. The members of the political parties in Slovakia which had been dissolved and outlawed turned to underground work. They found supporters among the more democratically-minded members of the Slovak People's Party itself. The Slovak Government, the totalitarian wing of the Separatists and the Hlinka Guards created an abyss between themselves and the rest of the nation, and the nation, in turn, deepened the chasm between them and itself. The State lacked the support of the Army and security organs, and could not command the loyalty of its own civil service. These conditions continued until the final disappearance of the Slovak State. The regime could survive solely by relying on German power. Whatever ideological and political views the Slovaks held, they were all united on the

one issue of wanting to help defeat national socialist Germany
and its vassal, the Slovak State and its undemocratic regime.
In Slovakia the majority of members of the second Czechoslovak resistance at home were recruited from the ranks of
democrats and non-Communists, whose views upon domestic
political problems, as well as questions of foreign policy
relative to the conduct of the war had been unequivocal from
the beginning to the end. The policy of the democratic underground in Slovakia did not undergo modifications according
to the changing fortunes of the battlefronts and it received no
orders from abroad. At the same time the Slovak Communists
were conducting their own underground movement according
to the shifting trends of Soviet policy and strictly in obedience
to orders from Moscow. Until the signing of the Nazi-Soviet
Pact, they had been in the resistance. From the outbreak of
the Second World War until the German attack on the USSR,
the Slovak Communists remained entirely passive. They denounced the war as imperialistic, they took note of the useful
relations which had been established between the Nazis and
the Soviets and considered it undesirable to produce difficulties between Bratislava, Berlin and Moscow. The entire burden of carrying the resistance during the critical period of
Hitler's continued victories, at the time of the capitulation of
France, and all through Britain's isolation, rested entirely on
the shoulders of the non-Communists. The years 1939-1941
were the most difficult ones for the resistance in Slovakia, and
most of the persons taken to the concentration camp at Ilava,
put into prison, or sentenced for forbidden political activities
were people of democratic and non-Communist ideals.

In the middle of March 1939 the second Czechoslovak
liberation movement abroad joined forces with the resistance
at home. It was brought into being by exiles whose numbers
grew from month to month, by Czechoslovak diplomats who
had refused to surrender their legations to the Germans, and

by Czechs and Slovaks abroad, above all in the United States.
The liberation movement at home and abroad drew much
strength and encouragement from the fact that neither the
American, nor the British, French and, to begin with, not
even the Soviet Government had recognized the state of affairs
created by Hitlerite and Magyar aggression in March 1939,
but continued to recognize the Czechoslovak Republic as
existing of right and permitted the Czechoslovak diplomatic
missions in their respective capitals to continue in existence.
Valuable assistance was also given by the broadcasting stations
of friendly powers, the Voice of America, the British Broadcasting Corporation, and the French Radio and, after 1941,
the Moscow Radio. These stations gave accurate information
on the military and political situation and by helping to
neutralize the effects of domestic and German propaganda,
they signally contributed toward "maintaining the spirit of
resistance and confidence in the eventual victory of the free
world."

At the beginning of the war, the liberation movement
abroad had its center in Paris. A National Committee was
founded in 1939, consisting of Czech and Slovak representatives in exile. In the following year the Slovak National Council was formed. Slovaks made up the majority of the Czechoslovak military units that were formed in France in 1939-
1940. After the capitulation of France, London became the
center of the Czechoslovak liberation movement abroad.
There Edvard Beneš once more assumed his presidential
functions, a Czechoslovak Government in exile was formed,
together with a State Council and essential administrative
offices. Numerous Slovak leaders participated, including Milan
Hodža, Štefan Osuský, Juraj Slávik, Ján Lichner, General
Rudolf Viest, Ján Bečko, Vladimír Clementis, Ján Paulíny-
Tóth, Vladimír Hurban, Ján Čaplovič and others. Slovaks
took part in the fighting as members of the Czechoslovak

Army at the side of the British, both on land and in the air. The Czechoslovak army corps which fought on the Russian front consisted almost exclusively of Slovaks, who had crossed over to the allied side from the divisions which the Slovak Government had sent to aid the Germans.

Czech and Slovak Communist leaders escaped to Moscow after the fall of Czechoslovakia. Very few of them went to Paris and then to London. The Moscow exiles acquired major significance only toward the end of World War II, when the Soviet Union became one of the decisive political and military factors of the world. From the Summer of 1941 on, the Czechoslovak Communists in Moscow established direct contact with the Communist underground in Slovakia, sent emissaries back home, and later also Soviet partisans and political commissars. They also sent political instructions. After war had started between Germany and Russia, resistance activities in Slovakia became more lively and intense. The Czechoslovak Resistance at Home could rely upon all classes of the population—on the intelligentsia, the civil service, the teachers, the churches, farmers, industrial workers, students, soldiers, police and customs officers, but above all upon the masses of the people, dissatisfied as they were with the state of affairs. Slovakia was entirely covered by clandestine networks, which were helping to guide Slovaks and Czechs out of the country, who were organizing help for persecuted or imprisoned Slovaks, Czechs and Jews, partisans and allied prisoners of war. The underground published clandestine newssheets, leaflets, conducted whispering campaigns, agitated against the government and the Germans, and organized a general disobedience to laws, decrees and government measures. The leaders of the resistance at home maintained secret communications by writing, couriers and radiotelegraphy with the leaders of the liberation movement abroad, first in Paris and later on in London. It was a systematic and dangerous work. It decidedly helped to weaken the position of the Germans and of the satellite regime in Slovakia and at the same time aided the allied war effort. The allies were supplied with valuable political, economic, and military intelligence from Slovakia.

Until the summer of 1943, the political and military resistance at home lacked unified leadership, but in September 1943 contact was established between representatives of the democratic and the Socialist groups. The former were represented by Ján Ursíny, Jozef Lettrich and Matej Josko, while the latter were led by Gustáv Husák, Ladislav Novomeský, and Karol Šmidke. The Socialist group comprised both Social Democrats and Communists. The outcome was the formation of a clandestine Slovak National Council in December 1943, consisting of the above six representatives. The Council became the joint political center of the resistance at home. Its program and objectives were stated in the so-called Christmas Agreement of 1943 (see Document No. 26). It proclaimed that "the purpose and objective of the Slovak National Council is the elimination of German dictation, which is being put into effect by the domestic usurpers of political power," to "take over all power in Slovakia" and ensure that the Slovak people be permitted "freely to appoint its representatives, to whom the Slovak National Council will hand over all power." The Slovak National Council "will conduct its affairs in agreement with the Czechoslovak Government and the liberation movement abroad." As regards matters of Czechoslovak domestic policy, the Agreement included the following stipulations: (1) The Slovak and Czech nations will let their future destiny within the Czechoslovak Republic, "that is, within the common state of Slovaks and Czechs, be governed by the principle of partnership between equals"; (2) the internal order of Czechoslovakia will be democratic and "all fascist, racialist and totalitarian tendencies" are to be eradicated; (3) the principles of democracy are to be introduced and deepened"; and (4) "the freedom of the several religious faiths" is to be maintained but "the influence of the churches upon the tendencies and leadership of the state" is to be eliminated. In the matter of Czechoslovak foreign policy the Agreement formulated the principle that "close cooperation with all the Slavic states and nations, especially with the USSR" was to be established. The Agreement was to have only temporary validity, because the final settlement of the questions involved, especially the settlement of the constitutional issues inherent in the relationship of the Slovak Nation to the Czech Nation, was to be reserved "entirely to the freely elected (appointed) representatives of the Slovak people."

The Christmas Agreement had farreaching political consequences. By unifying the leadership of the resistance at home, it concentrated much strength that was being dissipated and assured common success. It clarified views about the fundamental problems of the resistance and of life after the liberation. It bound the Slovak Communists to renounce their plan of attaching Slovakia to the Soviet Union and to accept the common objective of a reconstitution of the Czechoslovak Republic. The Agreement embodied the notion of two equal national partners. It established a common political and military leadership in the Slovak National Council and therefore made it impossible for the Communists to assume exclusive control of the resistance and to misuse it as an instrument of their own policy or of that of the Soviets. Had it not been for this agreement, with the possibility of controlling the activities of the Communist resistance, the way would have been open for the Slovak Communists to prepare the same fate for Slovakia, as was inflicted upon the Subcarpathian Ruthenia which, toward the end of the war, was, by "popular demand," annexed to the USSR.

The Christmas Agreement was concluded between the representatives of the democratic non-Socialist groups and those of the Socialist parties. Nobody spoke of any specific democratic parties as such, for nobody could estimate at that time which of the non-socialist parties would resume activities after the war. Nor was this of any importance for the resistance. While in the resistance, the representatives of the democratic group could rely on the unwavering support of the former Republican (Agrarian), the Czechoslovak Peoples', the Slovak National and the Tradesmen's Parties. Moreover, they enjoyed the approval of numerous social democrats and of democratically minded members of the governing Slovak People's Party. Three Communists acted on behalf of the Social Democratic Party, which, after Munich, had found itself isolated and inclined toward fusion with the Communists, a development which was completed after the war.

The first task after the Christmas Agreement and the creation of the clandestine Slovak National Council was to make preparations for an armed uprising of the Slovak people against the Germans and the domestic regime. For this the Slovak National Council created a military command of the resistance. Lt. Col. Ján Golian was appointed military commander. He organized his own military staff: Capt. Milan Polák, Lt. Col. Mikuláš Ferjenčík, Lt. Col. Jozef Marko, Lt. Col. Julius Nosko, Lt. Col. Mirko Vesel, Lt. Col. Dezider Kalina. The military command could call upon the entire staff of the gendarmes, especially Lt. Col. Vladimír Bodický, Lt. Col. Štefan Slezák, Lt. Col. Ján Plakinger, Major Andrej Martin Júny and Staff Captain Jozef Peterka. The political motive for an uprising was the desire to liberate Slovakia by its own efforts as soon as possible, to throw out the Germans, to destroy the dictatorship of the Slovak People's Party, reintroduce Czechoslovak democratic institutions, spare Slovakia the suffering of war and assure it its just place in a free Czechoslovakia. The Slovak National Council also considered the planned uprising a political and military contribution by democratic Slovakia to the allied war effort.

Within a short time the military staff submitted a plan for a military revolt. According to this, Central Slovakia was to be the focal point of the uprising, especially the regions of the Hron River Valley, the adjoining mountain ranges and the cities of Banská Bystrica, Zvolen and Brezno nad Hronom. The plan required the fulfilment of certain domestic and international conditions. The domestic precondition of the uprising was a thorough material, economic and financial preparation and the coordination of all the armed units in the country, the gendarmery, the partisan groups, customs officers and the army (especially two very well equipped divisions stationed in Eastern Slovakia). The international aspect of the preparations included the timely notification of the Czechoslovak Government in Exile in London and the coordination of the plans for an uprising with those of the Soviet Army. The latter was at that time approaching the opposite slopes of the Carpathian mountain ranges and was the only allied army which could be directly contacted from Slovakia. The Slovak National Council studied and discussed this plan very thoroughly, approved it, and started preparations for the uprising. It was to start either at the moment the Soviet troops would reach Cracow in Poland, regardless of conditions that would prevail in Slovakia at that time, or at an earlier date, if the German Army started occupying Slovakia. The Council was expanded to include another four members: Peter Zat'ko and Jozef Styk for the democratic bloc, and two Social Democrats with known pro-Communist attitudes, Ivan Horváth and Jozef Šoltész.

From the Spring of 1944 on, units of the Slovak Army were being inconspicuously concentrated in Central Slovakia, under the pretext of summer war-games, and army stores and food were being moved into the area. Matters were facilitated by the circumstances that the headquarters of the Slovak armed forces was at that time in Banská Bystrica and that Lt. Col. Ján Golian was Chief of Staff. Against this was the risk of discovery, as the country was in a state of war. The plans could easily have come to the notice of the Slovak Government authorities or the Germans who were maintaining a large military mission with the Ministry of National Defense in Bratislava and with headquarters in Banská Bystrica. Simultaneously with military preparations, financial reserves were being moved into the area from the National Bank in Bratislava and foodstuffs were being hoarded there. These transfers were made under the pretext of removing them from the capital to remote and more secure places. All these very widespread preparations could remain hidden from the Germans and from the governing clique only because the Slovak Army officers, NCOs and enlisted men, the state security organs, and the civil service, stood united against the Germans and the government and firmly on the side of the resistance at home.

Lt. Col. Golian got into touch with the commanders of Slovak and Russian partisan units, of whom a considerable number were operating in the mountains and forests, and enjoined them not to undertake any action that could not be completely coordinated with the military operations now being prepared. Lt. Col. Golian received assurances to this effect, but these were later disregarded. The Russian partisans were only obeying orders from their own Headquarters in Kiev, Ukraine, and these were frequently incompatible with the objectives of the Slovak National Council. Early in Spring 1944 President Edvard Beneš and the Czechoslovak Government in London were informed about the plans of the unified leadership of the resistance at home regarding the uprising. They approved and promised help. In order to maintain regular radio communications with Slovakia, the Czechoslovak military authorities in London parachuted Major Jaroslav Krátký into the vicinity of Banská Bystrica where he could be in permanent touch with Lt. Col. Golian. These matters were entirely beyond the control of the Communists who had no adherents in the Slovak Armed Forces.

After the successful invasion of the North of France by the American and British Forces, which began on June 6, 1944, and after the Soviets had launched a new offensive on June 22, 1944, Slovakia became a vital base for the German Army in its preparations for the defense of the Carpathian ranges against the advancing Russians. This greatly increased the danger of the occupation of all of Slovakia by German troops. As a result, the Slovak National Council met to discuss the political and military situation on June 27, 1944, approved certain preliminary measures and decided to report the situation to London and also to the commanders of the Soviet Forces. In order to establish direct contact with the Soviet High Command, the Slovak National Council dispatched two delegates, Karol Šmidke and Lt. Col. Mikuláš Ferjenčík, to the Soviet side of the front. They were flown out on August 4, 1944. Although these emissaries were given orders to return to Slovakia without delay, the Soviet authorities first confined them in complete isolation in Moscow and then kept postponing discussions with them. This resulted in the loss of priceless time, during which events began relentlessly to move forward in Slovakia.

Without informing the Slovak National Council or its military leaders, the Soviet partisan units suddenly became active in Slovakia. They started blowing up road and railroad bridges, blocking railroad tunnels, raiding military objectives, attacking police organs and threatening adherents of the regime and Germans. For the Slovak Government and the Germans this produced an unbearable situation. The local population, on the other hand, thought that this was the beginning of the armed uprising and began joining the partisans in large numbers. From then on no measures of the government, no extraordinary steps, nor the declaration of martial law could control the situation—a revolutionary wave had gripped Slovakia. The vital railroad lines from Bohumín to Košice, from Vrútky to Lučenec and from Žilina to Leopoldov were in the hands of the partisans, or blocked in several places and put out of operation. The German Army had lost the means of moving reinforcements into Slovakia. At this moment Romania defected from the Tripartite Pact and joined the Allies. On August 25, 1944, Turčiansky Svätý Martin was occupied by insurgent forces (partisans and soldiers), and the occupation of Vrútky, Ružomberok, Liptovský Svätý Mikuláš, Banská Bystrica and Zvolen followed. By August 28 all of Central and Eastern Slovakia had shaken off the control of the Slovak Government. The Slovak National Council viewed all these events with grave anxiety, because they were threatening the sweeping plans for a general military and national uprising. The Soviet and Slovak partisans lacked the means for putting up any sustained resistance to the Germans or for organizing a systematic defense against them. They were equipped only for hit-and-run raids, for causing confusion behind the lines and for sabotage.

The prevailing revolutionary conditions forced Jozef Tiso and the Slovak Government to take a desperate step. Their Minister of National Defense, General Ferdinand Čatloš, announced over the Bratislava radio on the evening of August 29, 1944, that "formations of the German Army are entering Slovakia" for the purpose of restoring peace and order. Čatloš called upon all Slovak soldiers and citizens "to welcome the German troops everywhere as our Allies." The German press agency, the *Deutsches Nachrichten-Bureau*, reported on August 30, 1944, "It is officially announced that, at the request of the Slovak Government, German troops have entered Slovakia to take part in the fighting against the partisan menace and to restore peace and order throughout the country." Tiso himself confirmed this report over the radio, on that same day. For the Slovak National Council as well as for the population of the country, this announcement meant that the Germans had started occupying Slovakia. The moment that had been foreseen for the start of the uprising had thus occurred. On August 29, 1944, over the Banská Bystrica radio, the Slovak National Council called Slovakia to arms against the German forces. Lt. Col. Ján Golian ordered the Slovak Army to start combat operations (See Document No. 27). The revolutionary National Committees ordered general mobilization. The Slovak troops, gendarmery, partisans and the population obeyed the call to arms with boundless enthusiasm. The Slovak national uprising had begun; Slovakia became a combat zone. Tiso's regime in Bratislava lost the ground under its feet. The Slovaks greeted the Germans with arms in their hands. The boundless elation over the freedom that had been granted, was, however, somewhat dimmed by anxiety as to the possibility of maintaining it. Everybody helped to the best of his abilities. The people volunteered to dig trenches, to carry ammunition for the troops, provide shelter and food and care for evacuees.

The German Army attacked the insurgents from the East where it disarmed the two divisions of the Slovak Army. This was an irreparable loss for the uprising. Although large numbers of troops of these divisions nevertheless managed to join the insurgents in Central Slovakia, they had lost their heavy equipment. The Germans attacked from the North, through the Spiš region, through the Orava Valley and through the Jablunkov Pass, toward Žilina. Other columns of German troops were advancing from the West and the South, especially from Bratislava, along the Nitra Valley. The insurgent forces

first held the natural barriers of Turiec, and when pushed
back from there, fell back upon the Hron Valley region. Their
forces included some 70,000 men, of whom some were in-
sufficiently armed. Twelve thousand partisans also took part
in the fighting, split into various units, of varying strength
and organization. The insurgent forces were under the Command of Lt. Col. Ján Golian, who had been promoted to the
rank of Brigadier-General. The German commander opposing
him was at first General Gotlob Berger and afterwards General
of the SS and of the Police Hermann Höffle. The Germans
sent the following formations against the insurgents: the crack
Adolf Hitler SS-Tank Division, four SS-Divisions, two Wehr-
macht Divisions, Units of Mountain Artillery, mountain infantry, independent tank battallions, air force units and the
Corps of General Vlasov.

Banská Bystrica became the political and military center
of the uprising. At the head of it stood the Slovak National
Council which proclaimed itself the representative of legislative and executive powers in insurgent territory in the name
of renewed Czechoslovak sovereignty. The Council published
a declaration on September 1, 1944 (see Document No. 28).
It stated that "all democratic and progressive elements of the
Slovak Nation have formed a Slovak National Council to be
the supreme organ of the liberation movement at home." It
"alone has the right to speak for the Slovak Nation." It assumed the "defense of Slovakia." It promised to lead the liberation movement at home "amidst unity and in close cooperation with the Czechoslovak liberation movement abroad." It
once more solemnly reaffirmed the wish "to live together in
brotherly unity with the Czech Nation in the new Czechoslovak Republic," and declared that "constitutional, social,
economic and cultural matters of the Republic will finally be
regulated by mutual agreement between elected representatives
of the Slovak and Czech people, in the spirit of democratic

principles, of progress and social justice." The Declaration "repudiates with the utmost vigor and condemns the anti-democratic and tyrannic abuses and theories of the Populist regime." It proclaimed that "the Slovak Nation had nothing to do with the alliance with Hitlerite Germany" and that "it had always been on the side of the allies, in all its ideals and convictions, of which it has given evidence on every occasion, at home and at the front." The Slovak National Council repudiated "the betrayal of the Slav family by Tiso and Tuka" and affirmed that "the Slovak Nation is overtly and ostentatiously joining the Allied Nations, whose struggle and great sacrifices are ensuring a free and democratic way of life for all nations of the world and therefore also for the (Slovak) Nation." In conclusion, the Declaration promised "to apply all its power to the early termination of the fight for freedom" and called "the entire nation to arms in the struggle against the enemy and his (domestic) servants." The Declaration of the Slovak National Council ended with a call of loyalty to the Czechoslovak Republic.

The Slovak National Council assumed its powers on that same day, September 1, 1944. Its two Chairmen were Dr. Vavro Srobár and Karol Šmidke. Members of its presidium were Ján Ursíny, Jozef Lettrich, Gustáv Husák and Daniel Ertl. At first the Council had 13 members (7 Democrats, 4 Communists and 2 Social Democrats) but this number was later increased to 41 and then to 50 (25 Democrats, 13 Communists, 10 Social Democrats and 2 military commanders with no political affiliations.) As of October 7, 1944, General Rudolf Viest assumed command of the Czechoslovak Army operating on Slovak insurgent territory. Gen. Viest was a member of the Czechoslovak Government in exile in London, who had been dispatched to the liberated territory. General Golian became his deputy.

The Slovak National Council exercised the legislative pow-

ers of a revolutionary national assembly by the plenary ses-
sions of all its members, the political functions through its
governing body, and executive powers by the ten Commissioners of the Slovak National Council, each appointed for one
of the branches of administration. The Slovak National Council adhered to the demand for a renewal of the Czechoslovak
Republic in its pre-Munich frontiers and consequently refused to accept any territorial or political changes that had
occurred in Czechoslovakia since Munich. As a logical consequence of this uncompromising attitude, the Slovak National Council equally refused to recognize the Slovak State,
its Constitution, President, Government, or executive organs.
The Slovak National Council ordered the dissolution of the
totalitarian Slovak Peoples' Party, the Nazi-German Party,
the totalitarian Magyar Nationalist Party, the Hlinka Guards,
Hlinka Youth, the German Freiwillige Schutzstaffel, Deutsche
Jugend, and all their elements and affiliated organizations.
Their property was declared as being confiscated by the
Czechoslovak State.

During the national uprising a new organization was also
being sought for the political life of the nation. The Democratic Party became the spokesman for all the non-socialist
insurgent elements of Slovakia. The *"Čas"* became its new
party daily, as well as the *"Národnie Noviny"* which had been
transferred to Banská Bystrica from Turčiansky Svätý Martin.
The socialist elements were represented by the Social Democrats and the Communists parties, but at a meeting held on
September 17, 1944, they decided to consolidate and together form a new Communist Party of Slovakia. This party's
official organ became the *"Pravda"*. Not all Social Democrats
agreed with the fusion of the two Socialist parties, but these
constituted a minority, some of whom decided to join the
Democratic Party while others assumed a wait-and-see atti-

[1] Order No. 4/1944 of September 1, 1944—Collection of Orders of the S.N.C.

tude. The Democratc Party was under the following leader-ship: Honorary Chairman Dr. Vavro Šrobár, Chairman Ján Ursíny, Deputy-Chairman Jozef Lettrich and Secretary-General Martin Kulich. The Communist Party had Karol Šmidke as Chairman, Gustav Husák and Daniel Ertl (a former Social Democrat) as Deputy-Chairman and Karol Bacílek as Secretary-General. Two other Communist leaders, Viliam Široký and Julius Ďuriš, more subservient to Moscow, were at that time in prison in Nitra and Bratislava, respectively. Co-operation between Democrats and Communists was, on the whole, satisfactory immediately after the start of the uprising and in the first half of its duration. After that, however, differences developed. Political appointments had been divided equally between the two parties, but this division could have only a limited validity, that is to say only until the first democratic elections after the war.

From the outset, the Slovak insurgents were at a disadvantage as against the attacking German Armies, supported by Hlinka Guards and German Ordners. There were several causes for this. The insurgents had not chosen the time for starting the uprising. They had to make the best of a situation that had been created by events beyond their control. The Germans entered Slovakia simultaneously from several directions with superior forces and succeeded immediately in disarming two well-equipped Slovak Divisions. The insurgents had to start fighting with what they had, not with what they needed. They lacked air-support, heavy and mechanized arms, and did not have enough light arms and ammunition. Allied aid had not been assured and the USSR showed little interest in the outcome of the uprising. It sent the delegates of the Slovak National Council back home, belatedly with only vague promises of help. Meanwhile the insurgents had applied for help to the Czechoslovak Government in London and to the High Command of the Soviet Army to the East.

The Czechoslovak Government in exile immediately under-took diplomatic action with the Allied Governments to obtain military and political support for the insurgents in Slovakia. The Czechoslovak Government itself had only one Czecho-slovak brigade within reach of Slovakia. This was in the Soviet Union and consisted almost entirely of men who had served with the Slovak units sent to the Russian front by the Slovak Government who had either crossed over to the Russian side or had been made prisoners of war. The Czechoslovak Government ordered the dropping of a Czechoslovak Para-chutist brigade from the USSR on insurgent territory. The Soviet Army was to fly them into Slovakia. President Beneš and the Czechoslovak Government also gave all possible moral encouragement to the Slovak insurgents.

How did the Allies react to the outbreak and subsequent fortunes of the Slovak uprising?

The uprising could have made it possible for the Soviet Armies to penetrate to the gates of Vienna and the upper reaches of the Danube as early as September 1944, instead of reaching those points in the Spring of 1945. It was clearly very much in the interest of the Allies and the Soviets to render the uprising the speediest and most effective assistance. Such assistance could most readily have been provided by the Soviet Union, whose forces were no more than 80 to 100 miles away. The Soviet Government promised material help, promised to fly in the Czechoslovak brigade, promised to change its original plans and launch an attack by the troops under Marshall Ivan Koniev against the Germans in the Car-pathians and on Slovak insurgent territory. It failed to fulfil any of these promises. As mentioned before, Moscow had unnecessarily detained the delegates sent by the Slovak Na-tional Council. Eventually military aid from Russia arrived, but too late, and in insignificant volume, and even this came only for the partisans and not for the army of the insurgents.

Throughout the entire uprising, the Soviet Union sent no more than 150 anti-tank rifles, 350 infantry rifles, a few thousand mines and a few aircraft, for which the insurgents had no fuel. Soviet reluctance to help the uprising was even more marked in the matter of flying in the Czechoslovak brigade. Although the weather in September 1944 was generally favorable, the Soviet Air Force took full six weeks to fly in 2,800 men. Meanwhile the shortage of arms and the long delay in the arrival of the brigade from the USSR had resulted in a marked deterioration of the military situation. Instead of troops, the Soviet aircraft were flying in Soviet partisan officers and political commissars, as well as Czech and Slovak Communist agitators and politicians who had been spending the war in exile in Moscow. Among the latter were the former Communist deputies Rudolf Slánský, Jan Šverma, Marek Čulen and others. Some Soviet troops did launch an attack toward the Carpathian ranges in the region of the Dukla Pass, but when they encountered stiff German opposition, they abandoned the project. This gave the uprising neither direct nor indirect relief. The Soviet Army failed to establish contact with the insurgent forces and also failed to pin down any German troops in order to relieve the pressure upon them. Although Soviet propaganda was making much capital of the uprising, words were not supported by deeds. On the contrary, the Soviet High Command inflicted deliberate and irreparable injury on the uprising by preventing the British and American armies from coming to their assistance. After the insurgent forces had been pushed up into the mountains, the Soviet officers insisted that the First Czechoslovak Army be disbanded and split up into partisan units which would be entirely under the control of Soviet Commanders or Communists. As it became clear later, all this was clearly motivated by Moscow's own political schemes. The Soviet Government found it undesirable for the Slovak people to free themselves from German domination by their own valiant efforts. The Soviets wanted to be the ones who would liberate Czechoslovakia, and by such liberation impose a Communist regime and Soviet domination upon the Republic.

As opposed to this, scarcely had the United States learned of the uprising than it wholeheartedly made common cause with it. A similar attitude was assumed by the British Government. On September 7, 1944, the Government of the United States issued a Declaration (see Document No. 29) which stated among others, "The soldiers of the Czechoslovak Army, including those in Slovakia and other parts of Czechoslovakia, constitute a combat force operating against Germans. . . . Reprisals by the German military authorities against the soldiers of the Czechoslovak Army violate the rules of war, by which Germany is bound. The United States Government, therefore, solemnly warns all Germans who take part in or are in any way responsible for such violations that they do so at their peril and will be held answerable for their crimes." In a message to President Edvard Beneš on October 28, 1944, President Franklin D. Roosevelt made the following reference to the Slovak insurgents, "The people and armed forces inside Czechoslovakia have joined actively and gloriously with their countrymen abroad in the ranks of the nations united against tyranny . . . We Americans salute our Czechoslovak comrades-in-arms who are today so bravely contributing to the liberation of their homeland and the rest of Europe." (See Document No. 30). On September 17, 1944, the American Army Command dispatched an American Military Mission to the Headquarters of the First Czechoslovak Army in Banská Bystrica. The Mission was under the command of the United States Navy Lieutenant James Holt Green of Pittsburgh, Pennsylvania. He was accompanied by five American servicemen, including an American of Czech descent, Sgt. J. G. Mičan of Chicago, Ill. The American Mission arrived with three aircraft, which brought much-needed arms, ammunition, drugs and other supplies. On their return they flew out American airmen who had bailed out over Slovakia or who had fled as prisoners of war from Germany during the war. On October 6, 1944, six more four-engined American planes arrived, with a cover of 30 fighters. At the same time the British Colonel Threlfall and the Czechoslovak Colonel Hynek Souhrada also landed on the Tri Duby airfield in insurgent territory. These planes again brought arms, especially antitank weapons, and medicines. The Associated Press correspondent A. Novak also arrived with this flight.

The British High Command sent a Military Mission to Banská Bystrica, under Major Sehmer. Some of the arms flown in were from British stores in Bari, Italy. The Anglo-American aid was being given as the result of instantaneous improvisation and "clandestinely." Col. Threlfall who discussed the possibilities of rendering aid to the insurgents with General R. Viest and General J. Golian admitted that the Western Allies were not permitted to make any military commitments to the Slovak insurgents, because Slovakia was in the sphere of Soviet military operations and there could be no Western interference in this sphere without Soviet permission. Because of this, one was to regard the aid rendered hitherto by the West as a gift, rather than military assistance. In fact, equipment for 10,000 men had been made ready in Bari and was to be flown to Slovakia, but the USSR had refused permission for the Western Allies to bring this aid to the insurgents.

On October 6, 1944, American planes flew out a three-man delegation of the Slovak National Council consisting of Ján Ursíny, Ladislav Novomeský and Lt. Colonel Miroslav Vesel. It proceeded to London to present a detailed report to the Czechoslovak President and Government, to give out all possible information to the Western press about the situation

in Slovakia, to discuss the problem of aid to the insurgents
with the Czechoslovak authorities abroad, as well as problems
of the internal organization of Czechoslovakia after the liberation.[2]

The Slovak insurgents were at all times on the defensive.
Because of the shortage of equipment, they were gradually
forced to retreat into the Hron Valley regions, to abandon
the strategically important valleys of the Váh, Nitra and
Turiec Rivers, and in the end of the Hron River Valley itself.
The well-equipped Czechoslovak brigade, commanded by
Colonel Vladimír Přikryl, which arrived from the USSR, ren-
dered signal services to the uprising. When in the middle of
October 1944 the regime in Hungary changed, the situation
of the insurgents became substantially worse. The German
Armies were able to attack insurgent territory from Hungary
and along several fronts. This created a threat to the three
key cities of Zvolen, Brezno nad Hronom and eventually to
Banská Bystrica. Under such pressure, the Slovak National
Council and the Military Command were forced to evacuate
these cities and to withdraw to the small settlement of Staré
Hory in the Great Fatra Mountain range. The German Air
Force repeatedly bombed this settlement and the German
troops followed close on the heels of the retreating insurgents.
On October 27, 1944, the political and military leaders of
the uprising resolved to withdraw still further into the forests
that cover the valleys of the Low Tatra, the Great Fatra and
the Slovak Ore-Mountain ranges and to reorganize the First
Czechoslovak Army into a number of smaller groups and combat teams. These would continue the fight until the moment
when contact could be made with the Soviet Armies, which
were approaching at snail's pace from the East. The military
units were joined by gendarme units which had shown extra-

---

[2] Dr. Jozef Lettrich: *O Slovenskej národnej rade* (About the Slovak National
Council) Bratislava, 1945, pp. 5-65.

ordinary discipline and prowess all through the uprising. Partisan units had been fighting on their own, not in coordination with military operations. Among them were Slovaks, Czechs, Russians, a group of Frenchmen who conducted themselves admirably under the command of Captain Georges de Lannurien, Yugoslavs commanded by Colonel Ilja Deretić, and some Bulgarian university students. The Frenchmen came from Hungary and Germany, the Yugoslavs from Yugoslavia and the Bulgarians were students from the Slovak University in Bratislava.

Regular military operations of the insurgents had been going on for two months when General R. Viest issued an order on October 28, 1944, to continue the fight "until the victorious end." As a result, the partisan type of fighting went on until the liberation of Slovakia at the end of April 1945, or another six months. During that time the Slovak liberation forces kept tens of thousands of German troops tied down in Slovakia and eliminated Slovakia from the German defensive system as early as August 1944. All the insurgents, whether they were members of the army, of the gendarmerie, partisan units, or civilians, suffered terrible hardships, deprivations, hunger, and cold all through that last winter of the struggle. The Germans treated them with barbarian cruelty.

German Gestapo units, aided by the Hlinka Guards and German Ordners, rounded up insurgent troops and partisans, and indiscriminately arrested civilians. They maltreated all of them, regardless whether they had participated in the uprising or not. A terrible terror gripped Slovakia. A wave of persecution was aimed at people of Czechoslovak orientation, at opponents of the Germans, and especially at Jews and Czechs. Wherever the Germans went, they plundered cattle, machines, and equipment. To satisfy their lust for revenge and also to prevent supplies from reaching the soldiers and partisans, the German Army put scores of communities to the torch, concentrated the inhabitants in certain places under the pretext of evacuating them or "for security reasons" and then shipped them off to Germany to concentration camps, to prison camps, or to forced labor. The Germans now systematically destroyed all communications, blew up all bridges and tunnels, and mechanically destroyed railroad tracks by smashing the sleepers and ploughing up the roadbed. The most revolting feature of this German revenge and terror was the mass-murders. Among the first victims were the insurgent Military Commanders, Generals Rudolf Viest and Ján Golian, who were captured by the Germans on November 3, 1944.

On December 9, 1944, the Commander of the German Sicherheitsdienst (Security Service) in Bratislava sent a top secret report (Geheime Reichssache) to Berlin about the bloody reprisatls against the participants in the uprising. (See Document No. 31). It mentions that five Slovak Special Commandos ("Einsatz, bzw. Sonderkommandos") with 24 liaison and affiliated organs were in charge of Slovakia. This was another name for firing-squads. According to this report, in the six weeks before December 9, the Germans had captured 18,947 persons. Of these 9,653 were reported to be Jews, 3,409 "bandits," 2,186 "deserters," 714 men who had offered resistance and 546 others. In fact, all these were insurgents. It was reported to Berlin that 2,257 persons had received the "special treatment" (Sonderbehandlung), which meant that they had been murdered on the spot, without hearing or sentence. The report further stated that 8,975 Jews and 530 other persons had been sent to German concentration camps. Both the insurgent generals, Viest and Golian, as well as Col. H. Souhrada, Major J. Krátky, First Lt. Várady, the Commissioner of Finance in the Slovak National Council, Viliam Pauliny, and 15 military members of the American Military Mission, referred to in the report as "Jews—American Citizens," had been taken away to Berlin. The report adds that both Slovak Protestant Bishops, Dr. Vladimír Čobrda and Dr. Samuel Š. Osuský, were among those imprisoned; that 14,062 persons had been checked in the course of controls of inns and hotels, and that 122 of these had been put in prison, that 485 motor vehicles had been held up; that railway travel had been controlled and that other security measures had been taken.

These figures are far from complete.[3] They do not include victims between December 9, 1944 and the end of April, 1945. The great majority of the 8,975 persons taken away to Germany were murdered. Among those killed by the Germans were besides Generals Viest and Golian, two other Slovak Generals, Imrich Jurech and Augustin Malár, Commissioners Viliam Paulíny, and Štefan Višňovský, Col. Souhrada, Maj. Krátký, and all 15 members of the American Military Mission, who had been captured wearing American uniforms. They were executed in Mauthausen. Among those executed were Navy Lieutenant J. H. Green, Sgt. J. H. Mičan, Captain E. V. Baransky, and the Associated Press Correspondents Joseph Morton and A. Novak. Colonel of the General Staff Karol Pekník was shot by the Germans in Slovakia. The German Government executed all these men notwithstanding the formal declaration of the American Government on November 19, 1944, (see Document No. 32) in which reference is made to its previous statement of September 7, 1944, regarding the consequences of crimes committed against captured Slovak insurgents. This declaration was issued in connection with reports received of the capture of Generals Viest and Golian and other Slovak officers and men.

Terrible evidence of retribution against the insurgents was uncovered after the war, evidence of crimes committed by the occupying Germans and the terrorist regime of Slovakia.

---

[3] Indictment against J. Tiso and Confederates and against V. Tuka before the National Tribunal in Bratislava, ("*Čas*", Bratislava, July 30, 1946, and December 3, 1946).

The first mass grave of 48 victims, who were murdered on October 3, 1944, was uncovered on the Bukoviny in Turčiansky Svätý Martin. (See Document No. 33). The corpses of a total of 4,316 victims were found, (see Document No. 34), most of them in the region around Banská Bystrica, the focal point of the uprising (1,654). In the village of Kremnička there were three mass graves with 533 victims. Not far from the village of Nemecká nad Hronom about 900 people were burned in a furnace. The Germans killed their victims by shooting, by hanging, by burning in lime-kilns, by beating to death. President Jozef Tiso, the Slovak Government and the representatives of the Populist regime, especially the members of the Hlinka Guard, were helpers and allies of the Germans.[4]

Yet the Slovak people continued to show their yearning for freedom, for the reconstitution of the Czechoslovak Republic and for membership in the world of democratic and non-totalitarian nations, even at the terrible cost of property and lives.[5] The overwhelming majority of the insurgents stood firmly on the side of the West. True, the people of Slovakia felt warm sympathies toward the Soviet Union because of the sacrifices it had made in the common cause, but communism and the Soviet regime were matters of which they would not hear. The Communists found practically no sympathizers among the troops, the police forces, or revenue and customs officers who participated in the uprising. Their only supporters were to be found among the partisans, though not among all of these either, and among their own party members. It is therefore a gross misrepresentation of facts when Communist propagandists now declare that the Communists

---

[4] D. Illek and J. Lánik: Nemecké a gardistické zverstvá (German and Gardist Atrocities) Bratislava, n.d. pp. 1-24.

[5] The Yearbook of the Union of Soldiers of the Slovak National Uprising, 1947, (Bratislava 1946) published a list of those killed in battle in the uprising, (pp. 75-96). It lists 1533 Slovaks, 15 Frenchmen and 7 Bulgarians. The list is incomplete and does not include those missing or wounded.

led the uprising, or that Communist leaders such as Klement Gottwald or Viliam Široký prepared and commanded it.[6]

The Slovak national uprising was a part of the Central European, non-Communist, democratic revolution, no less than the uprising of General Draža Mihajlović in Yugoslavia and the uprising of General Tadeusz Bór-Komorowski in Warsaw.

As of August 1944, the Slovak State was in the process of disintegration. When President Tiso and his government invited the German intervention and when the German Army began occupying the country, it had divested itself even of such meager remnants of sovereign prerogatives as Slovakia had enjoyed until them. From the international point of view, Slovakia had become an enemy occupied province, with a limited autonomous administration. The internal political situation of Slovakia was still worse. From the outbreak of the uprising, the Slovak Government was no longer master of Slovakia. Some, though not all, of its executive power the government could now exercise only in limited parts of the country, according to whether this or that part still remained outside the control of the insurgents, or whether it had not yet been liberated by Soviet and Czechoslovak troops, or whether the German Army had permitted it to exercise any control in an area. Without territory and without sovereignty, the regime of the Slovak State did no more than vegetate.

The Slovak Government was in a crisis and the leaders in utter confusion. The Minister of National Defense, General F. Čatloš, deserted to insurgent territory, where he was arrested. Prime Minister V. Tuka had been under medical treatment for some time. The Government arrested the Chairman of the Supreme Office of Supplies (NÚZ) and the Governor of the Slovak National Bank, Imrich Karvaš. Within the

6 See for example: Miloš Gosiorovsky: *Illegálny boj KSS a Slovenské národné povstanie* (The Illegal Struggle of the Slovak Communist Party and the Slovak National Uprising), Bratislava, 1949, p. 45.

Slovak People's Party everybody began suspecting everybody else of having been negligent in matters of security and of having been sympathetic with, and of having given aid to the insurgents. The German Army was conducting its own campaign of arrests and of purges among the Slovaks. The Slovak State was left without troops or police. On September 5, 1944, President Jozef Tiso appointed a new government: Štefan Tiso Prime Minister, Minister of Foreign Affairs and Minister of Justice; Alexander Mach, Minister of the Interior; Štefan Haššík, Minister of Defense; Mikuláš Pružinský, Minister of Finance; Aladár Kočiš, Minister of Education; Gejza Medrický, Minister of Economy; and Ludovít Lednár, Minister of Communications. Štefan Polakovič was appointed Deputy Chief of the Propaganda Office and Anton Mederly was made Governor of the Slovak National Bank. The new government proclaimed that its policy would emphasize a tightening of Slovak-German friendship and the continuance of the fight against the insurgents.

In helpless rage, President Tiso, the members of his government, and the official propagandists T. J. Gašpar, K. Čulen, J. Paučo, S. Polakovič, F. Ďurčanský and others, now centered their efforts on smearing, threatening, and trying to entice back the insurgents. They did their utmost to discredit the leaders of the uprising. On October 4, 1944, Štefan Tiso declared in the Diet, "We shall not hesitate for a moment to wipe out the treacherous clique and the small part of our population with utmost severity." At the same time the Slovak propaganda unit was outdoing itself in assertions of loyalty to Adolf Hitler and the Third Reich. J. Paučo wrote on September 17, 1944, "there is only one alliance, and that is the alliance with Germany." Prime Minister Štefan Tiso proclaimed on September 27, 1944, that "Small nations must realize that their free national life is assured only by the victory of the Powers of the Tripartite Pact," and on October 4, 1944, in the Diet, "In our foreign policy we will continue to be guided by the principles of Slovak-German alliance and friendship." T. J. Gašpar was trying to convince his listeners on October 14, 1944, that "Slovak-German collaboration is historically right, and faithful to these representatives of Slovak-German friendship, we shall collaborate even closer in order to achieve victory." Jozef Tiso, while celebrating the occupation of Banská Bystrica by German troops, called out on October 30, 1944, "Honor to the Protector Adolf Hitler! Glory to his Army and the SS, glory to General Höffle and other divisional commanders! . . . We have a protector in the German Reich, a magnanimous guardian, Adolf Hitler . . ." The dispatch expressing Jozef Tiso's gratitude to Adolf Hitler is couched in the same terms, (see Document No. 35), as is the one from Štefan Tiso to Joachim von Ribbentrop (see Document No. 36) and the one from Štefan Haššík to Heinrich Himmler (see Document No. 37). On October 27, 1944, the day Banská Bystrica fell to the Germans, President Jozef Tiso even went so far as to order a mass of thanksgiving in the presence of the German officers' corps at Banská Bystrica on October 30, 1944, at a time when tens of thousands of Slovak insurgents were suffering terrible hardships in the mountains, hounded by superior German Forces. He also personally decorated SS officers and SS troupers in Banská Bystrica. On October 27, 1944, the Slovak Government also issued a Proclamation of thanksgiving (see Document No. 38).

As the Slovak Government no longer possessed an army, it began organizing a Domobrana (Home Guard). In order to replace the Police Forces, which had joined the insurgents, the Hlinka Guards were given all police functions. Both were sent against the insurgents in support of the German Armies. When the first batallion of Hlinka Guards was leaving for the front on October 3, 1944, the Chief of the General Staff, Otomar Kubala, told them, "You are going to restore the honor of Slovak soldiers, of all Slovak men."

Neither the Slovak Government nor the leaders of the regime were prepared to recognize the hopeless international situation which now confronted Hitler, nor the desperate internal situation that prevailed in Slovakia. As a result, they never tried to compromise with and adjust to reality. On the contrary, their faith in a German victory on the battle fronts and in their own continued enjoyment of power knew no bounds. Indeed, the younger radicals of the Slovak People's Party, who had been the protagonists of Slovak Separatism and the propagators of totalitarianism, of collaboration with the Nazis, and of anti-Semitism, made one last desperate attempt to turn back the inexorable course of events. Ferdinand Ďurčanský, Štefan Polakovič, Stanislav Mečiar, Vojtech Š. Krajčovič, Karol Murgaš, Anton Macek, Jozef Mikula, Karol Murín, Jozef Paučo, Otomar Kubala, Alojz Krajčovič, Anton Vašek, Vendel Bezák, Jozef Magala, Ferdinand Jurčovič, Ľudovit Lednár, Koloman Geraldíni and others, sent a memorandum to President Jozef Tiso on September 20, 1944. (See Document No. 39). The memorandum bears all the hallmarks of the spirit of totalitarian Separatism. The authors of the Memorandum requested Tiso to bring about "a domestic rebirth" according to the slogan "Back to March 14, 1939." They demanded a "persistently authoritarian system within the (Slovak People's) Party and the state, a thorough purge in the Party, and riddance of all those who lack faith in the idea of the Slovak State." They further demanded "a purge in the state administration, immediate measures to be taken against the authors of the coup of August 29, 1944," and that "the principal culprits be specially punished." These radicals wished "to dissolve forever" all organizations and associations which helped to prepare the uprising, "to nationalize" the en-

terprises, to "deprive the cities of all municipal rights" and
"settle the problem of Jews and Czechs down to its final consequences."

The Bratislava regime complied with the request of these
radicals and decreed numerous measures of retribution against
the insurgents. It ordered a stiffening of penalties. It passed a
law of October 7, 1944, introducing the death penalty for
"acts of sabotage." [7] Almost simultaneously it announced that
48 insurgents had been executed. A law of October 13,
1944, extended the application of martial law to crimes not
usually considered as falling within its definition and also
provided that sentences of death could be carried out "by
shooting by security officers." [8] On October 26, 1944, ten
political leaders of the uprising were criminally indicted. Six
of these were members of the underground Slovak National
Council: Jan Ursíny, Jozef Lettrich, Jozef Styk, Vavro Šrobár,
Peter Zaťko and Jozef Šoltész. Apart from the last one, a
Social Democrat who had joined the Communists after the
consolidation of the Communist and Social Democratic parties, all were non-Communists. Ursíny, Lettrich, Šrobár, Zaťko, Soltész and Ivan Štefánik were sentenced to death in
absentia early in January, 1945.[9] Among the most rabid per-
secutors of the insurgents was the Editor in Chief of the
"Slovák", Jozef Paučo.[10] A Government decree of November
22, 1944, ordered the dismissal from the army and from the
various police forces of all officers and other personnel who
had participated in the uprising and provided for the forfeiture
of all their claims and rights.[11] A Government order of December 6, 1944 provided for more rigid punishment for a
group of further crimes, especially for the crime of "activities

[7] Law No. 226/1944, Slovak Code.
[8] Law No. 188/1944, Slovak Code.
[9] *"Gardista"*, Žilina, January 4, 1945.
[10] *"Slovák"*, Bratislava, November 19, 1944.
[11] Decree No. 215/1944, Slovak Code.

inimical to the state." [12] Towards the end of the year 1944, the
Slovak Government ordered the Ministry of Justice to review
all criminal sentences passed subsequent to September 1,
1944, to ascertain whether they were "in accordance with the
interest of the nation and the continued existence of the state."
This reviewing was carried out by a special bench of the
Supreme Court in Bratislava, consisting of one justice and
four lay-judges. The decree thus introduced "People's Trials"
into Slovakia while the Slovak State was still in existence.[13]
Jozef Paučo was a member of this special reviewing bench.

The radical Separatists were not content with these achievements. They wanted more. They held a rally in Piešt'any on
January 13, 1945, and drew up a manifesto. (See Document
No. 40). The manifesto stubbornly adhered to all the principles of totalitarian Separatism. It declared that the Slovak
State "is the highest expression of the sovereign Slovak
people," that the young Separatists were standing "irrevocable"
behind it. It insisted that discipline in the state be tightened
and demanded that the means of production be nationalized.
The manifesto also demanded "the increase of prosperity in
accordance with the irrepressible process of socialization."
Three months before the end of World War II, their manifesto
declared that "collaboration with Germany is the natural
result of the recognition of the Slovak State." These totalitarian Separatists could not renounce Hitler and his Third Reich.
They consequently declared that "by fighting at the side of
Germany, we are fighting for our natural right to a state and
for our place among the nations." The young radicals ended
by affirming that they wanted to "play their part in the defense of the European spirit, in order that they may enjoy its
blessings in their own Slovak State, after the termination of
the struggle between the two worlds" because "this fight can-

---

[12] Decree No. 228-229/1944, Slovak Code.
[13] *"Gardista"*, Žilina, January 9, 1945.

not end otherwise than with the victory of our and of the European spirit." [14]

But the regime's bombastic propaganda and cruel decrees were the last violent convulsions of the moribund Slovak State. In vain did Konštantín Čulen draw attention to conditions in liberated Italy in a speech on October 15, 1944, intended as a warning to the Slovak people. He announced that "after the breakdown of Fascism 35 anti-Fascist parties were founded." In vain Štefan Haššík issued an order on March 5, 1945, to draftees into the Army and threatened to deport to Germany anyone who disobeyed. In vain did General Höffle try to cheer up his audience on March 11, 1945, in Bratislava by declaring that "with iron nerve and firm resolve the Führer is preparing the great counter-blow which will mark the turning point of the war." The Army Order of J. Tiso and Š. Haššík of March 14, 1945, lauding the magnanimity and true friendship of the Great German Reich, was of no avail. The situation could no longer be saved. The days of the Slovak State and of its totalitarian rulers were numbered. The colossal contributions the Slovak people had to make to the Germans, who were taking away everything they could lay their hands on, were equally of little avail. Not only were the Germans taking everything, but they were also making the Slovak Government pay for their army of occupation. The financial expert Alexander Hrnčár testified before the National Tribunal on February 20, 1947, that the maintenance of German troops in Slovakia during the Slovak national uprising cost the Slovak taxpayer 700 million crowns per month. This, added to previous German exploitations, resulted in the complete financial ruin of the Slovak economy.

The representatives of the vanishing regime now tried to divert attention from the hopeless present and turn it toward

[14] Jozef Kosorín: *Za život národa, za trvanie štátu,* (For Life of The Nation, for Continuance of the State), Bratislava, 1945 (manuscript).

the future. Štefan Polakovič emphatically declared that the fate of the Slovak State was insolubly linked with that of Hitler. He wrote, "Even if we lose this war, we prefer to lose in honor with the German Nation, than to contribute by treachery toward helping our nation to come under a foreign yoke again." [15] "The Gardists" put it this way: "New revolutionary generations would grow up who would maintain the idea of Slovak independence." [16] Eventually President Tiso and his government were forced to flee from Slovakia, proceed to Germany under the protection of the German Army, and await the end of the war there. They settled in Kremsmünster, Austria, and from there continued to conduct political activities. On April 25, 1945, the Slovak Government still proclaimed that "it is resolved to continue its work and to fight for the victory of Slovak truth" and that "our friendly relations with the German Reich were and are based on the support which our great neighbor gave us in our just fight for the freedom of our nation." That is how they were still speaking five days before Hitler's suicide and two weeks before the Third Reich capitulated to the Allied Armies!

Thus ends the episode of the Slovak satellite state. Short as it had been, it left behind it great human suffering, bitter tears and much unnecessary spilling of blood, although its official propagandists, such as Konštantín Čulen, had shamelessly alleged that "the Government of President Tiso has never ordered any executions."

Except for a narrow strip of Western Bohemia, enclosed by the line Karlovy Vary, Plzeň and České Budějovice, which was liberated by the American Army, all the rest of Czechoslovakia, including the capital city of Prague and the other three provincial capitals of Brno, Bratislava, and Užhorod, were freed by the Soviet forces. The fighting between Soviet

---

15 "Slovák", Bratislava, November 13, 1944.
16 "Gardista", Žilina, November 26, 1944.

and German troops for the possession of Czechoslovakia lasted more than six months. The great Mid-European crisis which was the prologue to the Second World War had begun in Prague in 1938, and it was with the liberation of the ancient capital of Prague, on May 9, 1945, that the European chapter of this World War came to its close. More than six years of suffering of Czechoslovakia came to an end. The Protectorate of Bohemia-Moravia and the vassal state of Slovakia vanished from the earth. Czechoslovakia regained her formal sovereignty, although at this time neither her territory nor her independence were completely restored. The resistance to German domination had ended, but now the fight was on for a democratic way of life, in the shadow of the victorious Soviet Empire, in whose sphere of interest the Czechoslovak Republic had been placed, without the knowledge or consent of the Czechs, Slovaks or Subcarpathian Ruthenians. Scarcely had one tyrant been defeated, when another had stepped into his place.

Chapter Two

THE STRUGGLE FOR DEMOCRACY

Czechoslovak-Soviet Relations — The Communists in Czechoslovakia — The Košice Government Program — Communists in the Government — The Struggle of Democrats in Slovakia with the Communists — The Elections of 1946 — The Trial of Tiso — Political Crises in Slovakia — the Establishment of Communist Dictatorship in Czechoslovakia

The Soviet Union is quite unable ever to forget that the Czechoslovak Legions actively fought against the Bolsheviks in Russia during the revolutionary years 1917-1919. Nor can it forget that in 1919 Czechoslovakia offered armed resistance to the Magyar Bolshevik hordes that invaded Slovakia under Bela Kun. What is more, Moscow's fifth column, the Czechoslovak Communist Party, had never found things easy in the interval between the two World Wars. In 1920 the Czechoslovak Government succeeded in liquidating a general strike, which the Communists had organized to support an attempt at establishing a Communist regime in the country. From 1921, when the Communist Party of Czechoslovakia was formally created, until 1938, when the party was disbanded, the Communists never obtained a seat in the Czechoslovak Government. They never stopped their destructive opposition to the government. Although Czechoslovakia was highly developed industrially and had a well-organized industrial working class, which constituted one of the most important elements of the population, radical socialism and communism nevertheless remained alien doctrines to the large majority of the workers. Czechoslovakia did not recognize the Soviet Union, either *de jure* or *de facto,* until Hitler came to power with his National Socialism. Only when the growing pressure of Nazi Germany forced the Czechoslovak Republic to reassess its foreign policy did it accord the Soviet Union recognition and enter into diplomatic relations with it. Then, on May 16, 1935, Czechoslovakia concluded a treaty of friendship and mutual aid with the Soviets. Aid under this treaty was however subject to the conditions, that it would not be rendered unless France had supported her in the event of an attack on the Republic. During the Munich crisis the Soviet Government did nothing to give succour to Czechoslovakia, apart from a few protests. At first the USSR refused to recognize the changes which Hitler had brought about in Czechoslovakia by force and by blackmail in March 1939, but this, too, was not to last long. As soon as the Nazi-Soviet Pact had been signed, the Soviet Government granted recognition to the Slovak State and withdrew recognition from Czechoslovakia. After the German armies attacked the Soviet Union, the Soviet Government again recognized Czechoslovakia by establishing relations with the Czechoslovak Government in exile in London and, on July 18, 1941, it made a new agreement with the latter concerning united action in the war against Germany and its allies. On December 12, 1943, a new treaty of friendship, mutual assistance and post-war co-operation was signed in Moscow.

By the 20-year treaty of alliance, the Soviet Union undertook to respect Czechoslovak independence and sovereignty, not to interfere in domestic matters, to live in friendship and peace with her, to help defend her against any recurrence of German aggression, and to develop economic relations. The Soviet Union committed the grossest possible breaches of this solemn agreement. During the Slovak national uprising it clearly obstructed the rendering of military help to the hard-pressed insurgents. It went so far as to hamper the transport of the Czechoslovak brigade from the USSR to insurgent territory, which created a very serious situation for the insurgents. It also broke its solemn pledge to respect the territorial integrity of the Republic. When the Soviet troops entered into the Subcarpathian Ruthenia, Czechoslovakia's easternmost territory, the Soviets organized a rally of alleged delegates from National Committees which the Communists had set up under the protection of Russian troops. When the delegates convened in Užhorod, they were intimidated to vote in favor of annexing the province to the Soviet Union. Acting on this resolution, passed by fraud and duress, the Soviet forces immediately incorporated the territory into the USSR. By this coup, Czechoslovakia was deprived of 4,921 square miles of national territory and 725,357 unfortunate citizens. A formal Czechoslovak-Soviet agreement was concluded on June 29, 1945, while the rest of Czechoslovakia was still occupied by Soviet troops. By this treaty Czechoslovakia was forced to recognize what had in fact already been carried out earlier, by force. Moscow had also undertaken to respect Czechoslovakia's internal order and not to interfere in her domestic affairs. Yet Soviet soldiers and partisans comported themselves on Czechoslovak liberated territory with ruthless violence, as if they were in conquered enemy country. They arrested and deported from the country some 7,000 citizens of Slovakia. Many of them have not been returned to this day, although innumerable demarches were undertaken by the Czechoslovak Government. The Soviet military and political authorities shamelessly interfered with political life in Slovakia. Against the will of the people, they placed Communists at the head of the National Committees (i.e. the municipal administrations). In some places, as soon as the front had moved on, the Soviet NKVD, in cooperation with a few local

Communists, imposed a reign of unbearable terror. Most serious of all the interferences, however, was the Soviet role in helping Czechoslovak Communists to be admitted to the government and, later, to assume exclusive control of the country.

The strength of the Communist Party of Czechoslovakia between the years 1921 and 1938 is evidenced by the following election results: of 300 members of Parliament they had 41 in 1925 (13.7%), 30 in the year 1929 (10%), and again 30 (10%) in 1935. In Slovakia, the situation during the last ten years of the pre-Munich Czechoslovak Republic was as follows: of the above parliamentary seats, they received 152,242 votes and five seats in 1929 (10.9%), and 210,785 votes and six seats (13.7%) in 1935. Clearly the Communists were a minority both in the Republic and in Slovakia. Their loyalty to the Czechoslovak Republic was always subordinate to their loyalty to the Soviet Union. After Czechoslovakia had been occupied by the Germans, the Communist leaders escaped abroad—some went to Moscow, others to Paris, and thence to London. Their Headquarters, however, were always in Moscow, where party chairman Klement Gottwald had gone with the members of parliament for the Communist Party, Jan Šverma, Václav Kopecký, Rudolf Slánský, Marek Čulen, and, for a while, Viliam Široký, Karol Bacílek, Karol Šmidke, Professor Zdeněk Nejedlý and many more. Václav Nosek, Anna Hodinová-Spurná, Vladimír Clementis, Jozef Vallo and a few others went to London. The Czechoslovak Communists did not support the Czechoslovak Government in exile and were not represented in it but they refrained from any overt opposition to it during the war. They were biding their time, a time which did not fail to come. The Soviet Government saw to that.

By the Teheran agreement of November 28-December 1, 1943, between President Franklin D. Roosevelt, Prime Minister Winston Churchill and Marshal Josef V. Stalin concerning the unconditional surrender of Germany, the Soviet Union secured access to Germany through Eastern and Central Europe. By the time the Big Three met again at the Yalta conference, February 4-11, 1945, the Soviet Armies were already in control of all Eastern Europe and most of Central Europe, including about one third of Czechoslovakia. They were not only in military control but also in complete political control. Moscow regarded the states and nations which the Soviet forces had liberated as belonging to its own sphere of influence.[1] It assumed a dominant position in those states through its own occupation organs or by setting up Communist regimes, or by a combination of both.

The Yalta conference had scarcely ended when the Czechoslovak Communists in Moscow set out to invade the Czechoslovak Government, access to which had been refused to them for more than twenty years. They invited President Beneš and representatives of the Czechoslovak Government in exile in London, as well as representatives of the Slovak National Council in Košice to come to Moscow. The purpose of the discussions was to make the others accept a program of government which the Communists had prepared, and to constitute a new government, in which the Communists had reserved key positions for themselves. The Communists had by then become the masters of the situation. They could dictate their own terms while the others were faced with a difficult situation. Either they could try to control the Communist bid for total power, and thus be able to return to the liberated homeland where they could continue the struggle for democracy, or else throw up the sponge, not go home at all, and surrender the nation entirely to the Communists then and there. The discussions took place in the shadow of the Kremlin, while the advancing Soviet Armies were about to take control of the

---

[1] Chester Wilmot: *The Struggle for Europe*, New York, 1952, pp. 142 and 711.

western parts of Czechoslovakia as well as the eastern. The lesser evil, to return home and continue the relentless fight, was chosen.

After bitter arguments concerning the principles of the governmental program, which did produce a number of improvements from the non-Communist point of view, an agreement was reached. It was all the more difficult because the non-Communist parties were not united. As a reward for such services, the Social Democrat Zdeněk Fierlinger, who was at the time Czechoslovak ambassador to Moscow, was made Prime Minister of the first post-war government of Czechoslovakia. The program which had been agreed upon was made public in Košice on April 5, 1945, and thus came to be known as the Košice Program. It declared that the first Czechoslovak Government would have a provisional character only. Its task was to prepare democratic elections for a Constituent National Assembly, to help end the war as soon as possible, and to ensure the cooperation of the Czechoslovak Army with that of the Soviets. In matters of foreign policy, the program stipulated that Czechoslovakia was to rely primarily upon collaboration with the Soviet Union. The internal administration of the Republic was to rest upon a system of National Committees. The program recognized the Slovaks as a separate nation, whose relations with the Czechs were to be governed by the principle of "partnership between equals." The Subcarpathian Ruthenians were to decide their own future, Germans and Magyars were to lose their Czechoslovak citizenship and be transferred to Germany and Hungary respectively. Those guilty of collaboration with the enemy were to be tried by courts. Those political parties which had rendered aid to the enemy were to be banned. (In this respect the program mentions three democratic parties: the Republican, or Farmers Party, the National-Democratic Party, and the Party of Tradesmen). The property of Germans and traitors was to be confiscated and given to the poor, holdings of farm land were to be limited to a maximum of 50 hectares, the economic life of the country was to be rehabilitated. The means of production were to be placed "under general state control." Farmers were to be permitted to dispose freely of their surplus crops. The government would provide social security for all classes of the working population. Education was to be rehabilitated, expanded, and made accessible to the people. The interest of the people was to prevail above the interest of the individual.

Some of the above points were frought with hidden peril: the new orientation of foreign policy, the change in local administration, the decision concerning Subcarpathian Ruthenia, the banning of the three conservative political parties, and the proposed economic reforms, especially the nationalization of industry. The settlement of Slovak-Czech relations was to reflect the state of affairs that had developed during the national uprising in Slovakia. The difficulties were not confined to principles. The outstanding problem was the uncertainty as to whether or not the Communists would live up to their own promises.

Anxiety concerning future domestic developments in Czechoslovakia was increased by the composition of the new government, determined in Moscow, but made public on liberated Slovak territory at Košice, on April 4, 1945. It had 25 members. Of these, the Communists obtained eight: two deputy prime ministers, the Ministry of Interior (subordinated to which were the police and state security) and the Ministries of Agriculture, schools, information (including radio and propaganda), Social Welfare, and the post of Under-Secretary of State in the Ministry of Foreign Affairs. Moreover, Communist policies would receive the support of the Social Democrats who were given the posts of Prime Minister and Minister of Industry. The Minister of National Defense, a non-party man, had Communist leanings. After the return of the government to liberated Prague, the Communist Antonín Zapotocký became Chairman of the ÚRO, the single, unified trade-union organizatiōn. Another fellow-traveler, the Chairman of the State Planning Office, Edvard Outrata, also threw in his lot with the Communists. Before the war came to an end, the Czechoslovak Communists had achieved control of the army, police, internal administration, farming, schools, propaganda, trade unions, and to some extent foreign affairs. Against this, the non-Communists, who undoubtedly had the support of the great majority of Czechs and Slovaks, had been pushed into a defensive position. This unfavorable state of affairs was in no way improved by the otherwise free elections of 1946. They actually strengthened the position of the Communists still further in the Czech provinces.

It is quite wrong to compare the conditions of internal politics and power in Czechoslovakia after the Second World War with conditions after World War I, or with certain other countries, such as Finland, and to draw inferences which would place the blame for the deterioration upon the non-Communists. After World War I, Czechoslovakia was an independent state. She controlled her own internal policy, and was able to exclude the Communists from participation in the government for twenty years, without having to ask the permission of anyone. After World War II, the immense power of the USSR with its armies that had liberated the country was standing behind the Czechoslovak Communists. As a result, it was now the Communists who could decide at will who would and who would not be in the government.

Under the circumstances the Soviet Government could breach every stipulation of the treaty of alliance with Czechoslovakia. Instead of satisfactory economic relations, Czechoslovakia became the object of shameless exploitation by the USSR. Moscow could dictate its own terms for trade agreements, could order the kinds, quantities and delivery terms of all goods to be supplied to the Soviet. For negligible consideration Moscow also blackmailed Czechoslovakia into granting it unlimited privileges for mining uranium ore and obtained the gift of large hotels and houses in Karlovy Vary. In the political field, Soviet interference in internal matters was still more brazen. The Soviet Government prevented Czechoslovakia from concluding a treaty of alliance with France and from enjoying American economic aid under the Marshall Plan. In February 1948, a Communist *coup d'etat* was prepared and carried out, under the guidance of the Soviet Deputy Minister for Foreign Affairs, Valerian A. Zorin.

The Czechoslovak Communists behaved towards the non-Communists, and betrayed the principles laid down by the Košice program, in exactly the same manner as the Soviet Union behaved towards Czechoslovakia. They forced the non-Communists to accept the "National Front of Czechs and Slovaks" as a coalition of all political parties. The National Front was to discuss and to agree upon the solution of all controversial issues before these were to be presented to the government or to Parliament or, in Slovakia, to the Board of Commissioners or the Slovak National Council. The National Front was practically controlled by the Communists and Social Democrats, who had a formal majority of 51% at least in Parliament. Only such matters came to be submitted for discussion of the National Front as could not be settled outside of it. With the progressive liberation of Czechoslovak territory, the Communists also grabbed power in the majority of National Committees, thereby gaining a decisive influence in communal matters as well as in industrial enterprises and trade unions. As the police were also under Communist control, a hard struggle was fought within and outside the government for fundamental democratic rights and civil liberties. The transfers of Germans and Hungarians gave the Communists many opportunities to commit crimes and injustices, and to enrich themselves individually and as a party. They made use of the period of transition, that is while Parliament was not yet constituted, for pushing through the wholesale nationalization of industrial enterprises, banks and insurance companies, by means of orders embodied in presidential decrees. This was a breach of the Košice program which said nothing about nationalization, and only stipulated "placing enterprises under general government control." Nationalization amounted to confiscation, since the owners received no compensation. When the provisional National Assembly was constituted, the Communists insisted on prolonging its term of office, again in breach of the Košice program. The function of this Assembly was to prepare the elections for the Constituent National Assembly. Instead of preparing the Constitution, the Constituent National Assembly then devoted itself for 21 months to other legislative activities. By such tactics the Communists kept themselves in power, without a Constitution, without a regular parliament and without permitting political conditions to settle down in the country. It is clear evidence of the fact that Moscow and the Czechoslovak Communists had no intention of sharing power in the state with the non-Communist parties. They never took governmental co-operation with the non-Communists seriously. For them such co-operation was a necessary temporary expedient, to be in effect only until they could grab all power in the state. They believed that this would be most easily achieved through Slovakia.

Slovakia was the only part of the Republic which had a common frontier with the Soviet Union. The fighting spirit of the uprising was still very much alive. On April 5, 1945, Klement Gottwald proclaimed a Magna Charta of the Slovak Nation in Košice. The partisans in Slovakia had arms and were mostly Communists. The purging of political life of those who had collaborated with the enemy during the war had been carried out more thoroughly in Slovakia, because of the Slovak separatist movement, than in the Czech provinces. The Democratic Party in Slovakia became the protector of legal order and of those who were being attacked or persecuted. It was, in the Communist terminology, the representative of reaction, an obstacle to socialization, an enemy of popular-democratic order, and of friendship with the Soviet Union. Thanks to the aid rendered them by the Soviet Army, the Slovak Communists made much headway. They gained control of the security police and introduced the so-called National Security Corps No. 2, which was nothing but a corps of political commissars attached to the security organs. They became the masters of a large majority of National Committees, set up under battle-front conditions. With so many trump cards in their hands, they considered Slovakia as the most propitious set-up for liquidating the non-Communists and for establishing their brand of totalitarian dictatorship. They first tried to achieve this by democratic means: by obtaining a majority, and when this failed, they tried it by crude force.

One of the great problems of Slovak politics was the former membership of the disbanded Slovak People's Party, the majority of whom had never really forsaken their earlier loyalties to democratic principles and to the Czechoslovak Republic. These the Communists tried to win over. One of the inducements was the apparent Communist devotion to the idea of a privileged Slovak constitutional position within the Czechoslovak Republic in accordance with the Košice program and the so-called Magna Charta (Document No. 41). The Communists of Slovakia assumed a radical nationalistic attitude. Although formally there were two Communist parties in Czechoslovakia, the Communist Party of Czechoslovakia, led by Klement Gottwald, and the Communist Party of Slovakia, led first by Karol Šmidke and later by Viliam Široký, there was in reality but a single party, controlled by Gottwald and the Prague Politbureau, and subordinated to Moscow. In January 1946, the Slovak Communists began concerted action with a view to disorganizing the Democratic Party. They tried to provoke the creation of several non-Communist parties, of which one would co-operate with them and in reality be a mere front for the Communist Party, and to drive the Democratic Party into opposition which under the practices of the National Front would have been tantamount to dissolution and liquidation. They achieved the very opposite. A third party was formed in Slovakia, the Party of Labor (Strana Práce) whose members were mostly former Communist Party members, and this party became a branch of the Czechoslovak Social Democratic Party in 1947. The Democratic Party came out of this struggle with increased strength, especially after an intra-party agreement concerning Catholic matters, concluded on March 31, 1946. In Spring 1946, a fourth Slovak political party came into being, the Freedom Party (Strana Slobody) which was a non-socialist party, but this too, failed to change the political stratification of Slovakia to any significant extent. The Democratic Party became in fact the spokesman of the anti-Communists in Slovakia. Its political program included: maintenance of independence of Czechoslovakia, friendship with both East and West, equality of rights between Czechs and Slovaks, maintainance of Slovak national institutions with legislative, executive and administrative powers, an uncompromisingly democratic regime, maintenance of legal order, an economic system of private enterprise with limited participation of public enterprise, encouragement of cultural and material progress, and preservation of domestic, spiritual, national and political traditions. This program gained the support of the great majority of the Slovak people, which recognized that the Democratic Party was an effective force in fighting Communist intimidation and encroachments on liberties. The primary objective of Slovak politics was to wring from the Communists' grip all that which they had so unlawfully usurped, to regain the control of the National Committees and their key positions in the economy, to rid Slovakia of the terror of the Communist-controlled National Security Corps, to reestablish peace and confidence in the new conditions, and to prevent the Popular Tribunals from becoming instruments of liquidation of persons standing in the way of Communism. Most of this was achieved within the first few months after the war. The result of the elections of May 26, 1946, the first (and last) free postwar elections in Czechoslovakia, surprised the Communists, although it was no more than what the Democrats had expected. The Democratic Party obtained 999,622 votes (62%), 63 of the 100 seats in the Slovak National Council and 43 of the 69 Slovak members of the Czechoslovak Parliament in Prague. The Slovak Communist Party obtained 489,596 votes (30.3%) which gave them 31 members of the Slovak National Council and 21 members of the Prague Parliament. The Freedom Party got 60,195 votes (3.7%), 3 seats in the Slovak National Council and 3 representatives in Parliament after the second scrutinium. The Labor Party got 50,079 votes (3.1%), 3 seats in the Slovak National Council and 2 members of Parliament after the second scrutinium. There were 12,724 (0.8%) blank or invalid votes.

These election results proved several politically significant facts: (1) that 70% of the Slovak electorate repudiated communism; (2) that the Slovak people repudiated separatism and (3) that they voted in favor of the reborn Czechoslovak Republic. All these facts were relevant both with respect to the recent past and with regard to the immediate future of

Slovak politics. After the elections, the Communists completely changed their political line and their attitude to the Slovak non-Communists. In place of a program of Slovak nationalism, which they had been proclaiming until then, they now came out in favor of centralism. The reason for this aboutface was that in the Czech provinces the Communists had won the elections and had become the strongest party. They now embarked upon a course of open and ruthless attacks upon the Slovak Democratic Party, conducted with incessant and aggressive demagoguery.

Even though the Slovak Communists were defeated in the election, the 30.3% votes they obtained nevertheless represented a substantial increase in comparison with the 13.7% they got in 1935. Several causes contributed to this result: (1) the USSR had helped the Communists by liberating Slovakia from German domination; (2) the totalitarian regime of the Slovak State had made the people more radical and many of them now switched from one political extreme to the others; (3) a great many Social Democrats voted for the Communists notwithstanding the fact that the Party of Labor had put up its own candidates; and (4) the Communists went into the election with a professedly social-democratic (moderately socialist) and an extremely nationalistic program.

A very serious political crisis developed in Slovakia immediately after the elections. It was provoked by the Slovak Communists upon direct orders of the Prague Politbureau because of the election results. The Communists accused the Democrats of anti-Soviet attitudes, of anti-Communist agitation, of having misused the influence of the Roman Catholic hierarchy for their own ends, and of having rehabilitated the former members of the Slovak People's Party by admitting them to membership in the Democratic Party, and by letting several of them run as candidates for Parliament. The Communists launched an organized assault. The Communist Ladislav Holdoš declared on June 6, 1946, in Ružomberok, that "the leaders of the Communist Party of Czechoslovakia have prepared a plan, consisting of 15 points, aimed at destroying the Democratic Party and at taking power into our (Communist) hands. We must at all cost prove the Democratic Party guilty of treasonable activities and then disband it." In June 1946, the chairman of the Communist Party of Slovakia stated that the "Members of Parliament (for the Democratic Party) Kempný and Bugár will not receive clearance by the National Front," and will not be allowed to take their seats. Fanatical Communist printers refused to print the Democratic Party daily *"Čas"* for a while. This was an attempt at frightening, confusing, and disorganizing the anti-Communist forces in Slovakia. The new Prime Minister designate of the Czechoslovak Government, Klement Gottwald, was negotiating the forming of his government, in June 1946, in such a manner as to isolate the Slovak Democrats completely. He secured the collaboration of the Social Democrats and then concentrated on blackmailing the Slovak National Council into a new agreement which substantially reduced the powers of the Slovak national bodies, the Slovak National Council, the Board of Commissioners, and the individual departments of the Commissioners. It strengthened centralism in the Republic and produced a certain amount of dissatisfaction in Slovakia. After this agreement, which was concluded on June 28, 1946, the Board of Commissioners was constituted. In it the Communists had lost a very important department—that of the Commissioner of the Interior. A non-party man, General Mikuláš Ferjenčík, was appointed commissioner.

At the end of World War II, all nations that had temporarily fallen under the domination of the powers of the Berlin-Rome-Tokyo Axis tried those of their citizens who had committed crimes against the law of nations, especially crimes against peace and humanity and against the vital interests of their own people by voluntarily and willingly serving and aiding the enemy. Hugh Seton-Watson[2] has classified these as "Quislings," "puppets," "traitors" and "collaborators" with the Nazis in five classes of progressively greater responsibility and guilt. On May 15, 1945, the Slovak National Council also issued a "decree providing for the punishment of fascist criminals, foreign oppressors, traitors, and collaborationists, and for the creation of a National Tribunal and of People's Courts." [3] War criminals who had "no particular geographic location" were, under the Four-Power Agreement of August 8, 1945, tried by ad hoc International Military Tribunals in Nuremberg and in Tokyo.[4]

Jozef Tiso and his Slovak Government had escaped to Austria with the German Army on April 5, 1945. Early in November 1945 the American occupation authorities handed Tiso and his government back to the Czechoslovak Government in pursuance of the Declaration of the Great Powers in Moscow of November 1, 1943, and of the Potsdam Declaration of July 26, 1945. The Communists made improper use even of Tiso's trial for their own political purposes. The State Security organs which were under the orders of a Communist Minister of the Interior brought Tiso and his government back to Slovakia in chains. That was the first thing to cause much bad feeling among the population. When the time for the elections of Spring 1946 was approaching, the Communists demanded that Tiso's trial before the National Tribunal be held before the elections. By this they were hoping to anger the Slovak Catholics, as Tiso had originally served as a Catholic priest in Bánovce nad Beb-

2 Hugh Seton-Watson: *The East European Revolution*, New York, 1951, pp. 106-107.

3 Decree No. 33/1945, Coll. of Decrees of the Slov. Nat. Council amended by Decree No. 57/1946 of May 14, 1946.

4 Sheldon Glueck: The Nuremberg Trial and Aggressive War, New York, 1946, p. 3 and seq.

ravou. The Democrats prevented this. When the trial of Tiso, Ďurčanský and Mach was held in the end, it was started contrary to agreement. There could be little doubt that Jozef Tiso had been the most responsible political authority and that he was fully responsible, both in form and in substance for all that had happened in Slovakia during the existence of the Slovak State. It was therefore extremely probable that the National Tribunal would find all three men guilty and impose the heaviest sentence, death. Even before the trial the Communists repeatedly announced that Tiso must be executed. The Democrats opposed, arguing that apart from purely Slovak domestic considerations, Tiso's execution would reflect unfavorably upon Slovak-Czech relations. The Democrats had reason to fear a deterioration of Slovak-Czech relations if these protagonists of Slovak radical nationalism were executed and to fear serious disturbances in relations among Slovaks of different religions if a Catholic priest were put to death. There were also psychological arguments against an execution of a sentence of death as well as considerations of justice. It would have been a very nearsighted policy to give certain extremist elements an opportunity to make a martyr of this political offender. It also had to be considered that, however wrong his conduct had been in the totalitarian Slovak State, Tiso had nevertheless still led the more moderate faction of the regime. It would have been contrary to the people's sense of justice if relevant extenuating circumstances had been entirely ignored. Jozef Lettrich, the Chairman of the Democratic Party, therefore interceded, well in advance, with the President of the Republic, Edvard Beneš, to assure a Presidential reprieve for Tiso, if he were to be sentenced to death. Both before the trial and after it had started, the President promised to reprieve the death sentence. The trial began in December 1946 and ended on April 15, 1947. The National Tribunal in Bratislava, presided over by the Communist, Dr. Igor Daxner, pronounced the death sentence for Jozef Tiso and Ferdinand Ďurčanský (the latter having been tried in absentia) and sentenced Alexander Mach to 30 years in prison. Tiso requested a reprieve, the Commissioner of Justice and the Public Prosecutor of the National Tribunal—having been instructed to do so by the Chairman of the Slovak National council—recommended mercy, and the Presidium of the Slovak National Council submitted both the request and the recommendations that it be granted, through the Czechoslovak Government, to President Edvard Beneš.

The Communists could not, however, pass up this opportunity for creating extreme tension in Slovakia. They organized popular demonstrations against Tiso, sent deputations of partisans, former political prisoners, soldiers of the uprising, and workers to the Chairman of the Slovak National Council, Jozef Lettrich, in order to exert the maximum pressure upon him against procuring clemency for Tiso. Thousands of Communist inspired telegrams and resolutions flooded the offices of the leaders of the Slovak National Council, the Czechoslovak Government, and the President, all carefully calculated to intimidate non-Communist leaders. There also came cables and requests that mercy be exercised. The Papal Inter-Nuncio, Dr. Xaver Ritter, the Council of the Roman Catholic Bishops in Slovakia, the General Council of the Protestant Church in Slovakia, and others asked that mercy be shown Tiso. The former Minister of the Slovak State to the Vatican, Karol Sidor, who had obtained asylum after the collapse of the Slovak State, requested Pope Pius XII to intercede on behalf of Tiso. The Pope received Sidor in audience on June 29, 1945, informed him that he had done what was in his power, but at the same time reminded Sidor what he had told him in the course of his first audience "when, in July 1939, he pointed out that Tiso, since he was a priest ought not to have accepted the office of President of the Slovak State." The Pope had repeatedly warned Tiso and the Bishop Dr. Michal Buzalka, in 1939, to think twice before Tiso accepted the presidency and had expressed his serious misgivings as to the possible consequences of such an action. On September 17, 1939, Tiso had taken the opposite view from that of the Pope.[5] Events showed how right the Vatican and the Pope had been and how mistaken Tiso.

By a majority, the Czechoslovak Government decided that the President was not to grant a reprieve to Tiso. Even then Lettrich again telephoned to the President, asking that he decide in favor of Tiso. Several other members of the Democratic Party (Andrej Cvinček, Kornel Filo, Matej Josko, and Jozef Styk) did the same. The President refused a reprieve and Jozef Tiso was executed on April 18, 1947.[6]

The appointment of the presiding judge and the other members of the National Tribunal was one of the prerogatives of the Slovak National Council. The presiding judge, Dr. Igor Daxner, had repeatedly acted contrary to law. An exceptionally conspicuous instance was when, without justification other than the wish of the Communist Party, he separated the trial of Alexander Mach from the trial of Tiso, because the Communists had reason to want to give Mach a milder sentence, but did not want this to result in any leniency towards Tiso. In exercise of its constitutional powers, the Presidium of the Slovak National Council decided to relieve Daxner of his functions and duties with the Tribunal. The Czechoslovak Government, however, led by Gottwald, unconstitutionally interfered with this decision and ordered Daxner to remain in office. This created the absurd situation where an organ of the state who had no authority prevented

[5] Karol Sidor: *Šesť rokov pri Vatikáne* (Six Years at the Vatican) Scranton, Pa., 1947, pp. 61-63, 69, 84 and 273-4.
[6] *"Čas"*, Bratislava, April 23, 1947.

the carrying out of a decision of those who had full authority in the matter. This, too, was symptomatic of the approaching political storm.

After the Tiso trial, the Communists launched a general attack on the Democrats in Slovakia. They came out with such accusations as that the Democrats were bringing the Populists back into power and thereby threatened the security of the state. The Democratic Party, they alleged, permitted former members of the Slovak People's Party once more to assume responsible positions in politics and state administration. The Communist attacks were concentrated in particular upon three Democratic Members of the Parliament, Miloš Bugár, Jan Kempný and Jozef Staško, whom they accused of maintaining contacts with former Slovak Separatists in exile. The Democrats stood up for their three colleagues and the Communist accusations petered out.

This attempt having failed, the Communists tried again. The Prime Minister, K. Gottwald, accused the Democrats at a rally at Devín on July 6, 1947, of being reactionaries and aiding and abbeting antistate elements. The same accusations were repeated almost immediately by Antonin Zápotocký while on a political tour of Slovakia. The Democrats did not fail to reply in appropriate form to these accusations, attacks which clearly showed that it was the Czechoslovak Communists and not the Communists of Slovakia who were masterminding the campaign against the Slovak Democratic Party.

Scarcely had this storm blown over than the Communists provoked another incident. This occurred after the visit of a Czechoslovak government delegation to Moscow in July 1947, when the government had to accept Stalin's order that Czechoslovakia withdraw her acceptance of cooperation with the Marshall Plan and refrain from signing a treaty of alliance with France. A catastrophic drought and crop failure hit

Czechoslovakia in 1947. The Communists now pointed to the fact that the Department of Food and Supplies in Slovakia happened to be under a Democratic Commissioner. They made this a pretext for violent attacks upon the Democratic Party, in the press, at mass-rallies and at demonstrations; they sent workers' and partisans' delegations to importune the Democratic leaders; they created disorder, uncertainty, and tension. The Democrats succeeded in resisting these attacks. The Slovak people saw through these Communist tactics and refused to be swayed by them. So the Communists tried another trick.

The Communist-controlled organizations of former members of the resistance, especially the Union of Slovak Partisans, the Central Trade Unions organization of Slovakia, and the Slovak Trade Union Council, now presented demands in the form of an ultimatum, asking that by September 20, 1947, at the latest, they be granted representation in the Slovak National Front, that their material demands be met, and that public life be systematically purged of disloyal elements. Again the Democrats refused to give in.

The Communist Parties of Czechoslovakia and of Slovakia then, in close association with the Ministry of Interior, which was Communist controlled, attempted to compromise the Slovak Democratic political leaders with the aid of the secret State Police. By that time Communist terror and intimidations had also set in the Czech provinces where the fight between Czech National Socialists and the Communists was getting more and more acute. By an agreement of September 11, 1947, the Czech Communists secured the aid of the Social Democrats. A week later the Communists engineered an attempt to assassinate Peter Zenkl, Jan Masaryk, and Prokop Drtina. Hand in hand with the Secret Police, attempts at terrorization by Communist mobs were organized to terrorize the people. Such mobs were, for example, sent to attack the premises of the Slovak National Council and to threaten its Chairman that "he would not escape alive," if they caught him.

In the second half of September 1947 the State-Security organs "discovered" a number of widespread anti-state organizations in Žilina, Bratislava, and Prague. In each of these organizations evidence was "found" clearly incriminating some prominent Democratic leader. Apart from the three Members of Parliament who had been the object of earlier attacks, Bugár, Kempný, and Staško, accusations were now also aimed at the Chairman of the Party, Jozef Lettrich, the Deputy Prime Minister of the Czecho-Slovak Government and representative of the Democratic Party, Ján Ursíny, the Secretary General of the party, Fedor Hodža, and the Commissioner for Finance, (also a Democrat) Matej Josko. Bugár, Kempný, and Staško were accused of participating in a conspiracy against the state and indicted. As a result, the Czechoslovak Parliament deprived them of immunity and thus permitted their prosecution in court. All three were immediately arrested. Also arrested was one of Ursíny's personal aides. They searched his office and files, arrested and then fired several more of his employees. Officers of the State Security assaulted Commissioner Josko on September 27, 1947, in Žilina and charges were filed against Hodža on suspicion that he had helped to cover up the activities of an employee of the office of Deputy Prime Minister Ursíny. This was a direct, frontal attack by the Communists upon the Democratic Party, aimed at discrediting it, intimidating its members and seeking justification for outlawing the party.

The crisis reached utmost intensity towards the end of October 1947. The Communists invited delegates of industrial and employee's councils to convene in Bratislava on October 30, for the purpose of making the most radical demands upon the Democrats. On the following day all Communist members of the Board of Commissioners of Slovakia, with their Chairman Gustav Husák in the lead, resigned and thereby produced a crisis in the Board. The Democratic Commissioners, who were in the majority, refused to resign, however. Thereupon the leaders of the Communist-controlled Central Trade Union Council, František Zupka and Štefan Kušik, presented an ultimatum, demanding that all demands of the Slovak Trade Union Council be met by November 5, 1947. Somehow the Democrats succeeded in gaining more time. Meanwhile the Communist leaders in Prague, led by Klement Gottwald, managed to coerce and blackmail J. Ursíny into resigning. Prime Minister Gottwald and the Communist Minister of the Interior kept threatening Ursíny that they would prefer criminal charges against him for participation in treasonous activities if he did not resign at once. Although Ursíny was an outstanding patriot and national leader who would never have had anything to do with disloyal activities, he nevertheless resigned in order to relieve the pressure upon his Party. On November 8, 1947, Gottwald left for Slovakia to settle the crisis in the Board of Commissioners. The Communists made the following demands: (1) no political party was to have a majority on the Board, regardless of the election results; (2) grant representation to the Trade Union and Resistance Organizations (which were Communist controlled) as well as to the two small parties which had not hitherto been represented in the Board of Commissioners—the Party of Freedom and the Party of Labor; and (3) put Communists in charge of the Departments of Justice, Agriculture and Supplies, which had so far been under Democratic Commissioners. The Democrats refused. They were prepared to accept only the demand for admitting the two small parties to the Board. Gottwald also having failed, the Communists now called a conference of all Slovak Communist farmers at Bratislava for November 14. At the end of the conference, which levelled sharp accusations against the Democrats, the participants, reinforced by an organized mob of Communist rowdies, once more broke into the Headquarters of the Slovak National Council, having broken down the iron gates, and shouted that the Chairman should be hanged. The Democrats answered these attempts at intimidation by large anti-Communist demonstrations in many Slovak cities on November 16, 1947. The most impressive one occurred in Bratislava. The Communists recognizing that they were unable to subdue the Democrats agreed, on November 18, to a compromise solution of the crisis of the Board of Commissioners. Apart from gaining representation for the two small parties, which was given at the expense of the Democrats but was not of any benefit to the Communists, the Communists gained nothing. This brought to a happy ending the long and deep political crisis in Slovakia. It had been planned as a means of establishing a Communist dictatorship in Czechoslovakia. The crisis had been mastered only because the Democrats in Slovakia were able to rely upon the help of the solid common front of Czech democrats, especially the Czech National Socialist Party.

The crisis, once over, had its aftermath in the Prague Parliament and in the Slovak National Council. It produced a spontaneous outcry against the brutal methods of investigation practiced by the Communist State Police. It came to light that the security organs, in investigating democratic political prisoners, had committed gross breaches of the law and had deprived them of their constitutional civil rights. A number of prisoners had been kept under arrest for weeks without hearing and had been kept in police custody after preliminary hearings, which had failed to show any justification for holding them. A Member of Parliament, Jozef Staško, had been arrested without parliamentary assent. Prisoners were being forced to confess under physical coercion. When the Chairman of the Slovak National Council learned of these abuses, he publicly denounced them in an address at a rally in Bratislava on November 16, 1947. He handed the evidence he had obtained to the Democratic Members of the Parliament in Prague and to the Slovak National Council in Bratislava, in order that they might appoint members to bring up the matter in the Czechoslovak Parliament and the plenary assembly of the Slovak National Council. The Club of the Members of Parliament selected representative Štefan Blaško and Members of the Slovak National Council, Imrich Laurinec and Michal Géci. Blaško spoke in protest against Communist methods of investigation on December 18, 1947, and Laurinec and Géci on December 19, 1947. The Czech and Slovak Communists in Prague and Bratislava replied with vicious attacks on the Democrats and accused them of siding with conspirators and of smearing police organs. The Democratic Party moved both in Parliament and in the Slovak National Council that the excesses of the Communist police be investigated by a special commission of Parliament and of the Slovak National Council. Both these legislative bodies approved the motion. The Communist *coup d'etat* which was carried out soon afterwards prevented the investigation committees from performing their assignment. Following the *coup*, representative Štefan Blaško publicly declared that "he had not made that speech of his own free will and initiative, but upon the order and decision of the Club of the Deputies of the former Democratic Party, based upon unverified and scandalous material which had been supplied to him," a statement which the Communist press was happy to exploit.[7]

This incident was the last in the desperate struggle (a struggle which some political opponents now like to denounce as "collaboration") of the Slovak Democrats with the Czech and Slovak Communists, of the struggle for democracy, for

[7] *"Pravda"*, Bratislava, March 6, 1948.

the preservation of government by law, for respect for the will of the people and for their natural rights and liberties. This period, which lasted for three critical years following the termination of World War II, was the most dramatic in Slovak political history. The essence of the fight was the wish of a Communist minority in Slovakia to force its will upon the majority and to set up a totalitarian Communist regime. The Democrats resisted with every possible means at their disposal. It was of no avail. Democracy and Communism cannot co-exist, whether it be in the international or in the domestic field. The fault is certainly not that of the democrats or of democracy. It lies exclusively with the Communists. This became very evident during the last act of the struggle for democracy in Czechoslovakia, which transformed this drama into a tragedy. It happened in February 1948.

When all their efforts at grabbing power in Slovakia had failed, the Czechoslovak Communists decided to reach out for exclusive power by way of Prague. The Prime Minister of the Czechoslovak Government and Chairman of the Communist Party, Klement Gottwald, had announced over the radio on New Year's Day 1948, "We must at the same time see to it that the National Front, resolutely following the government program and the will of the people, rids itself of the reactionary elements which have infiltrated our political life and which are working against the program of the government, against the people and in the interest of subversion." Earlier Gottwald had declared at the meeting of the Central Committee of the Communist Party of Czechoslovakia, on November 28, 1947, that the objective of the Communist Party was "to win the majority of the nation." To win the majority and get rid of the reactionary elements—that was the aim the Communists had defined for 1948. The Communists had no majority and clear expressions of popular feeling left no doubt that the Czechoslovak people would never give them a majority. Indeed, nobody doubted that they would actually lose some of the strength they had shown in the 1946 elections. To "get rid of reactionary elements" therefore seemed to be the more realistic objective. Who were those reactionary elements, according to the Communists? All Czech and Slovak democrats and non-Communists, all anti-Communists. They included the National Socialists, who in 1946 had obtained 1,299,980 votes (18.3%) and 55 of the 300 seats in Parliament, the People's Party with 1,111,099 votes (15.6%) and 46 seats of Parliament and the Slovak Democrats with 999,622 votes (14.0%) and 43 seats in Parliament. The Communists considered only one part of the Social Democrats as reactionaries, the right wing of that party. The left-wing Social Democrats, led by Fierlinger, were regarded by them as good "progressives" because of their complete subservience to the Communists. In 1946 the Social Democrats had obtained 905,617 votes (12.7%) and 39 seats in Parliament. Although the Communists had not specifically mentioned the Freedom Party, because they held no cabinet appointments, they, too, belonged to the "reactionary" elements as they were a democratic party. The Communists had obtained 2,695,293 votes (37.9%) and 114 parliamentary seats. The 37.9% minority was faced with the problem of "getting rid of" a 61.5% majority. The problem had to be settled in favor of the Communists before the next elections, which were to be held not later than May 26, 1948. The Communists had only five months left. In this short period a mass of complicated legislation should have been enacted, legislation which, according to the Communist master-plan, would assure them the obtaining of a majority. The difficult problems that were to be settled included the completion and enactment of the new Czechoslovak Constitution, whose passage the Communists had been deliberately delaying for a long time and debate over vote-catching bills submitted by the Communist Party, such as the National Insurance Law, an amendment to the land reform law, tax-relief for farmers and tradesmen, changes in the distribution of consumers' goods, etc. The Communists, however, soon realized that they would not gain a majority in the elections by such means, partly because there was not enough time, and especially because of the now united resistance of all the non-Communist parties, including the Social Democrats. Their only hope lay in the application of undemocratic procedures, in the use of force, in a Communist *coup d'etat*.

This is how they engineered it.

The Communists started using the security organs for their own political purposes, and in particular against their political opponents in the Czech provinces. The police were prevented from investigating the attempt on the lives of certain members of the government, made in September 1947. The attempt was engineered by Communist officials in the Moravian village of Krčmany. Instead of investigating this affair, the Communist-controlled organs kept discovering sensational anti-state conspiracies, which invariably incriminated non-Communist political leaders. They filed charges against non-Communist members of Parliament. In Parliament, the Communist security methods were sharply condemned and their brutal methods of investigations were brought to public notice by the Democratic Party. Criticism centered around the person of the Minister of the Interior, Václav Nosek, to whom the police and security organs were subordinated. He was attacked also for failing to carry out the National Security Act of 1947, for his failure to reorganize the security forces according to that law, for failing to submit the name of a new appointee for the post of Commandant of National Security for the Land of Bohemia, and because he had fired nine commanders of the National Security who had been non-Communists and replaced them by Communist Party henchmen. As a result, political tension increased during January 1948. The Communists found themselves isolated both in Parliament and in the government. All the non-Communist members of Parliament and cabinet ministers stood against them. Press controversies also became more violent and the public expected a clash which would decide the political fate of Czechoslovakia.

The crisis began on February 13. The non-Communist members of the cabinet, who were in the majority, voted in favor of barring the appointment of security officers by the Minister of Interior, a move which was violently opposed by the Communist members of the government. The Communists countered with two moves according to the technique which they had already employed during the recent crisis in the Board of Slovak Commissioners. The Chairman of the Central Trade Unions Organization, Antonín Zápotocký, called a mass-meeting of the factory committees and employees' councils, which were Communist controlled. They were to meet in Prague on February 22, 1948, and voice their views regarding the government decisions about adjustment of civil and public service wages. The Minister of Agriculture, Julius Ďuriš, in turn, called a rally of representatives of the farmers' commissions, which were also Communist controlled, to meet in Prague on February 29, 1948, to voice the demands of the peasantry. In reality, both these moves were intended to camouflage the real intent of the Politbureau which was to grab power and to make the coup appear as the will of the "people." The Communist minority of the government, led by Prime Minister Gottwald, refused to submit to the will of the majority and lent its support to the illegal acts of the Minister of Interior. At a cabinet meeting on February 17, 1948, the non-Communist members of the government insisted that decisions taken at the last meeting be obeyed, whereupon Gottwald at once adjourned the meeting to February 20.

The cabinet members of the three non-Communist parties, the National Socialist, the Democrats and the People's Party, agreed that Communist maneuvers had brought the functioning of Parliament and of the government to a standstill and prevented them from exercising their legitimate functions. It had also become clear that the Communists were resolved to misuse the government and Parliament for the preparation of rigged elections. The non-Communists were consequently faced with the alternative of either to resist these attempts, to provoke a government crisis and demand new parliamentary elections, or to allow the Communists to continue their preparations for "obtaining the majority." The non-Communists chose the alternative of a government crisis. They arranged that it occur before February 22, when the rally of Communist workers was to take place. Before taking the step, they made sure of the approval of President Edvard Beneš and of his help in solving the crisis in the spirit of democratic traditions and of constitutional principles. The Social Democrats assumed a wait-and-see attitude. The non-Communists had counted on their active support, all the more since they had, of late, acted with the anti-Communist members.

On February 19, 1948, the former Soviet ambassador in Prague, who was now a Deputy Foreign Minister of the Moscow government, Valerian A. Zorin, suddenly arrived in Prague under the pretext of controlling shipments of Soviet wheat to Czechoslovakia. This puerile excuse was actually refuted by the Communist Gustav Husák, who threateningly declared to another member of the Board of Commissioners in Bratislava: "Surely you don't think that Zorin has come to Czechoslovakia to fool around with wheat." Zorin had, in fact, arrived to take a hand in the internal crisis which had now reached a critical phase. When Gottwald refused to give a clear-cut answer in the matter of the dismissal of security officers according to the earlier decision of the government, the cabinet ministers of the three non-Communist parties refused to participate in further government meetings and submitted their resignations to the President. Neither the Social Democratic ministers nor the two non-partisan ministers: the Minister of Foreign Affairs, Jan Masaryk, and the Minister of Defense, Gen. Ludvík Svoboda, handed in their resignation with the others. As a result, a majority of cabinet members were still in the government and from this the Communists could infer that the government as such had not resigned but that only some of its members had left. The Communists therefore remained adamant in their refusal to listen to reason and now stepped forward with a number of sweeping demands: the ministers who had resigned must not be permitted to return to the government, the President must accept their resignations, and "Action Committees" must be formed which will establish "the unity of workers, peasants, and intellectuals of cities and villages." The Communist Party proclaimed the "mobilization of all the resources of the working people" against the reactionaries, who were trying to destroy the National Front, to turn Czechoslovakia against the Soviet Union "upon orders and instigation of reactionaries abroad," to destroy the popular-democratic institutions, and so on. They claimed that the reactionaries were preparing to set up a care-taker government of civil servants, that they wanted Czechoslovakia to become "a free Eldorado for spies and saboteurs of foreign powers," as K. Gottwald alleged at a meeting in Prague on February 22. On that same day the Communists called upon the Social Democrats to "agree on further procedure and to prepare for filling the government vacancies." The Social Democrats did not accept this invitation. The Communists thereupon turned to the President and insisted that he accept the resignations of the ministers of the three anti-Communist parties and appoint a new government proposed by the Communists. The President resisted for a while, but in the end gave in.[8] On February 25, a new government was appointed, a non-democratic Czechoslovak government which was exclusively controlled by the Communists. That was the end of Czechoslovak democracy. Czechoslovakia had fallen under Communist domination. The Iron Curtain had dropped along her Western frontiers.

The government crisis also engulfed Slovakia. The Communists in Bratislava resorted to fraud and violence. One could no longer resist them by democratic means. They had controlled the army, the police, the partisans and the armed workers' militia from the instant the first Soviet troops had entered Czechoslovak territory. The Soviet historian, F. Petrov, concedes that in Moscow, in March 1945, the Communists "had been forced to retreat and to pretend to agree to the formation of a new democratic Czechoslovak Government, (the Košice government) "for they might otherwise have been thrown out of the political arena." [9] The fate of Czechoslovak democracy had been decided in Moscow, not in Prague; in 1945, not in 1948.

The new Communist Government had 23 members, 11 of whom were Communists, 4 Social Democrats, 2 of the People's Party, 2 National Socialists, 1 formerly a member of the Democratic Party, 1 of the Freedom Party and the 2 non-partisan ministers. All the members of this government had to enjoy the full confidence of the Communists even if they were not Communists themselves. In the Board of Commissioners of Slovakia, which consisted of 14 members,

---

[8] Klement Gottwald: *Ku předu zpátky ni krok* (Forward, Not a Step back) Prague, 1948, pp. 6-80.

[9] F. Petrov: *K voprosu o Sovetsko-čechoslovackich otnoseniach v gode velikoj otečestvennoj vojny Sovetskogo Sojuza* (To the Question of the Soviet-Czechoslovak Relations During the Great Patriotic War of the Soviet Union). (Voprosy istorii, Moskva, 1951, No. 10, pp. 22-41).

the Communists took 10 seats, gave 2 posts to former members of the Democratic Party and one each to the Freedom
Party and the Social Democrats. Even before the end of the
government crisis, the state security organs had prevented
the functioning of some political parties. In Slovakia they
stopped the printing of the Democratic Party Daily, *"Čas,"* of
the papers *"Demokrat,"* and *"Nové Prúdy,"* searched the
secretariat of the Democratic Party and the house of its
secretary and arrested a number of party functionaries, Members of Parliament and of the Slovak National Council. The
Democratic Party ceased to exist. Criminal indictments were
filed against its leaders, their residences were placed under
police surveillance, their movements were restricted, their
telephones disconnected, their mail censored. They were prisoners. The Action Committee that had been set up in Parliament refused clearance to 23 of its 43 members of Parliament.

German domination was replaced by Soviet and Communist tyranny. The struggle for Czechoslovak democracy had
ended in defeat. Now an underground struggle set in at home
and an open political fight abroad, a fight against Communist
domination.

Chapter Three

THE RESISTANCE AGAINST
COMMUNIST DOMINATION

Sovietization — Resistance — The Third Czechoslovak Liberation Movement Abroad — The Council of Free Czechoslovakia — Anti-Czechoslovak Groups among the Exiles.

The imposition of a Communist regime extinguished civil liberties and democratic institutions. Czechoslovakia was transformed into a police state, ruled by a secret police and a state and party bureaucracy, which in theory were subordinated to the Central Action Committee of the reconstituted National Front of Czechs and Slovaks, but in reality to the Politbureau of the Communist Party of Czechoslovakia. The Constitution of May 9, 1948, drafted according to the Soviet pattern, still maintains the separation of the legislative, executive, and judicial functions of the state, but it exists on paper only. To mid-1954 the regime only once held elections to Parliament, on May 30, 1948; there was then but a single list of candidates. Of the 7,204,256 votes cast 6,429,145 were for the candidates on the list. The Communist Party allocated itself 210 of the 300 seats in Parliament. The remaining 90 were divided as follows: Social Democrats 28, Czech Socialists (former adherents of the Czechoslovak National Socialist Party) 22, the Czech People's Party 22, the Party of Slovak Regeneration (former supporters of the Democratic Party) 12, and the Freedom Party 4. Within a

month after the elections, the Communists had liquidated
the Social Democratic Party and taken over their 28 seats in
Parliament. Currently there are 238 (79.3%) Communist
members in the Prague Parliament. As a legislative body, it
is devoid of powers. It meets only when ordered to do so and
performs only such work as the government wants it to do.
There is no opposition and no expressions of disapproval of
anything the government has presented to it. Since 1948
Czechoslovakia has had no independent foreign policy. As a
satellite of the Soviet Union it has faithfully carried out the
foreign policy of its Moscow masters. The regime has systematically introduced Soviet institutions. The sovietization
of Czechoslovak life has become its program. Official propaganda has been holding up Soviet experiences and examples
to Czechs and Slovaks for emulation. In its efforts to achieve
complete ideological and political reorientation of Czechoslovakia, the regime has persistently abused the West and
praised the East, falsifying history and suppressing national
and cultural traditions. Civil liberties and human rights have
been ruthlessly trampled down. Violence and terror have
been applied both to the democratic and anti-Communist
majority of the people and to those in the Communist Party
who have incurred the ire of the bosses. Wholesale purges,
persecutions, trials, executions, brutal methods of investigation, crowded prisons, labor camps, slave-labor in the Jáchymov uranium and other mines are the means whereby the
regime has kept itself in power. The state administration is
centralized. Even the function of the Slovak national institutions, the Slovak National Council and the Board of Commissioners, have been sacrificed to centralization. The National Committees, police, management of industrial enterprises and plant militia are subordinated to the central departments of the state. The Czechoslovak legal system has
been changed completely and made to conform to Soviet

principles of law. Cultural policies have also been made into instruments of sovietization. Schools have been infected with politics. Historical materialism and Marxism have become the official doctrines of the regime and the state. Propaganda to force the Russian language, Soviet opinions and Soviet ways of thinking upon the people has been incessant. Radio, periodicals, science and arts have been penetrated by politics. Since 1949, the regime has submitted the Churches to strict government controls. The State has usurped the right to remove Church dignitaries, to approve and appoint new ones. The autonomy of the Churches in matters of the faith is no longer recognized. In the economic field all private enterprise has been wiped out, with the exception of one part of farm production. Commerce, industry and trades have been entirely subjected to state control. National enterprises have taken the place of private enterprise. Gigantic distribution-centers, with networks of branch offices have replaced private wholesale and retail businesses. Trades and private workshops have been replaced by communal enterprises. The main economic preoccupation of the Communist government is industrialization, especially of Slovakia. Heavy industry is given priority, regardless of the real needs and interests of domestic industry or of economic conditions in the country. Such irrational industrialization is to serve Soviet economic and military plans. Planned economy and a cruel political regime have deprived even the industrial workers, from whom the regime claims to derive its power, of all freedom, of the right of free association, resistance to exploitation, the freedom to choose their place of work, of movement, etc. The regime is attempting to squeeze out of the workers the greatest possible effort without having to reward him for improvement in performance, by using "voluntary" work-brigades, output and production planning, counter-planning and reverse-planning, stiffening of norms, and stakhanovite shock-workers. An army of supervisors, commissars, block-superintendents, administrators and managers sees to it that any sign of resistance on the part of the workers is stifled at its inception and that the regime obtains at least approximately what it has planned. Still more brutal has been the treatment of the peasants. It has fixed wretchedly low prices for farm produce and intolerably high delivery quotas. It has forced the collectivization of agricultural production. It has established state farm-machinery stations, four types of unified farm cooperatives, and confiscated the farmers' land, buildings, livestock and equipment. At the same time the government has been fanning class hatred, has incited farmer against farmer, the small-holders against the so-called village rich, the farm-hand against the former employer, citizen against citizen.

This policy of sovietization has had several kinds of results. The regime has partly achieved its aim in that it has been able to fulfil Soviet demands to a substantial degree, that it has altered the structure of Czechoslovakia, has industrialized and rearmed the state. But it has failed to improve the individual's standard of living and to win the confidence and support of the people. The people of Czechoslovakia have had to pay dearly for the Communist experiment. They have paid with their freedom, with their former prosperity and with the interruption of their spiritual and material development. The answer to the Communist *coup* in 1948 and to the progressive sovietization of Czechoslovakia has been a persistent anti-Communist resistance in the country, a mass of escapes abroad and the creation in the free world of the third, anti-Communist, Czechoslovak liberation movement abroad.

All classes of the population which have been injured in any way by the Communist regime have joined the resistance against it. Members of the democratic and anti-Communist Czech and Slovak political parties have joined the resistance, parties which obtained a 62% majority in the 1946 elections. Communism has also alienated a large number of the pre-coup Communists, who have either been the victims of party purges or who have been disillusioned and disappointed in their hopes by discovering what the dictatorship of the proletariat really looks like when put into operation. The regime has lost the support of thousands of opportunists who joined the Communist Party for the sake of a career or to cover up a shady past. The greatest dissatisfaction has been created amongst the Communist industrial workers, who were made to feel the cruelty of this regime like all others. Those qualified to judge estimate the strength of communism in Czechoslovakia as no more than 12-15% of the population. An attitude of open hostility to the Communist government has been assumed by the Christian Churches in Czechoslovakia, especially by the Roman Catholic Church which holds a dominant position and which has been subjected to the hardest blows. The hard-hit classes of society, manufacturers, businessmen, tradesmen and, above all, farmers as well as workers and the intelligentsia, have recognized communism as their mortal enemy and have drawn the natural conclusion. The regime cannot even rely on the Army or on the students. All these together form one mighty anti-Communist force, ready to join in open battle against the regime. As long as conditions are favorable, they resist within the means presently at their disposal. Some specialize in spreading anti-Communist propaganda to demoralize the elements on which the regime must rely. Others have dared to commit acts of open defiance toward the hated rulers. The most powerful and most effective method of resistance is disobedience, passive resistance, failure to comply with orders, plans, working norms and farm delivery quotas. These tactics have been producing economic breakdowns of such proportions that the regime has been entirely helpless against them. Neither threats nor cajolery are of any help. The shrill calls for improvement in working morale, for political and national discipline and the entire gamut of governmental sanction and punishments have been of no avail. Absenteeism, fluctuations of the labor force, damage to equipment, wasting of raw materials, a high percentage of rejects, failure to comply with terms of deliveries, sabotage of work and of production both in industry and agriculture, all these are the results of the resistance to the Communists all over the nation and constitute a serious problem for the regime. The extent and intensity of anti-Communist resistance in Czechoslovakia has reached the point where the regime is threatened far more seriously from within than it is from the outside. The Soviet Union has not found a reliable ally in the Czechoslovak people. At the critical moment the people will turn against Soviet and Communist domination as they previously turned upon the Nazi invaders.

The regime in Czechoslovakia is fully aware of this situation and is doing its utmost to break the resistance by means of violence and terror. It has rounded up, imprisoned and sentenced to heavy terms in jail all those who had in any way been active against communism in the past, or who are likely to stand in the way of the sovietization of the country and the strengthening of the regime. The Secret State Police has been kept busy uncovering anti-state—that is to say anti-Communist—conspiracies and plots. The People's Courts are busy handing down vicious sentences of death or imprisonment. Hundreds of patriots have been sentenced to death and thousands to prison for life or long years. The administrative authorities are sending people they do not approve of to forced labor camps or to the mines. A new problem has arisen in Czechoslovakia under Communist rule, the problem of jails, because existing prison facilities have been unable to handle the prisoners whose numbers continue to grow from day to day. The government has therefore had to build a number of new prisons in great haste in Prague and Bratislava. The security organs have faithfully copied Soviet methods of investigations, down to the last details, methods which have been developed from the theories of the Russian biologist Pavlov; and the Communist courts have introduced the Soviet trial procedures of "spontaneous" confessions and self-incrimination of the accused. Communist justice has two objectives: to intimidate and to destroy. To intimidate potential enemies and to destroy enemies who have been caught committing acts inimical to the "popular democratic" regime. The Czechoslovak love of freedom, willingness to suffer for ideals, and resolution not to submit are boundless. Centuries of foreign domination and the recent German subjugation have taught the people to endure suffering with courage and not to lose faith in their liberation. The repressive measures of the government have therefore failed to break the anti-Communist resistance, even though they have succeeded in weakening it in certain places, for a certain time. The home front is holding firm.

There is endless proof of this in everyday life. Czechoslovak soldiers keep escaping to the West, in uniform and with their weapons, or else they fly out in army planes. Some Czechoslovak railroad employees once escaped across the frontier with an entire express train. Flying personnel of the Czechoslovak Airlines have repeatedly escaped with their planes and full complement of passengers to Germany. If one is to believe what Communist judges state in their judgments sentencing Czechoslovak anti-Communists, the regime can today no longer regard a single sector of its administration as fully reliable. All sectors are full of traitors, spies and agents of foreign powers—the government, the Communist Party, the Army, the Government offices, the nationalized industries, the schools. In a single political trial (the trial of

Rudolf Slánský and his associates) death sentences were passed and executed on the Deputy Prime Minister and Secretary-General of the Communist Party, on the Minister of Foreign Affairs, on four Deputy Ministers, and five high officials of the state and party. The Slovak Communist leaders Gustáv Husák, Ladislav Novomeský, and others also have been sentenced. Although these people had nothing to do with the Resistance, their case is nevertheless characteristic of conditions inside Czechoslovakia.

Perhaps the most significant of all anti-Communist acts of resistance were the demonstrations and revolts of industrial workers in Plzeň and other industrial centers in connection with the introduction of the so-called currency reform on June 1, 1953. These revolts were the signal for similar anti-Soviet demonstrations of workers in East Berlin and the Soviet zone of Germany. As a result, the Communist government had to give in on many issues for fear of revolutionary outbursts of such proportions that they could no longer be controlled. Following the revolts, the government revoked its orders for the criminal prosecution of workers for breaches of working regulations, reconsidered certain aspects of its farm policy, etc.

Another aspect of anti-Communist resistance is the wave of democratic escapees. Tens of thousands of men, women and children, of young people and old, of members of all classes and professions have faced the gravest possible dangers in their efforts to get away to the West. Their motives have been manifold. Some have left in order to be able to work more efficiently and successfully against Soviet imperialism and world communism than at home. Others have gone into exile because their life or liberty was in danger. Still others have left simply because they could no longer endure the stifling atmosphere of fear, terror, hypocrisy, falsehood and lies. Never in the history of Czechs and Slovaks have political exiles been more numerous than today, with the possible exception of the exile of Czech Protestants in the 17th century after the fateful battle of the White Mountain. Escapes abroad have become increasingly difficult because the Communist government has almost hermetically closed the frontier, beginning immediately after the Communist *coup* in February 1948. Especially the passages toward the American zones of Germany and Austria were carefully guarded and later made practically impassable by fortifications and other protective devices. Nevertheless, Czechoslovak democrats have found and are continuing to find ways of crossing the frontier to freedom. They have thought up means of escape that are almost unbelievable. Some have escaped through mountains and forests, after walking for days. Others have forded rivers along the frontiers, or chosen to escape by train, aircraft or other vehicles. In some cases political prisoners have dug tunnels from their prisons and have escaped in prison garb together with some of their guards. Some exiles have even dug a way out of the Jáchymov uranium mines. The Czechoslovak "Freedom Train" and "Freedom Tank" have become symbols of courage and of man's struggle for freedom. Czechoslovak democratic political exiles have waited for months and even years in displaced persons' camps in Germany, Austria or Italy for a chance to emigrate overseas. Except for the most recent arrivals or for those whose health, age, or other circumstances made emigration impossible, all have by now reached Great Britain, Canada, the United States or Latin American countries and have found new homes and jobs overseas. Many of them have been welcome as scientific or technical workers, as manufacturers, businessmen, radio employees, writers, workers or farmers. Czechoslovak exiles have their own publications, organizations and literature.

A very large number of persons who had played an im-

portant role in Czechoslovak political and public life before
the last war and after it have left the country. They include
six of the twelve members of the Czechoslovak Government
who resigned in February 1948 in protest against Communist
unlawfulness, scores of Members of Parliament, members of
the Slovak National Council, former Cabinet Ministers, Slovak Commissioners, political secretaries, newspapermen,
authors, army officers, professors, etc. Their numbers have
been swelled by Czechoslovak diplomats, heads of diplomatic
missions and their civilian and military personnel, who resigned their offices in protest against the setting up of Communist totalitarianism, who refused to serve the Communist
government of Czechoslovakia and applied for political asylum. The Czechoslovak Ambassador in Washington, Juraj
Slávik, was the first who resigned. Czechoslovak foreign
service was almost paralysed by these acts of protest. In the
years 1948-1949 the government could trust no one whom
it was sending abroad unless he happened to be one of the
Communist party-stalwarts, for the moment these political
workers crossed the borders to the west, they set to work
laying the foundations of the third Czechoslovak liberation
movement abroad. The former Czechoslovak representative
at the United Nations, Ambassador Ján Papánek, lodged a
complaint in March 1948 in the Security Council against the
Soviet Government for its part in the imposition of a Communist dictatorship in Czechoslovakia. The Security Council
was prevented from discussing the matter because the Soviet
delegate vetoed it. Other exiles did their best to inform the
governments and the public of the free world of what had
happened in Czechoslovakia. By discussions, lectures, articles
or publications they told the world how the Communists had
infiltrated Czechoslovakia, what changes they had forced
upon the country and what had been happening there since
February 1948. They also began organizing relief activities

for refugees, to alleviate the hardship they were enduring in the Displaced Persons camps and to help them find new homes in free countries overseas. They collected funds, intervened with officials, founded committees for social relief.

After prolonged preliminary discussions, representatives of four Czech and two Slovak political parties, the National Socialist, People's, Republican (Farmers), Social Democratic and the Slovak Democratic and Freedom Parties, together with other prominent individuals of Czechoslovak public life, such as diplomats, newspapermen, senior officers, etc., founded a joint exile organization in Washington, D.C., on the eve of the first anniversary of the Communist coup, February 20, 1949. It assumed the name of Council of Free Czechoslovakia and declared its aim to be "participation in the fight against communism, the restoration of a free, independent, democratic Czechoslovak Republic within its pre-Munich borders, the renewal of its democratic liberties, participation in efforts at creating a free and united Europe and a world order based on co-operation, peace and security, law and justice." The Council of Free Czechoslovakia therefore resolved to "unify Czechoslovak forces abroad, to lead them in accordance with the views of the homeland, to help the Nation in its resistance to communism, to keep the free world informed about conditions in Czechoslovakia and to represent Czechoslovak interests in the democratic world." The participation of Czechs, Slovaks and Subcarpathian Ruthenians in the Council of Free Czechoslovakia is governed by the principle of "equal rights and equal duties." At first, the Council had two organs: a 12-member Executive Board, consisting of an equal number of Czechs and Slovaks, and a 30-member Executive Committee, with 18 Czech and 12 Slovak members. Apart from these, the Council had Regional Organizations in London, Paris and Canada. The Council of Free Czechoslovakia was reorganized in April 1952 with: (1)

a 26-member Executive Committee, (2) a Central Committee consisting of former Members of Parliament, Members of the Slovak National Council, and of the National Committees of the Czech provinces, persons who had been otherwise prominent in Czechoslovak public life, (3) a Supervising Committee. From 1949 to 1951 Peter Zenkl was the President of the Council of Free Czechoslovakia and Jozef Lettrich its Vice-President. The same two persons were the Chairman and Deputy Chairman respectively of the Executive Committee between 1952 and 1954. Chairman of the Central Committee was Štefan Osuský, and Adolf Procházka and Václav Majer its Deputy Chairmen.

The Council of Free Czechoslovakia represents all the traditional democratic and anti-Communist political trends and parties that had been the moving powers of Czechoslovak public life until they were silenced by the Communist tyranny. This is demonstrated by the fact that ever since the creation of the Council of Free Czechoslovakia, Communist propaganda has aimed its most violent broadsides against it and its leaders. A great many members of the Resistance at Home have been persecuted for indicating approval of the Council's program or for helping to achieve its aims. Although the Council has to contend with numerous internal and external difficulties, it has nevertheless been able to perform some valuable political work in the interest of Czechoslovakia and of the defense of the free world against communism, particularly in connection with psychological warfare against the East. Thanks to the magnanimous understanding and support of the American public, the Czechoslovak exiles have been granted access to the efficient and modern Free Europe broadcasting station, which permits them to speak for several hours daily to the people inside Czechoslovakia. Under present conditions that is the most effective weapon for countering the effects of unceasing Communist and Soviet propaganda, for combating the Communist regime's efforts to consolidate its power, for telling the truth to the people in Czechoslovakia about the situation in the world, and for keeping alive the people's spirit of resistance. Radio Free Europe is also devoting its attention to the cultural and spiritual needs, and especially to the religious requirements of its Czechoslovak listeners.

In 1949 an American organization was created in New York under the name of National Committee for a Free Europe, Inc., which name was later changed to Free Europe Committee, Inc. The purposes of this organization include, apart from operating Radio Free Europe, the care of young exiles from behind the Iron Curtain and their education in the spirit of their free national and cultural traditions, the rendering of moral and material support to exile groups in the United States, and the gathering, analysis, and dissemination of information about conditions now prevailing in Communist dominated countries. The Council of Free Czechoslovakia and individual democratic political exiles have received invaluable assistance from this organization for their political, cultural and propaganda activities.

Standing aside from the body of Czechoslovak democratic exiles, represented by the Council of Free Czechoslovakia, is a group of Czech and Slovak exiles who are campaigning for an anti-Czechoslovak political program. They have declared themselves in favor of independent Czech and Slovak States, which would be members of a European Union. The Czech separatist exiles are grouped around the former Czechoslovak General Lev Prchala who embarked on an independent political activity during the last war, when he found himself in conflict with the Czechoslovak Government in exile in London. Gen. Prchala had never been politically active in Czechoslovakia. A number of individual Czechs of pronounced right-wing views have also been proclaiming a program similar to that of Gen. Prchala, or of Prchala's former adherents. Czech political separatism, an extremist movement, has been artificially created abroad, and has no support inside Czechoslovakia.

Slovak separatism, on the other hand, has some different aspects both at home and abroad. It has been shown earlier when and how the Slovak Autonomism of the Slovak People's Party transformed itself into Separatism. Its protagonists were the champions of Nazism and other anti-democratic trends within the Slovak People's Party, who disdained not only the political support of the Slovak people but even that of the membership of the Slovak People's Party, preferring to derive their powers and right to govern from the favor of Adolf Hitler and of the Third Reich. After they had acquired power in the state, the Slovak Separatists never once turned to the people for a vote of approval of their domestic and foreign policies. There was no free or democratic election in Slovakia from 1938 to 1945. The government was totalitarian, a police state. When the Second World War was nearing its end, the leaders of the Slovak State did not choose to remain in Slovakia, but elected to leave with the Germans. With them left a large number of the younger radical Separatists, especially those who had reaffirmed their Nazi, anti-democratic and anti-Semitic convictions as recently as September 20, 1944 and January 14, 1945. Tiso, his government and these young Separatists, renewed their activities abroad, on Hitlerite German soil, and even before the end of World War II. The program of the Slovak Separatist exiles is contained in the declaration issued by the Slovak Government in exile on April 25, 1945, and in the address of Jozef Tiso, made over the Austrian radio in Kremsmünster. Germany's military capitulation and its political consequences interrupted these activities for some time. The American occupation authorities arrested Jozef Tiso, his government and a number of other leaders of Slovak Separatism and turned them over to the Czechoslovak authorities for criminal prosecution. Other adherents of Slovak separatism, who were no less guilty, managed to hide or to flee from Austria and Germany. As soon as immediate danger of retribution receded, they assumed their Separatist and anti-Czechoslovak campaign. The only change was that they now suddenly began speaking of themselves as the representatives of "Tiso Democracy," that they conveniently and completely forgot their totalitarian political past. They stressed their anti-Soviet and anti-Communist policies. Thus they succeeded in gaining the support of some Americans of Slovak origin, especially in the Slovak League of America, who uncritically accepted the Separatist views, not only with respect to the origins, career and policies of the Slovak State, but also concerning Czechoslovakia and her future. The periodicals of the Slovak nationals in America favoring separatism have taken on the spirit of those Separatist papers which have been banned in Slovakia. Separatists in exile have become regular contributors and are responsible for their policies with regard to Slovak and Czechoslovak matters. All this is the unfortunate result of the lack of proper information and political orientation of this segment of Americans of Slovak descent.

Scarcely had the Slovak State disappeared, than the representatives of Slovak separatism in exile split into two distinct and antagonistic camps. One of these was led by the former Minister of the Slovak State to the Vatican, Karol Sidor, the other by Ferdinand Ďurčanský. Until 1949, Sidor evidenced a certain degree of embarrassment and political indecision. He failed to decide whether to insist on the theory of legal and political continuity of the Slovak State and of the vanished Slovak People's Party, or whether to come forth with a basically new concept of the Slovak State, and a new program. In December 1948, however, he founded a new politi-

cal party in Rome called Slovak Christian Democracy, which
had never existed in Slovakia. He himself became chairman
of the party. Its objectives were "the fight for the victory of
democracy and for the Slovak Republic, whether it be a
sovereign state, or a member state of a European, or Mid-
European Federation or Confederation." Sidor's Slovak Christian Democracy never even started to exist. It remained an
organization on paper only. In December 1949 Sidor came
to an agreement with Peter Prídavok in London. Prídavok
had escaped abroad while the Slovak State was still in existence, had quarrelled with all the Czech and Slovak leaders
of the second Czechoslovak liberation movement abroad during the war, and then joined the Separatist camp. He operated
in London under the name of Slovak National Council
Abroad, a paper organization, having the support of neither
people at home nor of Separatists in exile. Sidor and Prídavok
now reshaped this organization, retained its original name,
enlisted some further support, and agreed that Sidor should
be the chairman of the Council and Prídavok its secretary-
general. Their aim was "the liberation of Slovakia from Communist dictatorship and the domination of the Czech State."
Sidor moved from Rome to Canada in the Spring of 1950
and the headquarters of the Slovak National Council Abroad
transferred to Canada. Branch organizations were set up in
the United States and Germany. The office in Germany was
entrusted to Matúš Černák who had meanwhile also arrived
abroad and who, thanks to his personal contacts from Hitlerite days, has been able to establish a Slovak Separatist press
in Germany.

Sidor's rival, Ferdinand Ďurčanský, proved to be a livelier
and more active separatist leader. He formed a Slovak Action
Committee (Slovenský akčný výbor—SAV) in Germany in
1945, and when he transferred his activities to the Argentine,
he changed its name to Slovak Liberation Committee (Sloven-

ský oslobodzovací výbor—SOV). Ďurčanský opposed the
theory of continuity of the Slovak State and turned against
the Slovak People's Party. He, too, had founded a political
party on paper, the "Party of National Regeneration—The
Popular Movement of Freedom and Labor." Another radical,
a political mimic of Ďurčanský's, who had participated in
the Pieštany Convention of January 1945, Vojtech Krajčovič,
has also founded his own paper-organization in the United
States: the Slovak National Committee for the Liberation of
Slovakia. Krajčovič was never politically active in Slovakia
and is unknown there.

The two camps of Slovak Separatists are mutually com-
bating each other and the conflict has been extended to those
Americans of Slovak descent who favor the separatists. There
were a few attempts at cooperation between Ďurčanský and
Sidor, but they failed for personal and political reasons. Karol
Sidor died in October 1953 and the conflicts are currently
aggravated by a struggle for Sidor's succession in the Slovak
National Council Abroad.

*

*   *

*

The notion of unity of the Czechoslovak State has deep
historical and political justification.

Fifteen hundred years ago Czechs and Slovaks settled as
one racial unit on the territory occupied today by Czechoslovakia. Being a freedom-loving people, imbued with the
abilities required for statehood, they created a succession of
their own, common and independent states, which, however,
were later destroyed by invaders. These forced the separation
of the Czechs and Slovaks. Yet, not even separate historical
development could sever Czechoslovak cultural and spiritual
ties, nor suppress the yearning for a shared national and

political freedom. Czech and Slovak history has been decisively influenced by pressures from East and West. These pressures are still influencing their present life and will undoubtedly continue to influence them in the future. In the past Czechs and Slovaks have been able to resist the pressures only by leaning upon one another and by remaining together. Only thus will they be able to resist them in the future. All their strength and prospects lie in unity. United in one state they will remain free and independent, divided they will both fall under foreign domination. Czechs and Slovaks, and later the Subcarpathian Ruthenians, were proceeding on these assumptions during the First World War, when abroad and at home they laid the foundations of Czechoslovakia and they again accepted them as true when they were working for the restoration of Czechoslovak independence during the Second World War. The present Czechoslovak struggle abroad continues to draw its strength from these historical traditions.

In 1918 Czechoslovakia arose, and at the end of the Second World War it was renewed, by the free will of the Czech, Slovak and Ruthenian peoples exercising their natural right of self-determination. Czechs, Slovaks and Ruthenians regard the existence of the Czechoslovak state as a lofty ideal, worthy of any sacrifice. That is why they have defended it, why they continue to defend it, and will always defend it against any internal or external enemy. The Nazi occupation and the Communist domination of Czechoslovakia were both imposed against the will of a large majority of the Czechoslovak people. When the moment for action arrives, it will again be the people that will play the decisive role in renewing the independence of Czechoslovakia.

Czechoslovakia brought her three constituent nations incomparably greater political power, international respect, economic capacity, cultural level and standard of living, than did the Austro-Hungarian Monarchy before it or the Protectorate of Bohemia-Moravia and the Slovak State after it. As a result, Czechs, Slovaks and Subcarpathian Ruthenians are vitally interested in the Czechoslovak Republic. The more recent trends for European unity do not negative the justification for Czechoslovakia but, on the contrary, argue in its favor.

Czechoslovakia is a necessity, not only for the Czechs, Slovaks and Subcarpathian Ruthenians, but also for Europe. After the disintegration of the Austro-Hungarian Monarchy, it was the Czechoslovak Republic that assumed the vital function of setting up a barrier to Pan-Germanic ambitions aimed at Central Europe. It was a vital factor in the consolidation of the heart of the continent. Its international significance for the maintenance of a balance of power in Europe and for world peace became obvious at the time of the Munich crisis in 1938, which ushered in World War II, and after the Communist *coup* in February 1948, which led to the hasty marshalling of the defenses of the free world against Communist imperialism and to the Atlantic Pact. If Czechoslovakia were to disappear, a mass of new and extremely complicated problems of power-politics, territorial, frontier, minority and other difficulties would arise, which would dangerously complicate the situation of Europe and which would inevitably become the focal points of new and serious conflicts. A free Poland or even a free Central Europe is inconceivable without Czechoslovakia, because then the gates would be open to German expansion towards the East and the South.

When Europe is liberated from world communism and Bolshevik imperialism, Czechoslovakia will be the first to want to establish the most amicable neighborly relations with a free, united and democratic Germany, for such relations are in the national and political interest of both countries, as well as in the interest of the consolidation of Europe and of world peace. Germany, however, will have to renounce for ever the ambitions of Bismarck, Emperor Wilhelm and Hitler for the "expansion of its living space" at the expense of other nations, for these ambitions have twice within a generation plunged both the German nation and the rest of the world into terrible disaster. Humanity's present tribulations are all the proximate result of politically aggressive German nationalism. The unification of Europe will offer the Germans enough scope for development as a peaceful and great nation, in accordance with their numbers and abilities. The Czechs and Slovaks, who have lived as neighbors of the Germans for fifteen centuries, are vitally interested in a broader, European attitude and European cooperation of the German Nation.

As to the mutual relations between Czechs, Slovaks and Subcarpathian Ruthenians which have caused some internal difficulties, and which were the pretext for Hitler's interference in Czechoslovak affairs, these relations are and must remain domestic problems of the Czechoslovak Republic. These matters cannot be settled by Czech and Slovak nationals living abroad, nor by foreign powers, nor by ad hoc international committees. It cannot be said that a satisfactory solution has yet been found. Hitherto the schemes for managing Czech-Slovak relations have been in the nature of experiments. The Slovak National Uprising proclaimed the principle of equality of the partner-nations of Czechoslovakia and put this principle into effect by the creation of Slovak national institutions with legislative, executive and administrative powers. That was a reasonable basis for a permanent solution of the problem, because it fully respected the interests of the state as a whole as well as those of the Czech Nation and of the Slovaks. Communist dictatorship has destroyed these attempts and has turned back the wheel of development to a rigid system of centralization. The question of the in-

ternal organization of the Czechoslovak Republic is one of
regulating the relations within the common state of the
national elements, and of an appropriate division of state
powers between the organs of the state and those of the component nations. All experiences to date indicate clearly that
neither a centralized state nor national separatism are the
proper paths toward a permanent solution. Yet it is political
folly to agitate against the existence of the Czechoslovak
Republic only because it has not yet solved this internal problem. The Separatists can offer neither Czechs, nor Slovaks
nor Ruthenians anything that could satisfactorily replace
Czechoslovakia. In promising an independent Czech and an
independent Slovak States, they offer nothing to the Subcarpathian Ruthenians. The fateful days of March 1939 are
a warning of what would be the fate of Czechs, Slovaks, and
Ruthenians should they decide to part with the Czechoslovak
State. True, the Separatists are seeking an escape from these
dark perspectives into the hopes for a European Federation
which, they believe, will guarantee national independence to
both Czechs and Slovaks. This is nothing but political wishful
thinking. The idea of a Central-European Federation is still
in the state of theoretical planning and, alas, far from reality.
To renounce Czechoslovakia and instead rely entirely on
a federation, as if it existed in fact, is tantamount to political
suicide. Czechs, Slovaks and Subcarpathian Ruthenians dare
not run the terrible risk. Moreover, the lack of political logic
in the thinking of Separatists is remarkable. They would like
to break up Czechoslovakia—which was founded and existed
by agreement of its three component nations—pretending that
this would be in the interest of a future Central-European
Federation, which could, however, exist only on the basis of
a similar understanding and unity about its objectives and
means. European development is moving from the existing
small, medium and large states towards the formation of

regional entities and possibly European Union. The Separatists are moving counter to European development when they demand the destruction of the already existing Czechoslovak entity.

Insofar as Slovak separatism is attempting to renew the Slovak State of 1939-1945, we must remind ourselves of some relevant facts. First of all, the Slovak Separatists were much less interested in the nation or the state than in acquiring power. Throughout the existence of the Slovak State they governed without approval, against the will of the Slovak people. For twenty years the Slovaks had been demanding that the Czechs grant them a Diet in accordance with the Pittsburgh Agreement and when they obtained one, in 1938, they immediately degraded it to the role of a very unessential trimming of political dictatorship. Things were also much the same with respect to national independence. While Czechoslovakia existed, they clamored for a Slovak State, and the instant they got it, they immediately renounced it and were content to play the role of a German vassal. In 1944-1945 the Slovak people rose in arms against the Slovak State, against its President, its government and totalitarian regime, destroyed them and renewed Czechoslovak sovereignty. It will be equally impossible to force "independence" upon Slovakia in the future without first forcing political dictatorship upon it. The Slovak people will not permanently tolerate either dictatorship or "forced independence."

Anti-Czechoslovak and anti-democratic elements are on the march again, just as they were in the years 1938-1939. After Munich they grabbed all the power in Slovakia and helped to destroy the Czechoslovak Republic. It is no mere coincidence, that once again the center of anti-Czechoslovak and Separatist tendencies is in Germany. The leaders are Germans expellees from Czechoslovakia and Slovak emigrees. The names are familiar: Ferdinand Ďurčanský, Franz Karmasin, Rudolf Lodgman von Auen and Matúš Černák. These men are hoping to achieve their aims with the aid of the West-German State and those Americans of Slovak descent who are represented by the Slovak League of America. However, their hopes can only be justified if Germany abandons her present policy of cooperating in the building of a free Europe and returns to her unfortunate past policy of expansion. Although one can never entirely exclude any eventuality in world politics, it nevertheless appears unlikely that Germany will once again embrace a policy which has twice brought her disaster. Nor can the Separatists derive much comfort from the circumstances that American public opinion and American government leaders are not always well informed about East European affairs. The American leaders knew very well what they were doing during both World Wars when they put the entire weight of their mighty nation behind the efforts of Czechs, Slovaks and Subcarpathian Ruthenians, first to establish, and then to renew the independence of the Czechoslovak Republic. Neither Austro-Hungarian nor Nazi-German propaganda could confuse the issues for them. Czechoslovak democratic exiles in the free world and the Czechs, Slovaks, and Ruthenians who are today living under Communist slavery in the homeland, feel confident that the anti-Czechoslovak political propaganda of the Slovak totalitarian Separatists will fail to alter the traditionally friendly attitude of the American people and their Government toward Czechoslovakia.

The future of the Slovaks is at the side of the Czechs in Czechoslovakia. That is the meaning and the message of Slovakia's past.

DOCUMENTS

Number 1

Memorandum of the Slovak Nation

Adopted at the National Meeting of the Slovaks in Turčiansky Svätý Martin held June 7 1861

I. Be it resolved that a special delegation to the Hungarian Diet, with an expression of confidence in said diet, present this memorandum containing the request of the Slovak Nation for the purpose of securing justly instituted national equality and guaranteeing this equality by law.

These are the requests:

1. That the identity of the Slovak Nation and the Slovak national language be recognized by charters and law and be protected against malicious attacks of the enemies of harmony among nations.

2. That in that area occupied solidly by Slovaks, our national identity be recognized under the name of the Slovak Region of Upper Hungary, and that this area be formed by dividing the counties according to nationality.

3. That national rights and language rights be defined according to the principle of equality among nations. For this purpose it is proposed:

a. That in the region which represents our nation the Slovak language be the only channel through which the stream of public, civic, church, and cultural life should flow; so that in the future, through reorganization of government administration and of the counties of the region, one Court of Appeals and at least one Special Financial Court for the Slovaks be organized, at which the official language would be Slovak; that at the State Supreme Court and the Administrative Courts and at the Commission for Education men recognized by Slovak public opinion as Slovak patriots and cognizant of the Slovak language be admitted, (with the required personnel) as department heads in numbers corresponding to the size of the population; they are not only to perform official duties but also, if the need arises, defend the interests of the Slovak Nation.

b. That, while the Magyar language shall remain as the diplomatic language, that is, as a means of mutual communication in the correspondence with the non-Slav counties in internal affairs and in

285

the mutual official business of the highest administrative and judicial authorities, the Slovak national language should be used in performing all the acts of public life exclusive of the applications of the citizens, which should be always dealt with in the particular language of the applicant, and also at the common State Diet, not excluding, however, the use of other languages in the latter.

    c. That the articles of parliamentary procedure which are not in accordance with equality and freedom of nations, in particular Articles 16:1791, 7:1692, 4:1805, 3:1836, 6:1840, 2:1844, and 16/e:1848, be suspended by positive law.

    d. That a code of state laws in the Slovak language be compiled by the Diet.

    e. That, in the interest of the political and legal education of Slovak youth, an Academy of Laws be founded in a well-chosen Slovak city, and, in addition, that state funds be used to endow a Chair of Slovak Language and Literature at the University of Budapest.

    f. That the Slovaks be allowed to establish literary and educational associations and to solicit funds for that purpose.

    g. That Slovak communities in areas inhabited by foreign nationalities and foreign communities isolated in Slovak counties, which are to appear as distinct in the realm of civic life, be allowed to use their own language and freely cultivate and develop their nationality.

    h. That in the forthcoming reorganization of the Upper House, the legitimate interests of the nationalities and particularly the Slovak nationality be considered and proportionately represented.

    4. The Slovak National Meeting states that the interests of the Slovak Nation are identical with the interests of all nationalities in Hungary in regard to civil liberties, but that in regard to national freedom they are identical with those of the nationalities hitherto oppressed, namely, Ruthenians, Rumanians, Serbs, and Croats, inasmuch as that in the area which the Slovak Nation inhabits, it demands for itself (concerning national freedom) the same things which the Magyars already have, and that all the nationalities are willing to fight for them and guarantee them one for all and all for one.

II. It was resolved by the Slovak National Meeting to send to the nations of the Croats, Serbs, Rumanians, and Ruthenians addresses of sympathy, together with the declaration listed under point 4.

III. The national meeting appointed a standing committee for the purpose of taking necessary steps in connection with the demands contained in the Memorandum, and for bringing to life the literary and economic associations, and for stimulating national life in general and furthering its advancement.

Number 2

Resolution

Adopted at the Public Popular Meeting in Liptovský Sv. Mikuláš on
May 1, 1918

We, Slovak citizens and workers organized in the Slovak Social Democratic Party having heard the speakers at the public popular meeting
in Liptovský Sväty Mikuláš on the First Day of May, 1918, adopt the
following resolution:

The war which has been raging for four years has claimed from all
peoples of the world, including the Hungarian branch of the Czechoslovak people, immense sacrifices in fortune, blood and human life.
These immense sacrifices we have endured in the knowledge that we
were fighting for a just and sacred cause: for the highest human
values, for equal freedom of all fighting classes and nations of the
Austro-Hungarian Empire.

But we now state with regret that we have been disappointed in these
hopes, for the official policy is moving against democracy and the
present governments are using all pre-war antipopular means to deprive the popular masses, which bear the greatest burden of this world
war, of their well-deserved rights and freedoms.
We protest most earnestly against this deception and trickery by the
present governments and demand:

1. That the governments seize every opportunity to conclude a
just and lasting peace based on an honest solution of all problems of
international and domestic policy, a peace which will prevent the outbreak of new wars and bring the desired peace and freedom to nations of Europe.

2. As the natural consequence of the accorded freedom, we demand an unconditional recognition of the right of self-determination
not only outside the frontiers of our monarchy, but also for the nations of Austria-Hungary, among which is the Hungarian branch of
the Czechoslovak family.

We demand equality in everything, not only on the battlefields, where
life is at stake, but also behind the fronts.

Long live universal suffrage!

Long live world peace!

Long live equality and freedom of nations!

Number 3
Resolution

of the Slovak National Party with the Participation of Matúš Dula,
Dr. Emil Stodola, Andrej Hlinka, Vladimír Makovický, Ján Ružiak,
Dr. Vavro Šrobár, Andrej Devečka, Miloš Lacko, Dr. Metod Bella,
Juraj Janoška, Jan Vojtaššák, Ján Obuch, Dr. Dušan Halaša, Anton
Hromada, Štefan Mnohel, Otto Škrovina, Karol Medvecký, Jozef
Škultéty, Dr. Miloš Vančo, Viliam Paulíny, Gustáv Izák, Cyril Kre-
sák, Dr. Ľudovít Šimko, Dr. Igor Dula and Aurel Styk.

The Slovak National Party favors the unconditional and complete
right of self-determination for the Slovak Nation and on this ground
claims the right of participation of the Slovak Nation in the establishment of an independent state consisting of Slovakia, Bohemia, Moravia and Silesia.

The president, Matuš Dula, is authorized to bring this resolution to
the notice of the Czech representative in Prague.

Number 4
Declaration of the Slovak Nation

Representatives of all Slovak political parties assembled on October
30, 1918, in Turčiansky Svätý Martin and united in the National
Council of the Slovak branch of the united Czecho-Slovak Nation insist on the right of national self-determination accepted by the whole
world. The National Council declares that it alone is entitled to speak
in the name of the Czecho-Slovak Nation living within the frontiers
of Hungary.

The Hungarian Government is not entitled to speak thus for it has
done nothing for decades but suppress everything that is Slovak; it has
not built or even permitted a single school for our people; it has not
admitted the Slovak people to public office; it has destroyed our people
economically and exploited it through its medieval feudal system and
(policies).

Neither are the so-called representative bodies, composed on the
basis of limited suffrage, entitled to speak in the name of the Slovak
people for they do not permit the people to express their will and are
composed of men who, defying existing laws, do not permit the use
of one Slovak word in committees in purely Slovak counties.

Neither are popular meetings, which are under the pressure of
foreign influence, entitled to adopt resolutions in the name of the
Slovak people.

Therefore, the Slovak National Council alone is entitled to speak
in the name of the Slovak Nation in Slovakia.

The National Council of the Czecho-Slovak Nation living in Hungary declares:

1. The Slovak Nation is a part of the Czecho-Slovak Nation, united in language and in the history of its culture, in all the cultural struggles which the Czech Nation has fought and which have made it known throughout the world, the Slovak branch also participated.

2. For this Czecho-Slovak Nation we demand an unlimited right of self-determination on the basis of complete independence. On the basis of this principle, we express our consent with the new condition of international law accepted on October 28, 1918, by the Austro-Hungarian Minister of Foreign Affairs.

3. We demand an immediate conclusion of a peace based on humanitarian Christian principles, a peace which would prevent future wars and continuing armament through international safeguards.

We are convinced that our industrious and talented Slovak people, which despite unprecedented oppression have achieved such a degree of national culture, will not be excluded from the blessings of peace and from the community of nations, but that they will be given the opportunity to develop according to their character and contribute in the measure of their strength to the general progress of mankind.

From the session of the Slovak National Council in Turčiansky Svätý Martin on October 30, 1918

Matúš Dula,   *Karol A. Medvecký,*
President of the   Secretary of the
Slovak National Council   Slovak National Council

Number 5
Czecho-Slovak Agreement
agreed on in Pittsburgh, Pa., May 30, 1918

The representatives of the Slovak and Czech organizations in the United States, the Slovak League, the Czech National Alliance and the Federation of Czech Catholics deliberating in the presence of the Chairman of the Czechoslovak National Council, Professor Masaryk, on the Czechoslovak question and on our previous declaration of program, have passed the following resolution:

We approve of the political program which aims at the union of the Czechs and Slovaks in an independent State composed of the Czech Lands and Slovakia.

Slovakia shall have her own administrative system, her own diet and her own courts.

The Slovak language shall be the official language in the schools, in the public offices and in public affairs generally.

The Czechoslovak State shall be a republic, and its constitution a democratic one.

The organization of the collaboration between Czechs and Slovaks in the United States shall, according to need and the changing situation, be intensified and regulated by mutual consent.

Detailed provisions relating to the organization of the Czechoslovak State shall be left to the liberated Czechs and Slovaks and their duly accredited representatives.

Number 6

Telegram of the German Foreign Office in Berlin of September 19, 1938, to the German Legation in Prague

"No. 244 of September 19   Berlin, September 19, 1938
(e. o. Pol. IV 6210)

Drafting Officer: Counselor of Legation Dr. Altenburg.

Please inform Deputy Kundt, at the request of Konrad Henlein, that he should, without delay, get in touch with the Slovaks to persuade them to raise their demands for autonomy in the course of tomorrow.

Altenburg."

(Marginal note:) "Draft after consultation and in agreement with the Volksdeutsche Mittelstelle."

Number 7

Telegram of the German Legation in Prague of September 20, 1938, to the German Foreign Office in Berlin

"No. 404 of September 20   Prague, September 20, 1938-6:20 p.m.
Received September 20, 1938-8:30 p.m.

In reply to telegram No. 244 of the 19th, Pol. IV 6210.

Instructions to Deputy Kundt carried out this morning. Kundt stated he had already established contact a few days ago with the Slovaks People's Party on his own initiative on the lines of Henlein's wishes. The result was the communiqué of the Slovak People's Party, published today, announcing the following demands, decided on the 19th instant:

1) Full respect for the individuality of the Slovak people and the Slovak language.

2) Immediate and definite solution of the Slovak question on the basis of the Treaty of Pittsburgh and of the last parliamentary motion of the Slovak People's Party with legislative (group missing) might be Provincial Government (Landtag) for Slovakia."

The communiqué, which is doubtless influenced by strong consideration for the Prague Government, had concluded neither written nor verbal agreements in collaboration with non-Slovak political parties. Further attempts at a solution of the State's nationality problem by bloodshed of force are condemned in the communiqué and the conviction is expressed that eventually good relations would be established between the Czechs and the Slovaks and thus the Czechoslovak State would be strengthened within and without. The communiqué concludes:

"We want a free and satisfied Slovak people, autonomous and happy Slovakia, unified Czechoslovak Republic. May God help us to achieve this."

Kundt will try to establish contact again with the Slovak People's Party and to induce them to formulate their demands for autonomy more sharply. However, he is sceptical about the success of his efforts, as it is probable that the Slovaks People's Party wants continuance of close relations with the Government. Sidor, chief supporter of the autonomy movement, is at present completely without influence.

Hencke"

Number 8
Agreement Signed on September 29, 1938, at Munich between
Germany, the United Kingdom, France, and Italy

Germany, the United Kingdom, France and Italy, taking into consideration the agreement, which has been already reached in principle for the cession to Germany of the Sudeten German territory, have agreed on the following terms and conditions governing the said cession and the measures consequent theron, and by this agreement they each hold themselves responsible for the steps necessary to secure its fulfillment.

1) The evacuation will begin on October 1.

2) The United Kingdom, France, and Italy agree that the evacuation of the territory shall be completed by October 10, without any existing installation having been destroyed, and that the Czechoslovak Government will be held responsible for carrying out the evacuation without damage to the said installations.

3) The conditions governing the evacuation will be laid down in detail by an international commission composed of representatives of Germany, the United Kingdom, France, Italy, and Czechoslovakia.

4) The occupation by stages of the predominantly German territories marked on the attached map will be occupied by German troops in the following order: the territory marked number I on the 1st and 2nd of October, the territory marked number II on the 2nd and 3d

of October, the territory marked number III on the 3d, 4th, and 5th of October, the territory marked number IV on the 6th and 7th of October. The remaining territory of preponderantly German character will be ascertained by the aforesaid international commision forthwith and be occupied by German troops by the 10th of October.

5) The international commision referred to in paragraph 3) will determine the territories in which a plebiscite is to be held. These territories will be occupied by international bodies until the plebiscite has been completed. The same commission will fix the conditions in which the plebiscite is to be held, taking as a basis the conditions of the Saar plebiscite. The commission will also fix a date, not later than the end of November, on which the plebiscite will be held.

6) The final determination of the frontiers will be carried out by the international commission. This commission will also be entitled to recommend to the four Powers, Germany, the United Kingdom, France, and Italy, in certain exceptional cases, minor modifications in the strictly ethnographical determination of the zones which are to be transferred without plebiscite.

7) There will be a right of option into and out of the transferred territories, the option to be exercised within six months from the date of this agreement. A German-Czechoslovak commission shall determine the details of the option, consider ways of facilitating the transfer of population and settle questions of principle arising out of the said transfer.

8) The Czechoslovak Government will, within a period of four weeks from the date of this agreement, release from their military and police forces any Sudeten Germans who may wish to be released, and the Czechoslovak Government will within the same period release Sudeten German prisoners who are serving terms of imprisonment for political offenses.

Adolf Hitler
Ed. Daladier
Mussolini

Munich, September 29, 1938   *Neville Chamberlain*

Annex to the Agreement

His Majesty's Government in the United Kingdom and the French Government have entered into the above agreement on the basis that they stand by the offer, contained in paragraph 6 of the Anglo-French proposals of September 19, relating to an international guarantee of the new boundaries of the Czechoslovak State against unprovoked aggression.

When the question of the Polish and Hungarian minorities in Czechoslovakia has been settled, Germany and Italy for their part will give a guarantee to Czechoslovakia.

Adolf Hitler, Neville Chamberlain,
Munich, September 29, 1938. *Mussolini, Ed. Daladier*

Number 9
Note on the Secret Meeting of Field Marshal Hermann Göring on October 14, 1938

The Sudetenland has to be exploited by every means. General Field Marshal Göring counts upon a complete economic assimilation of of Slovakia. Czechs and Slovaks would become German dominions. Everything possible must be taken out. The Oder-Danube Canal has to be speeded up. Searches for oil and ore have to be conducted in Slovakia, notably by the State Secretary Keppler.

Number 10
Conversation between Field Marshal Göring and Ferdinand Ďurčanský in October 16 or 17, 1938

Also present:

Mach, Propaganda Chief of the Slovak Government
Karmasin, leader of the Germans in Slovakia
Reichsstatthalter Seyss-Inquart

Ďurčanský (Deputy Prime Minister) began by reading a statement. Contents: "Sympathy for the Führer; gratitude that, thanks to the Führer, the right of self-determination had been made possible for Slovaks." Slovaks never want union with Hungary. Slovaks want full independence, with very close political, economic, and military ties with Germany. Pressburg as capital. Execution of plan possible only if army and police are Slovak. At the meeting of the first Slovak Diet proclamation of independent Slovakia. In plebiscite, majority would be for separation from Prague. Jews vote for Hungary. Plebiscite to extend to the Morava River, where many Slovaks live.

Jewish problem will be solved as in Germany; Communist Party banned.

Germans in Slovakia do not want union with Hungary but to stay in Slovakia.

German influence on Slovak Government strong; a German Minister is promised.

Present negotiations with Hungary are being conducted by Slovaks. Czechs are more compliant toward Hungary than the Slovaks.

The Field Marshal is of the opinion that efforts of the Slovaks for independence should be suitably supported. A Czech State minus Slovakia is even more completely at our mercy. Air base in Slovakia for air force for operation against the east very important.

Number 11
From the Diary of Count Jan Szembek, Notes About a Visit by Sidor.

(Comte Jan Szembek, JOURNAL 1933-1939, Paris, 1952 pp. 359-362. With kind permission of the Librairie Plon, Paris.)

October, 19, 1938.

Discussion with Sidor

In the course of the luncheon I offered in honor of Sidor and at which Arciszewski and Kobylanski were also present, my guest described the present situation in Slovakia. He declared to us that his countrymen intended to create an entirely independent Slovak State, which, however, would lean politically, militarily, as well as from the cultural point of view on Poland, and economically on Germany and Hungary. The Slovaks do not want to admit German and Hungarian cultural influences but wish to place their country under a sort of Polish political and military protectorate. The entire Slovak people share this pro-Polish inclination.

I received Sidor in audience on October 20. I asked him what instruction he had been given by his government when he left for Warsaw and what was the real purpose of his journey. He replied that the Slovak Government had advised him to state in Warsaw what Mgr. Tiso as well as Papée had previously let us know, namely that his country planned an independent Slovak State. I then asked him to explain to me the present attitude of his government towards Prague.

Sidor answered me that his country was today still an integral part of the Czechoslovak Republic and that the Slovak ministers were part of the Czechoslovak Government although they did not actually participate in its deliberations. So far, Slovak ministers had taken part in only two meetings of that government. As far as foreign relations are concerned, the Slovaks are conducting their foreign policy themselves, and their emissaries who have recently gone to European capitals have been sent there by the Prime Minister Tiso and not by Prague.

I put the question to Sidor what method his countrymen wished to employ to obtain their complete independence. According to him, Tiso wishes to achieve his objective by legitimate means. His theory is as follows: under present circumstances, as a result of the chaos which prevails in the Republic and especially in view of the fact that a Czech army of more than half a million men is stationed in Slovakia, which itself has no army of its own, and whose Slovak recruits are still on the frontiers of Bohemia (a fact which constitutes a serious obstacle to the final separation of Slovakia from the Czechs, as Sidor has stressed with great insistance) there can be no question of applying more radical methods. Sidor would personally perhaps be of the opinion that such methods ought to be applied and he thinks it might be a good thing to employ what is called the "Hlinka Guards" and the National Committees which are subordinated to him. But in a spirit of loyality, he is obeying the government.

This is Tiso's political program which is inclined to adhere to legitimate methods: the election of the new President of the Czechoslovak Republic should take place not later than the 28th. The Slovaks demand that the one to be elected be a Catholic and that he should guarantee that the foreign policy of friendship with France and the Soviets be terminated. Chvalkovský is a candidate and the Hlinka Party will vote for him. This presidency will, however, be only of a temporary nature and will come to an end with the amendment of the constitution. The new constitution will create a federative regime by which Slovakia will obtain a special Diet and will enjoy broad autonomy. From then on the Slovaks will start discussing all their demands with Prague. Sidor is convinced that the Czechs will never accept these. The Slovak Diet will then proclaim the definite separation of Slovakia from the Czech Lands, as was the case between Sweden and Norway. Sidor estimates that it will mean waiting two months before matters reach this point. Meanwhile, the Slovak Government will complete its work of decentralization and will begin to organize the police, the gendarmes and the Army, a thing he has already started to do. The internal administration is already very largely in the hands of Slovaks. As to finances, the Slovaks will appropriate all state property on their territory. Tax receipts are already flowing to Bratislava. The State Bank is about to be instituted.

Number 12

From the Memorandum about the Conversation between Adolf Hitler, Vojtech Tuka, and Franz Karmasin in Berlin on February 12, 1939

After a short welcome Tuka thanked the Führer for granting him this interview. He adressed The Führer as "My Fűhrer" and said that he, although himself only a humble person, could nevertheless claim to speak in the name of the Slovak people. Czech courts and prisons gave him the right to make this assertion. He said that the Führer not only raised the Slovak question but also was the first to acknowledge the dignity of the Slovak people. The Slovaks wished too, under the leadership of the Fűhrer, to fight for the preservation of European civilization. It was obvious that for the Slovaks continued coexistence with the Czechs had become impossible, from a psychological as well as an economic point of view. The fact that today they were still part of the Czech State was made bearable only by the thought that the present government was a transitional phase, but he and his fellow-combatants were determined to follow the wishes of the Slovak people and to create an independent Slovakia. The fate of Slovakia lay in the Fűhrer's hands. Just as he had suffered in prison for his convictions, he was also ready to give his life for his ideals. Should it come to a revolt, Czechia would immediately try to suppress it with with bloodshed, but one word from the Fűhrer was enough to halt these efforts. The same applied to Hungarian and Polish aspirations, which could likewise be brought to a halt by a word from the Fűhrer. "I lay the destiny of my people in your hands, My Fűhrer; my people await their complete liberation by you." Today the Slovaks were still advancing with faltering steps, but their steps would become more and more determined.

Number 13
"Žilina Agreement" (Declaration)

I.

The undersigned accept the proposal of the Hlinka Slovak People's Party concerning the Constitutional Amendment of the Slovak Autonomy, as it was presented in the House of Deputies in 1938, and as it was published in No. 129 of "Slovák" on June 5, 1938. We are obliged to try with all our might to see that this Constitutional Amendment is agreed upon by the National Assembly not later than October 28, 1938. The constitutional position of Slovakia will be definitely resolved by agreement to that proposal.

II.

The governmental and the executive power in Slovakia should at once be put into the hands of the Slovak Government. Therefore, we ask to authorize immediately the Vice-President of the Hlinka Slovak People's Party, Dr. Jozef Tiso, as Premier-Designate, to form the first Slovak Government consisting of Premier and four Members (Ministers), and to propose them for nomination with the agreement of the undersigned political parties.

The undersigned accept the attached proposal of the law for decentralization of the governmental and executive power. This proposal should be approved and realized as soon as possible in order that the governmental and the executive power be transferred not only factually but also juridically into the hands of the Slovaks even before realization of the first paragraph of this Declaration.

Žilina, October 6, 1938

On behalf of the Republican Peasant and Smallholders' People's Party: Pavel Teplanský, Ján Ursíny, J. S. Vančo, Ján Petrovič, Ján Lichner, Karol Rybárik, Ondrej Devečka, Kornel Stodola, Adolf Šelmec, Ing. Jozef Styk, Milan Polák
On behalf of the Middle-Class Party: Ing. Ján Líška
On behalf of the Czechoslovak National Socialist Party: Dr. E. B. Lukáč
On behalf of the Fascists: Ján Ivák
On behalf of the Hlinka Slovak People's Party: Dr. Jozef Tiso, Dr. Jozef Buday, Jozef Sivák, Dr. Martin Sokol, Karol Sidor, Dr. Karol Mederly
On behalf of the Slovak National Party: Dr. Miloš Vančo, Dr. Ján Paulíny-Tóth

Number 14
Protest of the Slovak Legionnaries of March 14, 1939

Honorable Diet of Slovakia

Gentlemen,

If you are to decide today whether Slovakia is to be a part of the Czecho-Slovak Republic or an independent state by the side of some neighboring country bear in mind that:
——brave Slovak patriots fought and died together with the Czechs for the liberty of the Slovak Nation;
——that it was the Czechs who helped the Slovaks in the worst moments of their history and that all that we have from the spiritual and material point of view today we have acquired with Czech help during the last twenty years.

We implore you not to tarnish the national honor of the Slovaks and the memory of our fallen comrades, foremost among whom was General M. R. Štefánik.

For lack of time it is not possible for all Slovak Legionnaries and volunteers still living to join us in reminding you but we are certainly voicing the feeling of them all and of the great majority of the Slovak people.

Bratislava, March 14, 1939

Gen. Rudolf Viest   *Anton Granatier*
Lieut. Col. Aug. Malár   *Arch. Juro Tvarožek*
Staff-Capt. J. M. Kristin   *Dr. Ján Jesenský*
Josef Kustra   *Jozef Gregor-Tajovský*
M. Miškóci   *Králiček*
                 Ing Kalamen

Number 15
Telegram of Jozef Tiso to Adolf Hitler of March 15, 1938

"In the name of the legal Slovak Government I have the honor to inform Your Excellency that the sovereign Slovak Nation has today thrown off the intolerable Czech yoke and, in accordance with the wishes of the overwhelming majority of the population, the independence of our state has been proclaimed. Independent Slovakia is determined to live in peace and friendship with all her neighbors. In the early stages of her development, however, the young state requires strong protection. In the name of the people and of the Government of the new Slovakia, I request Your Excellency, as the Führer of the Great German Reich, which under your rule has always supported freedom and the self-determination of peoples, to take over the guarantee for the existence of our state and to take immediately all necessary measures for the protection of its frontiers.

Minister President of Independent Slovakia."

Number 16
Telegram of Adolf Hitler to Jozef Tiso of March 16, 1939

I confirm the receipt of your telegram of yesterday and I hereby undertake the protection of the Slovak State.

Adolf Hitler

Number 17
Treaty of Protection of the Slovak State by the German Reich

The German Government and the Slovak Government have agreed, after the Slovak State has placed itself under the protection of the German Reich, to regulate by treaty the consequences resulting from this fact. For this purpose, the undersigned representatives of the two governments have agreed on the following provisions:

Article 1

The German Reich undertakes to protect the political independence of the Slovak State and integrity of its territory.

Article 2

For the purpose of making effective the protection undertaken by the German Reich, the German Armed Forces shall have the right, at all times, to construct military installations and to keep them garrisoned in they strength they deem necessary, in an area delimited on its western side by the frontiers of the Slovak State, and on its eastern side by a line formed by the eastern rims of the Lower Carpathians, the White Carpathians, and the Javorník Mountains.

The Slovak Government will provide that the necessary soil and ground will be placed at the disposal of the German Armed Forces for those installations. The Slovak Government will also agree to a regulation which will be necessary to the appropriation of the German units without toll and to the deliveries for Army installations from the Reich without toll.

The German Armed Forces perform the Military Supreme Jurisdiction in the area described in Article 1.

The persons of German citizenship who are employed to build military installations in the described area in a private-obligation relation are subjected in this matter to the German jurisdiction.

Article 3

The Slovak Government will organize its military forces in close agreement with the German Armed Forces.

Article 4

In accordance with agreed relationship the Slovak Government will conduct its foreign policy in close understanding with the German Government.

Article 5

This agreement will be effective immediately after signing and is valid for a period of 25 years. Both governments will agree on an early prolongation of this treaty before the expiration of this time.

In proof of it the plenipotentiaries of both sides signed this treaty in two copies.

Vienna, March 18, 1939
Berlin, March 23, 1939

For the German Government: For the Slovak Government:
von Ribbentrop   Dr. Jozef Tiso
                                                      Dr. Vojtech Tuka
                                                      Dr. F. Ďurčanský

Number 18
Letter of Hungary's Regent, Admiral Nicholas Horthy, to Adolf Hitler of March 13, 1939

Your Excellency!

Heartfelt thanks! I cannot express how happy I am, for this head-water region is, in fact, for Hungary—I dislike using big words—a vital question.

Notwithstanding our recruits of but five weeks, we are tackling the matter with enthusiasm. The plans are already laid. On Thursday the 16th of this month a frontier incident will take place, to be followed on Saturday by the big thrust. I shall never forget this proof of friendship and Your Exellency can at all times ever rely steadfastly on my gratitude.

                                                        In friendly devotion,
Budapest, 13/III 939

                                                        Horthy

Number 19
Declaration of the Government of the United States of March 17, 1939, Concerning the Condemnation of the German Aggression against Czechoslovakia.

"The Government of the United States has on frequent occasions stated its conviction that only through international support of a program of order based upon law can world peace be assured.

This Government, founded upon and dedicated to the principles of human liberty and of democracy, cannot refrain from making known this country's condemnation of the acts which have resulted in the temporary extinguishment of the liberties of a free and independent people with whom, from the day when the Republic of Czechoslovakia attained its independence, the people of the United States have maintained specially close and friendly relations.

The position of the Government of the United States has been made consistently clear. It has emphasized the need for respect for the sanctity of treaties and of the pledged word, and for non-intervention by any nation in the domestic affairs of other nations; and it has on repeated occasions expressed its condemnation of a policy of military aggression.

It is manifest that acts of wanton lawlessness and of arbitrary force are threatening the world peace and the very structure of modern civilization. The imperative need for the observance of the principles advocated by this Government has been clearly demonstrated by the developments which have taken place during the past three days."

Number 20
Government Order of March 24, 1939, Concerning the Imprisonment of the Enemies of the Slovak State

(1) The Minister of Interior is authorized to arrange for the jailing of those persons whose activities until now have justified or justify

serious apprehensions that they will be an obstacle to the building of the Slovak State.

(2) The Minister of Interior will establish a security camp for the detention of such persons, in which camp the prisoners will also be compelled to perform physical labor.

(3) This order is effective on the day of its promulgation.

Dr. Tiso

Dr. Tuka   Dr. Fritz
Dr. Ďurčanský   Medrický
Dr. Pružinský   Stano
Sivák   Čatloš

Number 21

Manifesto

*of the Slovak Writers Issued in Tatranská Lomnica
on August 31, 1940*

On August 31, 1940, cultural workers met in Tatranská Lomnica to take a stand on the current problems of Slovak life. The participants were greeted in the name of the Propaganda Ministry by Dr Jozef Ambruš. The meetings were presided over by author Tido J. Gašpar. Writer Milo Urban clarified the position of the cultural workers on the present political reality. Reports were delivered by Representative Dr. František Hrušovský on the tasks of Slovak science, Dr. Stanislav Mečiar on the mission and importance of literary creativeness, Dr. Jozef Cincík on regulation of graphic arts, and Dr. Juraj Čečetka on the problems of schools and national education. After an exhaustive and thorough discussion of the problems presented, they adopted unanimously the following stand:

Slovak National Socialism and its application in our country means an organic continuation of the development of the Slovak national forces in the spirit of our traditions.

National Socialism is the system best fitted to the needs of Slovak life because it facilitates a complete solution of all political, economic, social, and cultural problems.

By this system he Slovak Nation frees itself from the sphere of liberalism and capitalism in which it has been kept by force by foreign regimes and integrates itself into a new economic, social, and cultural order upon which a new Europe is being built.

The representatives of the Slovak cultural and spiritual life empha--ically demand that this system, which is the best guarantee of Slovak statehood, be instituted immediately and uncompromisingly by the responsible factors in all the sectors of national life. They specifically point out the need of this being done primarily in building new economic and social institutions, but they emphatically add that the introduction of this system is to be followed through in the educational and cultural field.

In Tatranská Lomnica, August 31, 1940.

Tido J. Gašpar, Dr. Stanislav Mečiar, Dr. Jozef Ambruš, Valentín Beniak, Andrej Žarnov, Vladimir Rolko, Jozef Cincík, Dr. František Hrušovský, J. Čečetka, Frico Motoška, Ján Smrek, Milo Urban, Henrik Bartek.

Number 22
Telegram of Jozef Tiso to Adolf Hitler of June 24, 1941

To His Exellency the Führer and Reichskanzler A. Hitler in Berlin

At the moment when Slovakia joins with arms in its hands the fateful fight of the European community for the preservation of justice and civilization, I take the liberty to assure Your Excellency anew of the fidelity and alliance of the Slovak people and their Government and of their unshakable trust in the victory.

The President of the Slovak Republic—Tiso

Number 23
Telegram of Adolf Hitler to Jozef Tiso of June 24, 1941

I thank Your Excellency for the telegraphic report that Slovakia had entered into the fateful struggle for the future of Europe alongside Germany and for the assurance of its faithful alliance. With unshakable conviction in our cause I am sure that complete victory will be ours.

Adolf Hitler

Number 24
Note of the President of the United States Franklin D. Roosevelt to the Secretary of State, Mr. Cordell Hull, December 12, 1941

(From "The Memoirs of Cordell Hull", Volume II, New York, 1948, p. 1175, with kind permission of The Macmillan Company, Publishers, 60 Fifth Avenue, New York 11, N. Y.)

I see by tonight's bulletins that the Government of Slovakia has declared the existence of a state of war with the United States.

Also that the Government of Hungary has done so, or is about to do the same thing.

Other puppet Governments may join.

It is my present thought that the United States should pay no attention to any of these declarations of war against us by puppet Governments.

Number 25
Official Record

Prime Minister Dr. Vojtech Tuka conferred today with the deputy of Heinrich Himmler, the Reich's SS-Leader and Chief of the German Police, as the representative of Marshal Goering, who had direct orders from the Reichschancellor and Fuehrer Adolph Hitler to solve the problem of European Jews. It was stated at the meeting that the evacuation of the Slovak Jews was only a part of the program. The evacuation of half a million Jews from Europe to the East is now in progress. Slovakia is the first country whose Jews the German Reich has been willing to accept. Simultaneously, the evacuation of Jews from France (occupied), Holland, Belgium, the Protectorate, and the Reich is being effected. Jews from Slovakia will be placed in several locations near Lublin (district Lublin), where they will remain permanently. Families will stay together. The international legal and civic status of the Jews will be that of protegees (Schutzbefohlene) of the German Reich.

Jews, who have been baptized will be transported separately and settled in a special territory. (This refers to Jews qualified as baptized by the Jewish Codex and baptized before September 10, 1941. Jews baptized more recently do not belong in this category because they have been baptized for reasons of expediency.)

The German Government will take care of the Jews as humanely as possible. (In August, Department Chief, Koso, saw what a Jewish city was like; it had its self-government, a council of elders, and police.)

Bratislava, April 10, 1942

Number 26
Agreement

on the Founding of an Underground Slovak National Council Announced at Christmas, 1943

Those who represent the ideological trends in Slovakia which have remained faithful to the principles of anti-Fascist democracy even after October 6, 1938, and who have been conducting active resistance against the political, economic, and cultural coercion of the Slovak people, and who represent today the true opinions of all strata of the Slovak Nation, have agreed to create a common political leadership, the Slovak National Council, as the only representative of the political will of the Slovak Nation at home.

I. The tasks and aims of the Slovak National Council are:

1. To lead uniformly and centrally the fight of the Slovak Nation for the removal of the Nazi German dictatorship, which dictatorship was exercised also by the domestic usurpers of political power;

2. At the first propitious moment to take over all political, legislative, military, and administrative powers in Slovakia and exercise them according to the will of the people until freely elected representatives of the people are able to assume all power;

3. As soon as feasible after seizing power, the Slovak National Council will make it possible for the Slovak people to elect freely its representatives, to whom the Council will hand over all power.

4. The Slovak National Council will continue its activities in agreement with the Czechoslovak Government and the Liberation Movement Abroad, whose work in the international and military field it recognizes and supports.

II. The representatives of the united trends and groups then agreed on these principles:

1. It is our wish that the Slovak and Czech Nations, as the most closely related Slav nations, shape their destinies in the Czechoslovak Republic, in a common State of the Czechs and Slovaks built upon the principle of national equality.

2. We wish for close cooperation with all Slav countries and nations, especially with the USSR as the protector of the freedom and universal progress of small nations in general and Slav nations in particular.

3. The future Czechoslovak Republic is to direct its foreign policy in the spirit of these principles and is, therefore, to lean on USSR in the military and international fields.

4. The internal order of the future Czechoslovak Republic is to be democratic; all fascist, racist, totalitarian, and other tendencies which are contrary to these principles are to be rooted out. Prompted by this spirit the internal political regime is to be firm but democratic. The errors and mistakes of the past are to be avoided.

5. The ideas of democracy are to be applied and extended to the economic and social fields so that the national income would be divided equitably and justly as possible among all the people and the life of every citizen would have human dignity.

6. Culture, education, and learning are to be governed by the aforementioned principles. Religious freedom is to be retained, the

influence of the churches on policies and leadership of the state is to be excluded.

7. The definite solution of these problems—in particular the relation between the Slovak and Czech nations as assured by the Constitution—is to be decided by the freely elected representatives of the Slovak Nation.

Bratislava, Christmas, 1943

Number 27
Order of Lieut. Col. Ján Golian
to the Slovak Army on August 30, 1944, Concerning Military Resistance Against the Germans

Number 29,154 Sec./3 Div. 1944

Re: Struggles against the Germans—Order

Confirmation of orders issued by telephone

General Čatloš in the name of the traitorous Government of the Slovak Republic has called German units to Slovakia.

The Slovak units, as a part of the Czechoslovak Army faithful to the principles of democracy and freedom, will resist them with the support of the entire population.

All orders issued up until now by the Preparatory Committee remain in effect and must be carried out and respected.

Those Slovak orders which are contrary to the spirit and idea of the Czechoslovak Republic are hereby abolished.

Therefore, call together the officers and explain appropriately the situation to them.

Our aim, clear to us all, is: "Help defeat Germany."

Garrisons which as yet have not joined the struggle and operations already underway in our defense should henceforth be directed against the German and possibly also the Hungarian forces.

Arrange to listen to Radio Banská Bystrica.

By special distribution to garrisons and administration centers.

By order:
The Chief of Staff of the Czechoslovak Army in Slovakia
(S) *Lieut. Col. Ján Golian*

Number 28
Declaration of the Slovak National Council
in Banská Bystrica, September 1, 1944

All Democratic and progressive sections and movements of the Slovak Nation which have been engaged in a constant fight against the present Fascist regime in Slovakia and against its Nazi German allies have, on this day, set up a Slovak National Council which is to be the supreme representative of Slovak resistance on the home front.

Therefore, from this day on the Slovak National Council, which is the only authorized spokesman of the Slovak Nation, assumes the legislative and executive power throughout Slovakia, as well as the defense of Slovakia, and it will discharge these duties until the Slovak Nation has, by democratic methods, appointed its legitimate representatives.

Our resistance movement on the home front, which has hitherto been conducted in complete unity with the Czechoslovak resistance movement abroad, wishes to continue in unity and collaboration until the day of final victory.

We are in favor of a brotherly co-existence with the Czech Nation in the new Czechoslovak Republic. Constitutional, social, economic and cultural problems of the Republic will be settled definitely by elected representatives of the Slovak and Czech people in accordance with democratic principles, progress and social justice.

On achieving political liberation, our aim will be to ensure a better and happier life for the socially weak strata of the nation, that is for the Slovak worker and peasant. In order to secure a higher standard of living for the nation we are in favor of equitable distribution of national wealth, and a new land reform for the benefit of the small peasant. The worker shall have wages corresponding to a higher standard of living and share in the results of his labor.

We most emphatically reject and condemn the anti-democratic outrageous acts and ideas of the People Party's regime in our country. The Slovak Nation has had nothing to do with the alliance with Hitlerite Germany. On the contrary, in its way of thinking and in its conception it has always been entirely on the side of the Allies, as it has proved by its deeds at home and at the front on all possible occasions. The Slovak Nation, true to our national traditions, has rejected with indignation the Tiso-Tuka betrayal committed against Slavdom by the Populist regime which forced the Slovak Nation into the fight against the brotherly Russian Nation and other Slav nations.

Today the Slovak Nation openly and solemnly joins hands with the Allied nations, which by their struggle and great sacrifices will ensure a free, democratic life to all nations throughout the world— and to our small nation as well. We wish to contribute everything in our power toward the speedy conclusion of this fight for liberty.

In these historic moments we shall grant every moral and material support to our fighting Slovak Army and the partisans. We call on the entire nation to take up arms and to join in the fight against our traditional enemies and their henchmen at home, so that all Slovaks may be able to arrange their life in a free Czechoslovak Republic according to their own wishes.

May our just cause prevail!

Glory to our Czechoslovak Republic!

Banská Bystrica, September 1, 1944.

The Slovak National Council

Number 29

Declaration

of the Government of the United States of September 10, 1944, Concerning the Czechoslovak Army, Fighting in the Slovak National Uprising

The Czechoslovak Government in London on September 2, 1944, proclaimed all military forces fighting against the Germans in Czechoslovakia to be members of the regular Czechoslovak Army.

With reference to the operations of Czechoslovak forces in Europe, including the forces which have begun combat in Slovakia, the Government of the United States reiterates its view that all members of the armed forces of the countries at war with Germany which are engaged in active combat should be treated by the German military authorities in accordance with the laws and customs of war.

The Government of the United States therefore declares:

(1) The soldiers of the Czechoslovak Army, including those in Slovakia and other parts of Czechoslovakia, constitute a combat force operating against the Germans.

(2) The soldiers of the Czechoslovak Army are instructed to conduct their military operations in accordance with the rules of war and so doing they bear arms openly against the enemy and are provided with Czechoslovak uniforms or a distinctive emblem.

(3) In these circumstances reprisals by the German military authorities against the soldiers of the Czechoslovak Army violate the rules of war by which Germany is bound. The United States Government, therefore, solemnly warns all Germans who take part in or are in any way responsible for such violations that they do so at their peril and will be held answerable for their crimes.

Number 30

Message

of the President of the United States Franklin D. Roosevelt to President Edvard Beneš about the Slovak Insurgents.

This anniversary of the independence of Czechoslovakia is of special significance. The people and armed forces inside Czechoslovakia have joined actively and gloriously with their countrymen abroad in the ranks of the nations united against tyranny and can look forward confidently to the celebration of future anniversaries in the full enjoyment of unsuppressed freedom.

We Americans salute our Czechoslovak comrades-in-arms who are today so bravely contributing to the liberation of their homeland and the rest of Europe.

The close ties and deep sympathy between the democratic peoples of Czechoslovakia and the United States have never ceased to find concrete expression since the days of President Masaryk and President Wilson.

I look forward to the day when, victorious after a second great war for freedom they can continue to work in harmony for their mutual security and welfare in a peaceful world.

Franklin D. Roosevelt.

Number 31
Secret Report

of the Commandant of the German Security Service of December 9, 1944, on the Reprisals against the Insurgents

Bratislava, December 9, 1944

SECRET REICH AFFAIR!
IV L

1.) Security of Slovak area is assured at present by five shock *(Einsatz)*, i.e. Special Commandos' in Bratislava, Ružomberok, Trenčín, Banská Bystrica and Nitra with 24 contacting and adjoining units.

2.) Up to now 18,937 persons have been arrested:

9,653	Jews
3,409	Bandits
2,186	Deserters
714	Resistants
172	Gypsies
546	Others

The remainder 2,257 were specially treated (executed).

| 8,975 | Jews and |
| 530 | others were transferred to German concentration camps. |

3.) The following leaders of the insurgents were delivered to the Reich Security Office in Berlin:

General Viest
General Golian
Lieut. Col. Souhrada
Major Krátký
First Lieutenant Várady

As a leading insurgent, Paulíny-Tóth, also was arrested, who has not yet been delivered to the Reich Security Service Office.

4.) Lutheran Bishops, Dr. Prof. Osuský
Dr. Čobrda

outstanding clergymen in Slovakia, were also arrested.

5.) Fifteen Jews, American citizens, were transferred to the Reich and are to be exchanged.

6.) In hotel and restaurant inspections and controls
14,062 persons were investigated and of these
122 were arrested.

In addition to above, 485 motor-vehicles were checked.

7.) In trains a careful check is made of passengers traveling without permission.

8.) To safeguard contact on the frontier with the Slovak Security Guards, special units have been stationed at Strelenka, the Vlára Pass, Čadca, the Bratislava-Petržalka bridge, Devínska Nová Ves and Kúty by Special Commands of the Security Service.

9.) At this time steps are taken against persons returning from the territory of the insurgents.

The Commandant
*of the Security Office and the Security
Service*

Number 32

Declaration

of the Government of the United States of November 19, 1944 Concerning the Capture of General Rudolf Viest, General Ján Golian and Other Insurgent Officers and Soldiers

In connection with recent German radio reports of the capture of General Viest, General Golian, and other Czechoslovak officers and soldiers in Slovakia, attention is again called to the declaration made by the United States Government on September 7, 1944, as printed in the Bulletin on September 10, 1944, page 263.

Number 33
First Grave

Names of the Victims of the Slovak National Uprising, Murdered in Turćiansky Svätý Martin (Na Bukovinách) Without Trial and Without Sentence on October 3, 1944

1. Achin, Peter, 30,
2. Baka, Ján, 60,
3. Barkovicy, Bartolomej, 33,
4. Belička, Ján, 38
5. Bobček, Ján, 38
6. Bobček, Ján, 22,
7. Bobček, Jozef, 22,
8. Bozin, Jozef, 36,
9. Bratsa, Fridrich, 23,
10. Brna, Andrej, 47,
11. Brna, Juraj, 40,
12. Dostál, František, 49,
13. Doubek, František Jozef, 36,
14. Duratrich, Jozef,20
15. Dzurian, Andrej, 41,
16. Facuna, Rudolf, 18,
17. Filip, Ján, 44,
18. Hajči, Ambróz, 44,
19. Hanušák, Alojz, 41,
20. Herz, Otto, 15
21. Horský, Oskar, 40,
22. Hynek, Karol, 55,
23. Huculák, Ján Otomar, 19,
24. Juríček, Imrich, 39,
25. Keračík, František, 52,
26. Keračík, Ladislav, 21,
27. Kollár, Ján, 32,
28. Kováč, Jozef, 29,
29. Král, Gustáv, 20,
30. Krenek, Metodej, 21,
31. Kučera, Jozef, 20,
32. Kucma, Jozef, 42,
33. Majer, Ján, 39,
34. Majer, Miloš, 31,
35. Majerčík, Michal, 35,
36. Majerčík, Juraj, 47,
37. Meyer, František, 47,
38. Michalík, Ambróz, 36,
39. Petráš, Jozef, 33,
40. Pulec, Ladislav, 53,
41. Samčík, Emil, 25,
42. Samčík, Vladimir, 22,
43. Šarkan, Ján, 30
44. Štreklan, Ján, 49,
45. Taranza, František, 29,
46. Tschelko, Anton, 20,
47. Turček, Ján, 29,
48. Velich, Jozef, 49,

Number 34

List of Mass Graves of the Victims of the Slovak National Uprising, Murdered from August 30, 1944, up to May 1, 1945

District	Town	Number of Victims
Turčiansky Svätý Martin	Turčiansky Svätý Martin	
	—Na Bukovinách I.	48
	—Na Bukovinách II.	28
	—Pod Stráňami	21
	—individual graves	28
	Turček	180 305

Banská Bystrica	Banská Bystrica		
	—Pri Mičínskej ceste	48	
	Kremnička		
	—Protitankový zákop	325	
	—Pod akátovým hájom	93	
	—Pod Stráňou	115	
	Nemecká		
	—Rástocká dolina		
	(estimate)	900	
	Poniky	31	
	Hriadel—Les Príslop	69	
	Slovenská Lupča	34	
	Donovaly	19	
	Motyčky	20	1,654
Zvolen	Kováčová		108
Nová Baňa	Nová Baňa		60
Kremnica	Kremnica		
	—on the road to Piargy	44	
	—on the road to Skalca	11	55
Prievidza	Handlová	14	
	Prievidza	92	106
Topoľčany	Nemčice		53
Bánovce nad Bebravou	(45 individual and mass graves)		142
Ilava	Dubnica nad Váhom		
	—mass grave	26	
	—individual graves	3	
	Ladce	20	49
Žilina	Žilina—3 mass graves		
	(15, 16 a 7)		38
Trenčín	Trenčín—Na Brezine		
	(7 mass graves)		64
Ružomberok	Ružomberok		22
Trstená	Trstená		15
Bratislava	Petržalka		460
			3,131

Number 35

Telegram of Jozef Tiso to Adolf Hitler of October 27, 1944

With great joy and deep gratitude I have the honor to inform you that troops under the command of SS-Obergruppenführer General of the Police, Höffle, today liberated Banská Bystrica, the seat of the putchist Czechoslovak National Council; and that, cooperating with units of the Slovak Domobrana, the HG and the HM, they are sucessfully clearing Slovak territory of the Czecho-Bolshevik bandits. The entire Slovak Nation joins with me in rejoicing and conveys to Your Excellency the hope that similar blessed successes may accompany the heroic struggle of the Greater German Reich for the life and honor of its nation and for the protection of European culture.

Number 36

Telegram of Štefan Tiso to Joachim von Ribbentrop of October 27, 1944

To his Excellency the Reich Minister of Foreign Affairs, Joachim von Ribbentrop, Berlin.—Having just received the gratifying news of the destruction of the centre, in the heart of Slovakia, of the Bolshevik advance guard which had menaced the independence of the Slovak State and Europe's culture, I beg Your Execellency to convey to the Reich Government the most heartfelt gratitude of myself and of the Slovak Government for the help which the Greater German Reich and its Leader have nobly given for the future of the Slovak Nation.

Number 37

Telegram of Štefan Hasšík to Heinrich Himmler of October 27, 1944

Units fighting under the command of SS-Obergruppenfűhrer General of the Police, Höffle, have just captured the seat of the putchist National Council, Banská Bystrica. On this day of joy, so memorable for the Slovak Nation and State, I thank Your Excellency for the aid granted, in the conviction that the heroic struggle of the German Nation will be crowned by the victory it deserves.

Number 38

Proclamation

of the Slovak Government Issued on the Occasion of the Fall of Banská Bystrica on October 27, 1944

Slovaks, citizens. The enemy, resorting to treachery, committed a shameful attack against the Slovak State. Taking possession of a certain area, the enemy attempted to exercise foreign government control on Slovak territory by forming an illegal Government at Banská Bystrica and proclaiming a Czechoslovak Republic. The legitimate Government of the Slovak Republic and the entire loyal population were never in doubt that this disgraceful undertaking would fail.

Therefore everything was done by our own authorities, with the help of German troops, to break up this attack of enemy usurpers and Slovak traitors and to restore Slovak sovereignty throughout the country. The Slovak Government has been victorious in its determination. Today Banská Bystrica, the seat of the insurgents, has fallen. Thus the last remnant of Slovak territory violated by the enemy has been freed and brought back under the administration of the Slovak State. The Slovak Government rejoices in this historic success which foiled the devilish intentions of the enemy and brought victory to Slovakia. Slovaks, citizens! Carry out the mottos of our Leader. Be loyal to him and the nation and be united in deed and thought in the realization that your liberation from the Czecho-Bolshevik plague, so long awaited by everyone, is telling evidence of Germany's loyal fulfilment of her Treaty of Protection.

At this moment of joy we think with sincere gratitude of the Führer of the Greater German Reich and his heroic Army. We appeal to the population of the liberated territory to fulfil loyally all orders of the Government and the authorities, and to assist the German Army. We assure you that the Government of the Slovak Republic is determined to punish the traitors severely. The Government will again help the innocent population, which suffered under the terrorist regime of the Czecho-Bolshevik usurpers. It will make it possible for the people to share in the blessings of our own state.

The Government, therefore, calls upon all loyal Slovak citizens of the State to return calmly to their work and participate actively in restoring order and prosperity in our free homeland, the Slovak Republic. The Slovak State lives and shall live on! The traitorous clique stabbed the Slovak State in the back but was not able to destroy it by this satanic attempt, for it is founded on our inalienable right and historical justice. With firm faith and trust in God's help, the Government sends its greetings to the liberated areas and, assisted by all loyal citizens, sets out to heal the wounds and to continue the work of building the Slovak State, the free home of all Slovaks.

Number 39

Memorandum

of the Representatives of the Young Generation of the People's Party to Dr. J. Tiso of September 20, 1944

Our Leader:

Prompted by anxiety and interest in our nation and state, we take the liberty of presenting you in the name of the young generation of the People's Party a number of proposals which we believe to be vital to the internal reconstruction of our state. In all our requests, we want to adhere to your motto: Back to March 14, 1939.

Therefore we propose that:

1. A genuine authoritarian system be introduced in the Party and State;

2. All faithful members of the Party be rehabilitated who for five years have been forced into the background by anti-state elements and that there be a thorough purge in the Hlinka People's Party;

a) All resign from the Praesidium of the Party and from government departments who do not believe in Slovak statehood, who are easily influenced by hostile propaganda and capitulate far in advance, also those who have shown themselves weak in performing their official duties. The first to resign shall be Dr. Gejza Medrický, Julius Stano, and Aladár Kočiš. The first two are responsible for the fact that in their ministries the interests of the Party have been neglected or sabotaged and that anti-state elements have been organized there.

b) in the third case, Dr. Aladár Kočiš, as Secretary General of the Hlinka Slovak People's Party has proved himself so weak that the Party has begun to disintegrate because of his lack of determination and perseverance and because of insufficient defense of the movement's interests until it has begun to take on the character of a mere society. He tolerated former centralists in the general secretariat. The situation is not better among the regional secretaries, and there are even several old adversaries of the Party among the functionaries.

All three are unfit to hold a ministerial office.

c) All organs and components of the Party must be headed by unencumbered and uncorrupted Slovaks, completely devoted to the movement and to the state.

d) All members of the People's Party who have been exposed as being of an other orientation than purely Slovak and national are to resign from every responsible public function.

e) There is an urgent need of a revision of all Diet seats. The Deputies to the Diet of the Slovak Republic are subject to the requirement stated in point 3, article a) of this memorandum.

3. That a purge in the state apparatus be carried out.

a) The entire administration of our state must be taken over by old Party members who support exclusively the Slovak statehood and are ready to work and fight for it without compromise.

b) There must be a change in the position of the Chairman of the State Agricultural Agency.

c) There must be a revision of all Aryanizors and business licenses.

d) There must be immediate reprisals against all direct and indirect organizers of the coup of August 29, 1944. Guilty members of the People's Party must be punished with special severity.

e) Political indoctrination is to be introduced in the entire military apparatus.

4. That the principal instigators of the August coup must be punished:

a) Individuals are to be tried by the nation.

b) Institutions and societies which participated in any way in the organization of the coup are to be permanently disbanded and their property confiscated for cultural and social purposes.

c) The property of individuals who joined the insurgents is to be confiscated and used to pay for the losses caused by the uprising. Large industries, that either organized their own uprising or spontaneously joined the insurgents or financed the uprising (i.e. the Bat'a Works, the Turiec Brewery, etc.) are to be nationalized.

d) If at least five leading personalities in a city have taken part in the uprising, the city is to be deprived of all city rights, administrative agencies are to be permanently shifted elsewhere, as well as cultural, economic and social institutions of national or regional importance.

5. That the Jewish and Czech problem be definitely solved with all consequences.

We hereby reaffirm that in submitting these proposals we are prompted solely by love for our nation and state in the knowledge that a nation stands and falls with its state and also because we are inspired by an active will to help the nation and the state in these difficult times.

Because of our love for the people's movement and the idea of the Slovak State, we shall always work with devotion. Unfortunately, it is impossible to work properly under present conditions with those in leading positions. Our Leader, please understand that we can perform the tasks only if such conditions are created as set forth in this request. This is the opinion of all collaborators devoted to our movement and of the entire activistic young generation.

If these requests should go unheeded, we respectfully suggest that we be freed from any direct resposibility pertaining to our present functions and that it be made possible for us to work as rank and file fighters; we add that we shall always work for the principles set forth here and under all conditions, and with the utmost sacrifices by ourselves.

If necessary, we shall gladly help to select persons and to decide the means to be used in putting our proposals to practice.

Having the utmost confidence in you, our Leader, we turn to you alone in these turbulent times. In the name of the young Slovak generation which has grown up in the idea of Slovak statehood and which follows you we beg you to free yourself of the influence of people who are opposed to the idea of a Slovak State, who are against you because you embody the will of the Slovak people to have its own independent state (we remind you of the first meeting of the Praesidium of the Party after the declaration of Slovak independence) and who have made the present conditions possible through their attitude.

We are led by selfless motives, as selfless as is our devotion to the Church, the nation, the state, and yourself, our Leader.

Bratislava, September 20, 1944

On guard!

Number 40
Manifesto

of the Young Slovak Separatists' Meeting in Piešťany on January 14, 1945

To ensure the life of our nation and to preserve the Slovak Republic, we, cognizant of our responsibility for the present and future development of the Slovak Nation and of our bond with the preceding generations, do declare:

The Slovak Republic expresses fully the sovereignty of the Slovak Nation. As such, it is the only state form in which we want to live and to work, in which we can best develop our aptitudes and thus contribute nobly to the great work of European culture. No member of cultural mankind can demand that we betray the laws which all nations of the world consider sacred.

Therefore, we are irrevocably for the Slovak State. We can do but one thing: Stand up and fight against anyone who would deprive us of the Slovak State, whether in the name of Czechoslovakism, Bolshevism, or the St. Stephen ideology. In this fight for our existence we are, therefore, for using the entire fighting potential of the Slovak Nation.

It is in the supreme interest of the State that civic discipline be augmented and severe measures be taken against those who, either through their activity or negligence in performing their duties, have hurt the vital interests of the State and the work in the field of domestic policies.

The ideas of the People's movement should always be embodied in the program of the endeavors and struggle of the whole nation, and the Party itself should remain a constant source of the revitalizing forces of Slovak life. Only chosen individuals, utterly devoted to the nation, can be members of the Party.

To give assistance in cultural endeavor will be the supreme task in the Slovak State. Access to cultural values will be open to every citizen.

Labor and capital must serve everyone, the entire national community. It is in the vital interest of the nation that it own all the sources of production and that everyone find employment at home. The economic functions of political power must be put to work toward this end.

The solidarity to the entire national community in all its strata—and not class struggle—will form the basis of the social structure and progress of the nation. We want all strata of the nation to prosper and advance in the inevitable process of socialization so that every man may live in the way best suited to his position and in human dignity. Every man has a natural right to work and the duty to work.

Common sense dictates that we cooperate with those who recognize our right to our own state and to freedom. Our cooperation with Germany is a self-evident consequence. Fighting side by side with Germany, we fight for our state and for our place among nations.

We know there is sufficient moral strength in the Slovak Nation, even at this time of great tribulations during wartime, to resist the cruel fate which would overtake us should we fall victim to foreign domination. As a self-respecting European nation, we wish to play our part in the defense of the European spirit so that, after this struggle is ended, we can share the blessings in our own Slovak State. We bow before our nation's greatest sons who have given their life-blood. For us this is an obligation and challenge to continue the struggle for our nation's rights. This fight can end only in victory for us and for the European spirit.

Number 41

The Relation Between the Czechs and Slovaks Stated in the Program of the First Government of the National Front of the Czechs and Slovaks, Promulgated in Košice April 5, 1945

The first home government of the Republic shall embody the Czechoslovak Commonwealth based on new principles. To end old differences and in recognition of the Slovaks as an independent nation ethnically, the Government shall endeavor to put into practice, from the outset, the principle of equality in Czecho-Slovak relations and to practice real brotherhood between the two nations.

In recognition of the right of the Slovaks to be masters in their own land and of the Czechs in theirs, the Republic shall be renewed as a common state with equal rights for the two nations—the Czech and the Slovak. This recognition of equality shall find expression in important political state acts. The Slovak National Council, founded on the National Committees in villages and counties, shall be not only the legal representative of the independent Slovak Nation but also the representative of state power in the territory of Slovakia (of legislative, governmental, and executive power) in accordance with the special agreement between the Slovak National Council on the one hand and the President of the Republic and the Czechoslovak Government in London. The Government as a central government of the Republic shall perform the common state functions in close cooperation with the Slovak National Council and with the Board of Commissioners as an executive organ of the Slovak National Council.

Within the framework of the newly built unified Czechoslovak Armed Forces, and in accordance with unified service regulations, there will be formed Slovak military units (regiments, divisions, etc.), composed predominantly of troops, non-commissioned officers, and officers of Slovak nationality; Slovak shall be the official language. The officers and persons of the former Slovak Army with a fixed salary will be reinstated in the Czechoslovak Army in their present rank on condition that they have not committed an offense against Slovak national honor and that they are not subject to criminal procedure for their past activities under the former traitorous regime and on condition that they are recommended by the Slovak National Council.

The new Government of the Republic shall incorporate into the Constitution dealing with the Czecho-Slovak relations, the Slovak legislative, governmental, and executive organs, as they already exist in the Slovak National Council.

The legitimate representatives of the Czech and Slovak Nations will agree how the powers shall be divided between the central and Slovak organs. The Slovaks will be adequately represented, both as in the central state offices, institutions and economic agencies, both as to number and the importance of their functions.

BIBLIOGRAPHY

Slovakia—properly speaking—has been a terra incognita in English literature. With the exception of the pioneer works by R. W. Seton-Watson: *Racial Problems in Hungary, Slovakia Then and Now—The New Slovakia* (1924), *Slovakia Then and Now,* (1931), *A History of the Czechs and Slovaks* and the excellent book *Czechoslovakia in European History* by S. Harrison Thomson, there are no exhaustive English books about Slovaks and Slovakia. Original documents and sources and the greatest part of literature regarding the history of Slovakia in general and its modern history in particular were published in Slovak, Czech, Magyar or Latin. I intentionally do not list them because they are of little value to the American or English student of history. I limit myself, therefore, to books published only in English and to some published in French and in German. Some of the following books have only brief references to Slovaks and Slovakia. For these reasons I also omit the titles of periodicals and scholarly journals in English and in foreign languages which contain only short articles concerning events in Slovak history.

Acta Academiae Scientiarium et Artium Slovacae, Vol. X., Bratislava, 1943/44

Aulneau, J., Histoire de l'Europe Centrale, Paris, 1926

Bartlett, Vernon, East of the Iron Curtain, London, 1949

Beck, Colonel Joseph, Dernier Rapport, Neuchâtel, 1951

Beneš, Edvard, Memoirs, London, 1954

Beneš, Edvard, My War Memoirs, New York, 1928

Bett, R. R., Central and South East Europe, London, 1950

Borovička, J., Ten Years of Czechoslovak Politics, Prague, 1929

Brown, John, Who's Next? The Lesson of Czechoslovakia, London, 1951

Bruce-Lockhardt, R. H., Guns or Butter, London, 1938

Čapek, Thomas, The Slovaks of Hungary, New York, 1906
Childress, P., Soviet Methods of Domination in Czechoslovakia, Washington, 1951
Churchill, Winston S., The Second World War, Vols. I-IV, New York, 1949-50
Ciano, Galeazzo, The Ciano Diaries, 1939-1943, New York, 1945
Czechoslovak Ministry of Foreign Affairs, Department of Information, Two Years of German Oppression in Czechoslovakia, London, 1941,
Four Fighting Years, London, 1943

Denis, Ernest, Les Slovaques, Paris, 1917
Dérer, Ivan, The Unity of the Czechs and Slovaks, Prague, 1938
Diamond, William, Czechoslovakia between East and West, London, 1947
Documents on German Foreign Policy, 1918-1945, Series D, Volume II, IV, Washington, 1949, 1951
Douglas, Dorothy W., Transitional Economic Systems, The Polish-Czech Example, London, 1953
Dvornik, Francis, The Making of Central and Eastern Europe, London, 1949
Dvornik, František, Les Slaves, Byzance et Rome au IXe siècle, Paris, 1926

Eisenhower, General Dwight D., Crusade in Europe, New York, 1948
Encyclopedia Britannica, Vol. VI (Czechoslovakia), Vol. XX (Slovakia, Slovaks), Chicago-London-Toronto, 1954

Friedman, Otto, The Break-Up of Czech Democracy, London, 1950
Gadourek, Ivan, The Political Control of Czechoslovakia, Leyden, 1953
George, Pierre, Le problème allemand en Tchécoslovaquie (1919-1946), Paris, 1947
Geschichte des zweiten Weltkrieges in Dokumenten, I, Der Weg zum Kriege, 1938-1939, München, 1953
Gunther, John, Behind the Curtain, New York, 1948-49

Hadley, W. W., Munich, Before and After, London, 1944
Healey, Denis, The Curtain Falls. The Story of Socialists in Eastern Europe, London, 1951
Hodža, Milan, Federation in Central Europe, London, 1942

Hoetzl, L. and Joachim, V., The Constitution of the Czechoslovak Republic, Berkeley, 1940

Jászi, O., The Dissolution of the Hapsburg Monarchy, Chicago, 1929
Josten, Josef, Oh, My Country, London, 1949

Kerner, Robert J., Czechoslovakia, Berkeley, 1949
Krofta, Kamil, Histoire de la Tchécoslovaquie, Bruxelles, 1930
Krofta, Kamil, A Short History of Czechoslovakia, New York, 1934
Kunoši, Alexander, The Basis of Czechoslovak Unity, London, 1944
Kybal, Vlastimil, Les origines diplomatiques d'État Tchécoslovaque, Prague, 1929

Lederer, Ed., Björnson et Apponyi, Prague, 1921
Le Monde Slave, La Tchécoslovaquie, 1918-1930, Paris, 1930
Levée, Madeleine, Les précurseurs de l'independence tchéque et slovaque à Paris, Paris, 1936
Lewis, Breckett, Democracy in Czechoslovakia, New York, 1941

Macartney, C. A., Hungary and Her Successors, London, 1937
Macartney, C. A., Problems of the Danube Basin, Cambridge, 1944
Manhattan, Avro, The Vatican in World Politics, New York, 1949
Markham, R. H., Communists Crush Churches in Eastern Europe, Boston, (1950)
Masaryk, Jan, Speaking to My Country, London, 1944
Masaryk, T. G., The Making of A State, London, 1927
Masaryk, T. G., La résurrection d'un État: souvenirs et reflexions, 1914-1918, Paris, 1930
May, J. Arthur, The Hapsburg Monarchy, 1867-1914, Cambridge, Mass., 1951
Meissner, Otto, Staatssekretär unter Ebert-Hindenburg-Hitler, Hamburg, 1950
Muran, J. B., We Fight On. Slovak Rising in the German Rear, London, 1945

Namier, L. B., Diplomatic Prelude, 1938-39, London, 1948
Namier, L. B., Europe in Decay, London, 1950
Namier, Sir Lewis, In the Nazi Era, London, 1952
Nowak, Karl Friedrich, Der Sturz der Mittelmächte, München, 1921

Opočenský, J., The Collapse of the Austro-Hungarian Monarchy and the Rise of the Czechoslovak State, Prague, 1928

Pogue, Forest C., Why Eisenhower's Forces Stopped at the Elbe (World Politics, IV, April, 1952), Princeton, N. J.

Ripka, Hubert, Czechoslovakia Enslaved (translation of Le Coup de Prague, Paris, 1949), London, 1950

Ripka, Hubert, Munich: Before and After, London, 1939

Roucek, Joseph S., Central-Eastern Europe, New York, 1946

Roucek, Joseph S., Czechoslovakia (People's Encyclopedia, Vol. VI), New York, 1950

Seton-Watson, Hugh, The East European Revolution, New York, 1951

Seton-Watson, Hugh, Eastern Europe, London, 1945

Seton-Watson, Hugh, From Lenin to Malenkov, New York, 1953

Seton-Watson, R. W., Munich and the Dictators, London, 1939

Seton-Watson, R. W., A History of the Czechs and Slovaks, London, 1943

Seton-Watson, R. W., Racial Problems in Hungary, London, 1908

Seton-Watson, R. W., Slovakia Then and Now—The New Slovakia, Prague, 1924

Seton-Watson, R. W., Slovakia Then and Now, London, 1931

Schmidt, Dana Adams, Anatomy of a Satellite, Boston, 1953

Schmidt, Dr. Paul, Statist auf diplomatischer Bühne 1923-1945, Bonn, 1950

Smith, Howard K., The State of Europe, New York, 1949

Stanoyevich, Milivoy S., Slavonic Nations of Yesterday and Today, New York, 1925

Statistical Digest of the Czechoslovak Republic, 1948, Prague, 1948

Street, C. J. C., Hungary and Democracy, London, 1923

Street, C. J. C., Slovakia Past and Present, London, 1928

Student of Affairs: How Did the Satellites Happen?, London, 1952

Štúr, L'dovít, Das Slaventhum und die Welt der Zunkunft, Bratislava, 1931

Survey of International Affairs (Royal Institute of International Affairs), 1938, Vol. III., London-New York-Toronto, 1953

Szana, Alexander, Die Geschichte der Slowakei, Bratislava, 1930-31

Szekfü, Jules, État et nation, Paris, 1945

Szembek, Comte Jean, Journal, 1933-1939, Paris, 1952

The New Funk & Wagnalls Encyclopedia, Vol. 10 (Czechoslovakia), Vol. 30 (Slovakia, Slovaks), New York, 1950-51

Thomson, S. Harrison, Czechoslovakia in European History, Princeton, N. J., 1953

Thourtzer, H., Louis Štúr et l'idée de l'independence slovaque (1815-1856), Cahors, 1913

Toynbee, Arnold,-Ashton Gwatkin, Frank I., The World in March 1939, Oxford, 1952

Trial of the Major War Criminals Before the International Military Tribunal, Nuremberg, 1947

Vambéry, Rustem, Hungary—To Be or Not to Be, New York, 1946

Wanklyn, Harriet, Czechoslovakia, New York, 1954

Walsh, Edmund A., S. J., Total Empire, Milwaukee, 1951

Warriner, Doreen, Revolution in Eastern Europe, London, 1950

Wheeler-Bennett, J. W., Munich: Prologue to Tragedy, New York, 1948

Wilmot, Chester, The Struggle for Europe, New York, 1952

Wynne, Waller Jr., The Population of Czechoslovakia, Washington, 1953

Yurchak, Peter P., The Slovaks, Whiting, Ind., 1946

INDEX

Adalram, Archbishop, 13
Altenburg, Günther, 89
Ambruš, Jozef, 155
Andrej, Saint, 186
Apponyi, Count Albert, 36
Arnulf, Emperor, 16

Bacílek, Karol, 209, 231
Bačinský, Edmund, 100
Baransky, E. V., 217
Bartek, Henrik, 156
Beck, Col. Joseph, 5, 84, 102
Bečko, Ján, 196
Bella, Metod, 47
Benda, Ferdinand, 144
Beneš, Edvard, 51, 82, 92, 95, 119, 196, 202, 210, 212, 232, 244-245, 257
Beniak, Valentin, 155
Beňadik, Saint, 186
Beran, Rudolf, 108, 118, 129
Berger, Gen. Gotlob, 206
Bethlen, Count Gábor, 23
Beust, Count Fridrich Ferdinand, 41
Bezák, Vendel, 222
Blaško, Štefan, 252
Bočkay, Count Stephen, 23
Bodický, Lt. Col. Vladimír, 200
Bór-Komorowski, General Tadeusz, 219
Boris, Czar, 161
Brauchitsch, Gen.-Col. Walter von, 136
Buday, Jozef, 108
Bugár, Miloš, 242, 247, 249
Buzalka, Msgr. Michal, 246
Bürckel, Joseph, 106, 126

Cablk, Ján, 46
Čaplovič, Ján, 196
Carbus, Lorenz, 125

Čatloš, General Ferdinand, 130-131, 160, 204, 219
Čečetka, Juraj, 155
Černák, Matúš, 85, 94-95, 103, 112, 117-118, 157-159, 162, 167, 276, 283
Černák, Vladimír, 117
Černoch, Ján Cardinal, 68
Chamberlain, Neville, 1-2, 91, 93
Charles III, Emperor, 16
Charles IV, King, 21, 44
Churchill, Sir Winston S., 232
Ciano, Count Galeazzo, 103
Cincík, Jozef, 156
Clementis, Vladimír, 196, 231
Čobrda, Vladimír, 156, 217
Constantine-Cyril, 11, 14-15, 186
Čulen, Konštantín, 151, 153, 220, 225-226
Čulen, Marek, 211, 231
Čunderlík, Col. Alexander, 117
Cvinček, Andrej, 246

Dafčík, Ján, 127
Daladier, Edouard, 93
Danihel, Štefan, 127
Daxner, Igor, 245-246
Daxner, Štefan Marko, 32
Deynek, Professor, 164
Dérer, Ivan, 46
Deretić, Col. Ilja, 215
Dietrich, Otto, 128
Djuračka, Andrej, 144
Dobrjansky, Adolf I., 32
Drtina, Prokop, 248
Drüffel, Ernst von, 127
Dula, Matúš, 47, 50
Ďurčanský, Ján, 77
Ďurčanský, Ferdinand, 77, 88-89, 96, 99-107, 112, 118, 122, 123-127, 130-131, 135, 137, 142, 157, 165-166, 176, 220, 222,

244-245, 275-277, 282
Ďuriš, Julius, 209, 256

Egolin, Professor, 164
Eichmann, Adolph, 184
Eisenlohr, Ernst, 87
Ertl, Daniel, 207,209

Fábry, Pavel, 144
Farkaš, Ján, 104
Ferenčík, Ján, 134, 153
Ferjenčík, Gen. Dr. Mikuláš, 200, 203, 242
Fierlinger, Zdeněk, 162-163, 233, 254
Filo, Dr. Emanuel, 164
Filo, Kornel, 246
Francis, Ferdinand, 41
Francis, Joseph I, 31
Frank, Karl Hermann, 82, 88
Fransoni, Francesco, 132
Fritz, Gejza, 130
Fundárek, Jozef, 164

Gajdoš-Breza, Juraj, 181
Galan, František, 165
Gašpar, Tido J., 151, 154-155, 170, 173, 181, 220-221
Gažík, Marko, 77
Géci, Michal, 252
Geraldíni, Koloman, 222
Golian, General Ján, 8, 200, 202-203, 205-207, 213, 216-217
Gottwald, Klement, 219, 231, 237, 239, 242, 246-247, 250, 253, 256-258
Göring, Marshal Hermann, 99-100, 103-105, 124, 159, 171, 176, 182
Granatier, Anton, 133
Green, Lt. James Holt, 212, 217
Gregor-Tajovský, Jozef, 133

Habsburgs, 3, 23, 28, 41, 54
Hácha, Emil, 108, 118, 123, 129, 132

Hadrian II, Pope, 14
Hammerschmidt, 107
Haššík, Štefan, 89, 220-221, 225
Hegel, G.W.F., 25
Henlein, Konrad, 2, 4, 67, 77-78, 82-85, 87-91
Herder, J. G., 25
Hermann, 136
Heydrich, Reinhold, 107
Himmler, Heinrich, 180, 182, 221
Hitler, Adolf, 1, 2, 4-6, 9, 77-78, 80, 82-93, 97, 99-100, 105, 107-109, 123-124, 126-128, 130-133, 135, 137, 139-141, 146, 151-153, 155-159, 161, 164-168, 171, 173, 175, 178, 182, 194-196, 206, 220-222, 224-225, 229, 274, 276, 280
Hletko, Dr. Peter P., 83, 101, 134
Hlinka, Andrej, 4, 5, 38-39, 47, 49, 61, 63, 67-70, 72-74, 76-78, 80-84, 88-89, 91, 96, 109, 111, 113, 115-117, 120, 127, 129, 134, 136, 142, 144, 146, 149-150, 152, 156, 160, 166, 170, 175, 178, 180, 182-183, 185, 189-190, 194, 208-209, 218, 221
Hodinová-Spurná, Anna, 231
Hodža, Fedor, 249
Hodža, Michal Miloslav, 31
Hodža, Milan, 39, 45-48, 61, 80, 92, 84, 196
Holdoš, Ladislav, 242
Horthy, Admiral Nicolas, 5, 139-140
Horváth, Ivan, 201
Höffle, General Hermann, 206, 221, 225
Hrnčár, Alexander, 225
Hrušovský, František, 155
Hull, Cordell, 169
Hurban, Jozef Miloslav, 31, 35
Hurban, Vladimír, 51, 196

Hurban-Vajanský, Svetozár, 44, 46
Husák, Gustáv, 198, 207, 209, 250, 257, 268
Hušek, Jozef, 101, 134
Hušek, Karol, 144
Chvalkovský, František, 123, 132

Imrédy, Béla, 139
Ištvánčin, Jozef, 117
Ivanka, Milan, 46

John VIII, Pope, 15
Jehlička, František, 73
Jesenský, Fedor, 150
Jesenský, Ján, 51, 133, 156
Jiskra z Brandýsa, Jan, 22
Joseph II., Emperor, 25
Josko, Matej, 9, 198, 246, 249
Joštiak, Jozef, 104
Júny, Lt. Col. Ján Martin, 200
Jurech, General Imrich, 217
Jurčovič, Ferdinand, 222
Juriga, Ferdiš, 50, 77

Kaftanov, Professor, 164
Kalina, Dezider, 200
Kánya, Kálmán, 139
Karmasin, Franz, 82-85, 89, 97-100, 103-104, 107, 125-127, 136, 139, 142, 153, 282
Karvaš, Imrich, 171, 219
Keitel, Marshal Wilhelm, 86, 124, 128, 136
Kempný, Ján, 242, 247, 249
Keppler, Wilhelm, 103-104, 106, 125, 127-128
Kirschbaum, Jozef, 107, 117, 125, 142, 158
Kobylanski, Tadeusz, 101
Kočiš, Aladár, 146-147, 220
Kollár, Ján, 26
Komenský, Ján Ámos, 45
Konev, Marshal Ivan, 210
Kopecký, Václav, 231

Kossuth, Louis, 29
Košík, Gustáv, 52
Körper, Karol, 117
Krajčovič, Alojz, 222
Krajčovič, Vojtech, 222, 277
Kramář, Karol, 54
Krátký, Major Jaroslav, 203, 216-217
Kreisel, 82
Krofta, Kamil, 132
Kubala, Otomar, 222
Kulich, Martin, 209
Kún, Béla, 55, 228
Kundt, Ernst, 82, 91-92
Kušík, Štefan, 250
Kuzmány, Karol, 33-34

Labaj L'udovít, 77
Lacroix, Victor Léopold de, 132
Lannurien, Georges de, 215
Laurinec, Imrich, 252
Lednár, L'udovít, 220, 222
Lettrich, Jozef, 144, 198, 207, 209, 223, 244-245, 249, 272
Lichner, Ján, 112, 196
Lodgmann von Auen, Rudolf, 283
Louis II, King, 22
Louis, the German, 13-14
Ludin, Hans Elard, 153
Luther, Martin, 22

Macek, Anton, 222
Magala, Jozef, 222
Mach, Alexander, 88, 99-101, 104, 107, 112-113, 117, 135, 137, 142, 151, 153, 164-166, 170, 180-182, 220, 244-246
Majer, Václav, 272
Makovický, Vladimír, 47
Malár, General August, 133, 217
Marko, Gen. Jozef, 200
Markovič, Ivan, 51
Masaryk, Ján, 248, 258
Masaryk, Tomáš G., 44, 51-53, 56-57, 79, 82

Mečiar, Stanislav, 154-155, 181, 222
Mederly, Anton, 220
Medrický, Gejza, 131, 220
Meissner, Otto, 128
Messík-Vajda, Msgr. Alexander, 153
Methodius, Archbishop, 11, 14-15, 185
Mičan, J. G., 212, 217
Mihajlović, General Draža, 219
Mihalus, Vinco, 144
Michael, III., Emperor, 14
Mikula, Jozef, 222
Mojmír I., 11, 13
Mojmír II., 16
Moravčík, Vladimir, 117
Morávek, Anton, 180
Morton, Joseph, 217
Motoška, Frico, 155
Moyses, Štefan, 33-34
Murgaš, Karol, 104, 107, 117, 125, 127, 222
Murín, Karol, 222
Mussolini, Benito, 80
Mutňanský, L'udovít, 104, 127

Nebe, 107
Nejedlý, Zdeněk, 231
Neujoks, Alfred Helmut, 107
Newton, Basil, 132
Nicholas, Czar, 52
Nicolas I., Pope, 14
Nosek, Václav, 231, 255
Nosko, Lt. Col. Julius, 200
Novak, A., 217
Novikov, Professor, 164
Novomeský, Ladislav, 198, 213, 268

Országh, Jozef Sr., 51-52
Országh-Hviezdoslav, Pavel, 49
Osuský, Samuel Š., 156, 217
Osuský, Štefan, 52, 196, 272
Otto I., Emperor, 18

Outrata, Edvard, 235

Palacký, František, 26, 29
Paučo, Jozef, 189, 220, 222-224
Paulíny, Viliam, 216-217
Paulíny-Tóth, Ján, 144, 196
Párvy, Alexander, 38, 39
Pavelić, Ante, 161
Pavlov, Ivan P., 267
Papánek, Ján, 270
Peacock, Virgil L., 9
Pekník, Col. Karol, 217
Peterka, Cpt. Jozef, 200
Petrov, E., 259
Pilfousek, Col. 172
Pilsudski, Marshal Józef, 85
Pius XII., Pope, 245
Plakinger, Lt. Col. Ján, 200
Plato, 6
Pocisk, Ján, 144
Polak, Cpt. Milan, 200
Polakovič, Štefan, 154-155, 220, 222, 226
Prchala, General Lev, 273-274
Pribina, 11, 13
Prídavok, Peter, 276
Přikryl, Col. Vladimír, 214
Procházka, Adolf, 272
Pružinský, Mikuláš, 105, 130, 220
Pulanich, Col. Anton, 117
Puškin, Juraj Maximovič, 163
Pyšný, Eduard, 171

Rákóczy II., Count Francis, 23
Rastislav, 11, 13-14, 16
Rátz, General Eugen, 139
Rázus, Martin, 77-78, 81
Reis, R., 185
Révays, 23
Ribbentrop, Joachim von, 88, 100, 103, 124, 128-130, 138, 165-166, 221
Ries-Javor, Viliam, 98, 155
Ritter, Xaver, 245
Rolík, Rev. Andrej. 101

Rolko, Vladimír, 155
Roosevelt, Franklin Delano, 169, 212, 231
Rudinský, Jozef, 144

Samo, 3, 11-12
Sehmer, Major, 213
Seton-Watson, Hugh, 243
Seton-Watson, R. W., 38
Seyss-Inquart, Arthur, 99, 106-108, 126
Schirach, Baldur von, 159
Shkarcev, Alexander, 162
Sidor, Karol, 84, 96, 101-102, 107-108, 113, 117-118, 122-127, 129-131, 133-135, 142, 166, 187, 245, 275-277
Sinčák, Michal, 101
Sivák, Jozef, 130, 164
Slánský, Rudolf, 211, 231, 268
Slávik, Juraj, 9, 196, 270
Slezák, Col. Štefan, 200
Smrek, Ján, 155
Sokol, Martin, 81, 92, 108, 118
Souhrada, Col. Hynek, 212, 216-217
Stalin, Joseph V., 232
Staněk, František, 47
Stanislav, Ján, 164
Stano, Julius, 108, 130
Staško, Jozef, 247, 249, 251
Stephen, King Saint, 18-19
Stodola, Emil, 68
Stodola, Kornel, 46
Styk, Jozef, 201, 223, 246
Styková, Hana, 144
Syrový, General Jan, 94
Svätopluk I., 11, 16
Svätopluk II., 16
Svoboda, General Ludvík, 258
Szembek, Count Jean, 101-102
Sztójay, Döme, 137
Šafárik, Pavel Jozef, 26
Šeliga, Dr. Michal, 164

Široký, Viliam, 209, 219, 231, 239
Škrábik, Andrej, 186
Škultéty, Jozef, 47
Šmidke, Karol, 198, 203, 207, 209, 231, 239
Šoltész, Jozef, 201, 223
Šrámek, Msgr. Jan, 72
Šrobár, Dr. Vavro, 47-49, 54-55, 61-62, 67, 69-70, 72-73, 207-209, 223
Štefánek, Anton, 46, 144
Štefánek, Ivan, 223
Štefánek, Gen. Milan R., 51, 55, 57, 74, 134
Štúr, L'udovít, 27, 30
Šubík, Dr. František (Andrej Žarnov), 155
Šverma, Ján, 211, 231

Teplanský, Pavel, 112, 117, 118
Threlfall, Col., 212
Thurzo's, 23
Tiso, Fraňo, 162
Tiso, Jozef, 5-7, 77, 80-81, 84, 88, 92, 95-96, 100-103, 105-109, 111-115, 118 - 119, 123, 125, 127-133, 135-137, 142, 146, 148, 151-152, 155, 161, 163, 165-166, 168-169, 173, 178, 181, 186-187, 204-205, 207, 218-222, 225, 228, 243-247, 274
Tiso, Štefan, 189, 220-221
Tisza, Count Kálmán, 36
Tománek, Florián, 77
Tököly, Count Emery, 23
Tranovský, Juraj, 45
Třešňák, František, 144
Tuka, Vojtech, 67, 74-77, 84, 96, 103-106, 117, 130, 135, 137, 142-144, 152-153, 155, 163, 165-167, 170, 178, 181, 207, 219

Urban, Milo, 155
Ursíny, Ján, 111, 144, 198, 207, 209, 213, 223, 249, 250
Vallo, Jozef, 231
Vančo, Miloš, 118, 120, 150
Vanovič, Ján, 47
Várady, First Lt., 216
Váša, Helen Kiernan-, 9
Vašek, Anton, 181, 185, 188-189, 222
Vávra, Rudolf, 88, 107, 127
Vesel, Lt. Col. Mirko, 200, 213
Veselý, Ján, 170
Vesselényi, Count Francis, 23
Vessenmeyer, Edmund, 103
Viest, General Rudolf, 8, 133, 196, 207, 213, 215, 217
Vilenskij, Professor, 164
Višňovský, Štefan, 217

Vlasov, General, 206
Vlček, Jaroslav, 46
Vojtaššák, Ján, 186
Votruba, František, 46, 47
Vráz, Vlasta, 9
Weizsäcker, Baron Ernst von, 137
Wilhelm II, Emperor, 280
Wilson, Woodrow, 54
Wisliczeny, Dieter, 180-181, 183-184
Wodráška, Tibor, 125
Zápotocký, Antonín, 235, 247, 256
Zaťko, Peter, 201, 223
Zenkl, Peter, 9, 248, 272
Zimák, František, 144
Zorin, Valerian A., 236, 257
Zupka, František, 250
Žižka z Trocnova, Jan, 22

Jozef Tiso visiting with Adolf Hitler in Berlin on March 13, 1939.

ozef Tiso receives the Order of the German Eagle, awarded him by Adolf Hitler.

Jozef Tiso greets the German Minister with the Nazi salute.

Matúš Černák with Adolf Hitler.

Joseph Goebbels with Jozef Tiso in Bratislava. Also shown are Vojtech Tuka, J. Gašpar and Gejza Medrický.

Adolf Hitler welcomes V. Tuka.

Alexander Mach greets J. Goebbels in the presence of T. J. Gašpar.

Field Marshal Wilhelm Keitel with Jozef Tiso.

Reichs-Fuehrer Robert Ley with Jozef Tiso in Topolčianky.
(Also shown is Franz Karmasin, second from right).

Vojtech Tuka with members of the Soviet delegation in Bratislava.

Vojtech Tuka, accompanied by Matúš Černák, after calling on Hitler.

Vojtech Tuka and Matúš Černák with Joachim von Ribbentrop and the Japanese Ambassador Kurusu
at the signing of the document of Slovak accession to the Tripartite Pact.

The head of the Soviet delegation, professor Kaftanov, in Bratislava.

Karol Sidor, Commander-in-Chief of the Hlinka Gua

Matúš Černák, Commander of the Hlinka Youth.

Jozef Kirschbaum, Commander of the Hlinka Academic Guard.

Arming of Guardists in Bratislava during the events of March, 1939.

Demonstration of HG and FS co-operation.

The Freiwillige Schutzstaffel (FS).

Armed Hlinka Guards (HG).

Konštantin Čulen speaks in the shadow of Nazi and Guardist flags.

Canon Karol Körper wearing a Hlinka Guard cap while speaking.

Ferdinand Ďurčanský before the assembled HG.

Ferdinand Ďurčanský and Jozef Kirschbaum greet the HG with the Nazi salute.

Synagogues demolished by the HG and FS.

Marking of Jewish houses.

Hlinka Guardists publicly cut off the beards of orthodox Jews.

Jews at collecting point waiting for deportation.

Jews sentenced to deportation await further orders.

The same fate awaits the Jewish aged and children—deportation.

The last moments in the homeland.

Carrying only the most essential belongings.

Under the eyes of Hlinka Guard, Jews board cattle cars for the voyage to death.

One remained alive of this family—the first one on the right.

he end of their suffering—the bodies of deported Jewish women after mass-execution in the gas-chambers.

The first insurgent Military Commander, General Ján Golian.

The second insurgent Military Commander, Gene Rudolf Viest.

The Slovak people help the insurgent troops by digging tank ditches.

About to leave for the unknown.

The Americans, J. G. Mičan and Lieut. J. H. Green-Haul, U.S.N., with British Major Sehmer among the insurgents.

American flying fortresses brought armaments to the Slovak insurgents.

French partisans in combat during the uprising in Slovakia.

More gallows and mass graves.

Jozef Tiso speaks, in the presence of Gen. Höffle, in Banska Bystrica.

Jozef Tiso decorates German soldiers for beating down the uprising.

Revenge on Slovak insurgents—the gallows.

Jozef Tiso accompanied by Štefan Tiso and the SS-Obergruppenfuehrer, General Hermann Höffle, leaving the church in Banská Bystrica where Jozef Tiso had celebrated Mass to honor the German occupation of the insurgent city.

Exhumed corpses of insurgent victims found in mass grave near Turčiansky Svätý Martin.

They even murdered children.